# A Greater Unity

# A Greater Unity

## Foundational Patterns of the Bible

MATTHEW JEAN TURGEON

RESOURCE *Publications* · Eugene, Oregon

A GREATER UNITY
Foundational Patterns of the Bible



Resource Publications
An Imprint of Wipf and Stock Publishers
199 W. 8th Ave., Suite 3
Eugene, OR 97401

www.wipfandstock.com

PAPERBACK ISBN: 979-8-3852-6303-5
HARDCOVER ISBN: 979-8-3852-6304-2
EBOOK ISBN: 979-8-3852-6305-9

VERSION NUMBER 04/21/26

# Contents

# Introduction

THIS BOOK BEGAN AS a journey into understanding patterns between the Old and New Testaments, particularly how Gen 1–4 provides insights for reading all of Scripture. Like many believers, I find Old Testament narratives puzzling. But what if the Bible's earliest stories establish interpretive patterns that illuminate everything that follows—patterns ancient readers recognized instinctively, but modern readers often miss? This book explores how Gen 1–4 establishes foundational patterns, providing practical tools for recognizing them throughout Scripture and revealing the coherence of the Bible from Genesis to Revelation.

We often read the Gospel narratives as moral stories—lessons about how to behave. But Scripture invites us into something deeper: a restored cosmic communion with God through Christ, where the broken communion introduced in Eden—affecting not just individual souls but the entire created order—is being restored through his mediation. The Gospels reveal not merely how Jesus lived, but how he restores the structure through which divine life flows into humanity. When the modern Christian doesn't understand Genesis, they end up reading the Gospels as surface-level moralism only—or in a literalist sense, where everything is flattened to just a blow-by-blow account. When we do engage these Old Testament stories, especially Genesis, we often read them primarily as pointers to Christ, searching backward from the New Testament to find where he fits in the Old Testament. This approach has real value. The early church consistently read the Old Testament in light of Christ's revelation, and rightly so. But when this becomes our only approach, we can miss something important: the depth of the questions that Christ came to answer. Consider this idea: that an answer is only as significant as the question it addresses. We have an answer (Christ) before we understand the questions and problems (Old Testament), which has led us to discount the answer.

We as Christians affirm Christ is present in every Old Testament story, yet often we don't understand how and in what manner he can relate in every story. To fully appreciate the redemption and life he brings for Christians, we benefit from understanding the context, struggles, and brokenness that necessitate his incarnation. As St. Gregory of Nazianzus argues in response to the Christological controversies of his day, what Christ does not assume, he does not redeem.[1] Christ assumes our hunger, grief, and all the travail of a fallen world precisely to redeem them. The Old Testament not only conveys these human struggles in vivid detail but also prepares us by highlighting the patterns He will fulfill. The New Testament authors lived in a world already shaped by the stories of Abraham, Moses, David, and the prophets. They experienced the corruption and struggles inherited from Adam. When they encountered Christ's teaching and redemptive work, they could see that it addressed real human questions, needs, and suffering that these ancient stories had illuminated—all highlighting how reading the Old Testament on its own terms reveals the struggles Christ came to redeem, deepening our understanding of his works in the New Testament.

When I first read the story of Adam and Eve, I admit I leaned toward a literal reading. After all, it describes the beginning of humanity—the garden, the tree of knowledge and the tree of life, a talking serpent, and what seems like catastrophic consequences for Adam and Eve's disobedience. On the surface, a literal approach seems straightforward: it tells us what happened at the beginning of history. But the more I studied it, the more I realized that this is more than an origin story. It is a foundational narrative, a worldview, and a frame through which we can understand the rest of Scripture.

One thing I have noticed in my own reading is that I often want to come to the text fresh, without any preconceived notions, but still think I am getting all the depth from my study somehow. At first, this may sound like an advantage, allowing the Bible to tell you what you need to know without having someone else tell you what it says—after all, it's reasonable to come with an open mind, allowing the Bible to tell you what it means? There is more honesty in our interpretations by not having another source of truth that tries to tell us what something means. But what tends to happen instead is that I unconsciously bring my modern lens of culture and

1. Paraphrased from Gregory of Nazianzus, *On God and Christ*, 158.

social norms into the story. I begin interpreting ancient narratives as though they were written yesterday, in my world, under my assumptions. Without realizing it, I project my expectations onto the text. The problem with this approach is that it prevents me from seeing the story within its own world and, more importantly, within the larger flow of the Bible's grand narrative. I may be able to pull out a moral lesson or a bit of encouragement, but I miss how this story fits into God's unfolding plan from Genesis to Revelation. In other words, I reduce the Bible to a series of isolated episodes rather than recognizing it as a unified story that reveals God's will. "The Elder of blessed memory [St. Sophrony] always stressed that our aim is fulfillment of God's will, eternal life and knowledge of God, not moral improvement."[2]

## SPECIFIC PRINCIPLES/FRAMEWORKS FROM GENESIS 1–4

A lens does more than guide interpretation, it establishes a hierarchy of value. It determines what we treat as central and what we treat as secondary. Every reading of Scripture already operates with such a hierarchy, whether acknowledged or not. The question is not whether we have a hierarchy, but whether it is drawn from Scripture itself. And having a lens from Genesis, the beginning, the foundation of the world seems appropriate. From the first stories, Gen 1–4, there are principles one should draw from for our lives today and further reading of the Bible, since opening chapters of unified works establish the thematic and interpretive frameworks that help readers understand all later material, something common in unified works. Most Christians sense that the Bible is unified but cannot say how—they feel the coherence without being able to demonstrate it. Because I believe the Bible is divinely inspired and has a grand narrative, we can see the greater unity that the Bible can convey. The following example shows how this operates throughout Scripture.

For example, in one's study of the Adam and Eve story, one narrative instruction, acting as an interpretive principle, is when Adam receives God's command directly but fails when he "heeded the voice" (Gen 3:17) of Eve rather than maintaining obedience to God. This same pattern appears repeatedly: when those called to mediate between God and people yield to pressures from those they're meant to lead, order collapses and consequences follow. We see this pattern recur with Aaron and the golden

2. Vlachos, *"I Know a Man,"* 14.

calf (yielding to the people's demands), with Saul and the Amalekite spoils (yielding to the people), and with Solomon and his foreign wives (yielding to relational influence over divine command). Paul even references this Genesis pattern directly when addressing church leadership issues: "And Adam was not deceived, but the woman being deceived, fell into transgression" (1 Tim 2:14). This suggests the biblical authors expected readers to apply these patterns forward through history and the Bible, not just discover them through backward reflection from Christ. We are to read later texts through earlier patterns.

Throughout this book, I'll use "pattern," "principle," and "framework" in related but distinct ways.

- A principle is the foundational instance of that pattern, found in Gen 1–4, that serves as a template for understanding later occurrences. In this book, it is the Adam and Eve principle, the tilling/rain/yield principle, and the inheritor/renewer principle. Principles precede patterns.
- A pattern is a recurring occurrence of the initial principle across multiple biblical stories—like leaders yielding to pressure from those they're meant to lead.
- A framework is a lens or interpretive method. In this book, I use the three principles together in a framework that I call the Genesis Conflict Framework.

Most see patterns but not the principles those patterns derive from, so ultimately they miss the meaning the repeated pattern is communicating. The goal is not to impose an external grid, but to uncover the exegetically observable framework and structure that the Bible itself seems to establish in its opening chapters. These patterns are not just literary devices—they reflect how the biblical authors structured narrative and expected it to be read and lived by, being narrative instruction. This book offers interpretive tools for ordinary Christians seeking to read Scripture as a unified narrative. I highlight principles from Gen 1–4 that communicate the unity of the Bible, giving readers more tools in their Bible study and practical wisdom for their lives. Each principle first appears in Gen 1–4 and then recurs throughout Scripture, ultimately finding its fulfillment in Christ. This framework explains how the three curses of Gen 3 structure all biblical narrative from Genesis to Revelation, providing interpretive tools for the majority of Scripture.

Understanding these principles and patterns doesn't replace reading the Old Testament with a Christological lens—it enriches it. When we see how consistently human leaders fail in their mediating roles, Christ's perfect mediation becomes more remarkable. When we understand the recurring breakdown of order, Christ's establishment of the new covenant carries greater weight. This approach treats the Bible as a unified story rather than isolated episodes. Stories engage our imagination and teach through example. When we carefully enter these narratives, we see ourselves reflected in them and understand both recurring human behaviors and the consequences of our choices.

Another question I often have is, why does the Old Testament often seem disconnected from Jesus? When we isolate biblical stories, we blind ourselves to the deeper patterns and connections woven throughout both the Old and New Testaments. We fail to see, for instance, how the struggle between Cain and Abel sets a pattern that reappears in Jacob and Esau, Joseph and his brothers, and ultimately finds its fulfillment in Christ. What looks like a random conflict between brothers is part of a larger design, revealing the contrast between human inheritance and divine renewal. When you understand Genesis as foundational for understanding the rest of the Bible, you'll discover why biblical brothers consistently conflict, how marriage passages illuminate Christ's relationship with the church, and why God repeatedly chooses the unlikely over the obvious. Without this lens, we miss the rhythm and consistency of God's ways in history. My goal is to communicate the structure of the Bible that one can see across multiple stories, highlighting the coherence embedded. This is the difference between:

- Information: knowing facts about biblical events
- Understanding: seeing how events connect and cohere
- Wisdom: recognizing the structure and principles that generate the events—i.e., recognizing ontological truths, truths about the nature of reality itself

## MY PURPOSE AND LIMITATIONS

My aim is modest: to show how understanding Gen 1–4 can provide one with a lens for reading Scripture and understanding the internal logic in most biblical narratives. The goal is to highlight these patterns that start in Genesis that pervade later stories. This won't solve every interpretive question or replace other valid approaches—it's simply one tool that has enriched my own reading of Scripture. But I have found it to be a particularly powerful tool, one that reveals connections and makes the Bible readable as a unified story. I do not aim merely to explain biblical texts, but to invite you into a deeper way of reading the Bible—one that discerns a common logic running through its stories. Since Scripture is divinely inspired and ultimately has one Author, coherence is not only reasonable to expect but essential to understanding that God's actions are not arbitrary.

The questions that Adam and Eve's story introduces—about authority, responsibility, temptation, participation with God's will, and obedience—aren't merely ancient history. They're questions we face in our relationships and spiritual struggles today. For those whose faith has been shaken by science and the common literal readings of Genesis, this book's goal is to inspire you to see the Bible anew. For this reason, I frequently include application sections, since these spiritual interpretations are intended to highlight the life application and instruction one should draw from these stories. I write not as a professional but as someone who has wrestled with these texts; everything is my opinion, and any shortcomings are solely my own. My hope is that this book helps you see Scripture's coherence, depth, and unity—revealing the greater unity God designed from Genesis to Revelation.

# 1

# A Worldview from Genesis

This chapter will review how a Genesis worldview aligns with how ancient Israelites understood the Torah, allowing the stories to be embodied by reading them literally but living them as a constitution and worldview. One of the great debates surrounding Genesis is how we should approach it, whether literally or spiritually. Is it the story of humanity's literal beginnings, or a symbolic narrative conveying enduring truths for our lives? For many readers, myself included, this question can feel overwhelming. A literal reading might focus on the physical location of the garden of Eden, while a spiritual reading delves into what the "garden" represents—a place of communion, abundance, and divine presence.

However, the more I wrestled with leaning on the literal perspective, the more I realized its limits. Without understanding the deeper significance or understanding the spiritual meaning, it is easy either to dismiss the story altogether or to cling solely to a literal interpretation that risks losing its life-giving meaning. It becomes a historical fact, a mythic explanation for our origins, rather than a source of guidance for living faithfully. When science, history, or modern scholarship challenged this overly literal reading that many Christians take, I felt my belief in Scripture begin to falter, since all I had were these "facts" that have been significantly challenged.

## SPIRITUAL READING

The church fathers taught us to read Genesis both literally and spiritually. Literally: There was a garden, disobedience occurred, and exile happened. Real history. Spiritually: These events reveal enduring patterns—highlighting that the deepest spiritual interpretations reveal ontological truths. Timeless truth. Both matter. This book focuses on the spiritual reading—the patterns Genesis establishes that recur throughout Scripture. The literal and spiritual readings are complementary; the literal anchors the text, while the spiritual unlocks its transformative meaning. Paul states, "The letter kills, but the spirit gives life" (2 Cor 3:6). In other words, understanding the spiritual meaning of Scripture gives it life and guidance for our spiritual benefit, beyond just knowing the historical facts of the narrative stories in the Bible.

Observing Old Testament laws and narratives literally without recognizing their typology and deeper meaning risks missing their ultimate purpose. This perspective also helped me reconcile the tension between modernity and Scripture. Science, history, and textual criticism can challenge a purely literal reading, but a spiritual life application interpretation allows the story to retain its power and relevance. It is not about proving when or how events occurred; it is about understanding the principles embedded in the narrative and applying them in life. The transformative power that emerges through embodying these biblical narratives—regardless of their precise historical details—provides its own form of evidence. When the Adam and Eve story teaches me to recognize authority breakdowns in my own relationships, or when the tilling/rain/yield principle, which we will go over, helps me understand divine-human cooperation in my spiritual life, these stories prove their truth through their practical wisdom. I hold to the worldview that these stories, the Bible, and the church communicate not because I can scientifically verify every detail, but because living according to their principles produces genuine spiritual fruit. This is the bridge of why both literal and spiritual are important.

More importantly, this is how the church acts today: the liturgical year and the feasts and services we participate in are all meant to highlight that we are there at Christ's death, resurrection, and triumph. We are there celebrating the life of the saints and the works they performed for the kingdom of God. Without a literal reading, we can lose this faithfulness to the real historical element of the church. Put together, the literal and spiritual offer a powerful resource for our faithfulness to Christ. One question I have: Is there a way of still having a literal reading that aligns with how the ancient Israelites believed these stories, and what benefit does it give us? This spiritual reading of the text was not an invention of the church fathers; it was rooted in the way the ancient Israelites themselves viewed their foundational texts, particularly the Torah, as their constitution. Understanding Genesis as their foundational worldview requires grasping how they used these texts constitutionally, as living principles rather than historical records alone.

## TORAH AS CONSTITUTION

Using a lens from the Bible, specifically Genesis, aligns with the authority of the Torah, as it already served this function as a constitution, providing the worldview for the Israelites, giving them ideals to uphold. This approach aligns with the Torah's function of giving instruction and warning to its followers. Themes such as communion with God, temptation, corruption, and repentance, which are evident in the Adam and Eve story, are universal patterns throughout the Bible. Gary Anderson, in *The Genesis of Perfection*, writes,

> Religious texts are not just for reading and rereading; they are meant to be lived. Crucial to every piece of Jewish and Christian interpretation that we have encountered is some sort of dramatic enactment, be it liturgy, prayer, or almsgiving. How we perform the Scriptures is just as important a vehicle for understanding as how we read.[1]

This makes the Adam and Eve narrative a key for interpreting the rest of the Bible. Given the significance of the story of Adam and Eve, creating a lens through which to view the rest of the Bible seems appropriate. As Nahum Sarna emphasizes,

> It must be remembered that the Mesopotamian and Hebrew cosmologies, each in its own way, express through their symbolism the worldviews and values that shaped the civilizations each represents. The opening chapters of the Bible unveil the main pillars upon which the Israelite worldview rests.[2]

The Genesis account functions as more than just historical narrative; it served for the ancient Israelites as the constitutional stories and

1. Anderson, *Genesis of Perfection*, 177.
2. Sarna, *Understanding Genesis*, 8.

worldview governing all subsequent divine-human interaction, just as a nation's constitution provides the pattern for interpreting all subsequent laws and policies. Jesus himself performs this constitutional reading in Matt 19 when the Pharisees ask about Mosaic divorce law and he bypasses Moses entirely to appeal to Gen 2: "from the beginning it was not so." His reasoning is explicitly constitutional—the foundational text establishes the norm, Moses' concession is a departure from that norm, and when the two conflict Genesis governs, exactly as a constitution governs later statutes. The constitutional reading of Genesis is therefore not a framework imposed on Scripture but the hermeneutical method Jesus himself uses in his dispute. For Israel, history was not just a record of the past but the foundation of identity. Remembering God's actions shaped how they lived in the present. This is why so much of the Torah commands Israel to "remember"—the Exodus, the covenant at Sinai, the wilderness journey. Festivals such as Passover, Pentecost, and Tabernacles were not simply cultural celebrations but acts of historical memory: they represented God's mighty works so that each generation could participate as if they themselves had been there. Genesis, in particular, served as a memory of beginnings—who God is, who humanity is, and what happens when we allow pride and self-determination to become our God. Without this collective memory, Israel risked assimilation and forgetting their unique vocation. For Christians, the same principle applies: liturgy, Eucharist, and the church year anchor us in salvation history, making the past a living reality that guides the present. Living these stories and their worldview can draw us closer to God.

Spiritual reading shifts attention from external compliance to inner transformation and principled application in our lives and that of the church. Christ redirects attention to the heart, teaching that true purity is transforming and spiritual rather than merely external. The approach I take in this book does not ignore historical or textual realities; rather, it asks a deeper question: What is this story teaching us about life, God, and the choices we face? This leads to the question of how I should "perform the Scriptures," specifically Gen 1–4. The Adam and Eve story, seen through a spiritual lens, becomes a guide for understanding the structure of reality as ordered communion with God. When that order fractures, the consequences that follow are not arbitrary, but follow the logic embedded in creation itself.

## APPLICATION: THE ADAM AND EVE STORY IN LITURGICAL LIFE

I want to highlight that, just as the ancient Israelites embodied the Torah as a constitution, the Orthodox Church and the liturgical calendar don't simply commemorate past events—they make them present. During Holy Week, the faithful don't just remember Christ's passion; they participate in it. The services of Great and Holy Friday place the congregation at the foot of the cross. The matins of Holy Saturday descends with Christ into Hades. The Paschal vigil witnesses the resurrection. Through carefully structured worship, Scripture becomes embodied experience rather than historical memory. This same principle applies to the Genesis narratives. The Orthodox understanding of humanity's fall and redemption isn't merely a theological doctrine—it's liturgically enacted. Every Divine Liturgy begins with the recognition that we approach God's throne as fallen beings in need of mercy: "With fear of God, faith, and love, draw near."[3] Yet through the Eucharist, we participate in the restoration of communion that Adam lost, receiving life in Christ's body and blood.

Perhaps nowhere is the Genesis pattern more clearly "performed" than in Orthodox fasting disciplines. The Church doesn't simply prohibit certain foods arbitrarily; fasting recreates the essential dynamic of Gen 2–3. Just as Adam faced the test of the forbidden tree, Orthodox Christians regularly confront the choice between immediate desire and divine command. The Wednesday and Friday fasts, the Lenten periods, and preparation before receiving Communion all place believers in Adam's position: will we trust God's ordering or follow our appetites? These aren't merely dietary rules but liturgical performances of the fundamental human choice between obedience and self-will.

Orthodox wedding services connect marriage to Genesis and the ideal established in chapter 2, as well as its fulfillment in Christ. The crowning ceremony doesn't just bless a social contract—it establishes a liturgical reality where husband and wife become living icons of Christ and the church. Marriage becomes a way of "performing" the corrected Genesis pattern. This liturgical embodiment transforms abstract biblical principles into lived experience. Through regular participation in Orthodox worship, believers don't just learn about authority and obedience—they practice it. They don't simply study temptation and response—they experience both

3. Holy Transfiguration Monastery, *Prayer Book*, 130.

regularly and learn to choose correctly. The truths of the Bible become internalized not through intellectual analysis alone but through repeated liturgical performance.

The Orthodox tradition encourages the faithful to remember that we are Adam, as Adam is our common forefather. Equally important for this study is the understanding that the other characters in the Bible also originate from Adam, and their experiences can be interpreted through the lens of his story. The ideal state Adam enjoyed in the garden—communion with God—was lost through his failure to overcome temptation and his disobedience. Bishop Nikolai Velimirović offers a prayer that invites reflection on this shared history, concluding with the words, "For all the history of mankind from Adam to me, a sinner, I repent; for all history is in my blood. For I am in Adam and Adam is in me."[4] St. Symeon the New Theologian also emphasizes this concept: "If any of us does not recognize that he is Adam, the one who sinned before God in Paradise, how can he recognize and believe that the coming of the Son and Word of God was for him?"[5] This statement further emphasizes the need to see the biblical characters as Adam figures, each encountering temptation that must be overcome. This perspective provides us, just as it did for the ancient Israelites, a way to embody these stories. The Orthodox Church has preserved this wisdom for centuries, recognizing that biblical narratives achieve their full meaning only when they become the lived reality of the believing community. Through liturgy, Genesis ceases to be ancient history and becomes the present pattern through which we encounter God, understand ourselves, and learn to respond faithfully to divine grace. Bridging the application of Scripture with understanding Scripture leads to our use of typology in our study of the Bible.

## TYPOLOGY AND PATTERN

Typology refers to "persons, institutions, or events divinely intended in the Old Testament to serve as models, previews, or representations of something yet to come."[6] This study will use typology to explore how Jesus connects with Old Testament figures, but also how Jesus recapitulates the temptations that occurred in the garden, and instead of disobedience

4. Manley, *Grace for Grace*, 39.

5. Symeon, *First-Created Man*, 79.

6. Kaiser, *Messiah*, 38.

and separation from God, Jesus overcomes and obeys. The Bible comprises many different books, and since Christians believe it is inspired by God and possesses intertextual unity, we can rely on Christ in the New Testament to answer the questions posed by the Old Testament. "Intertextual dialogue deepens and enriches the reading experience, bringing multiple layers of meaning to the text, some of which readers may not even consciously notice."[7] Typology isn't just a gimmick one can use to try to see how Christ fits into the Old Testament. Bruce Beck states,

> Typology has been, and is, the language of the Church as it expresses its identity as the people of the New Covenant, instituted by the blood of Jesus, God's Son. It is, therefore, a literary technique, but more essentially a theological language, which sees the present as ever instantiating the great deliverances, institutions, and persons of the past.[8]

Christ shares similarities with many individuals in the Bible, since most stories usually have a conflict, problem, or issue where a character must act, overcoming temptation or failing.

One helpful technique in typological analysis is the convention of repetition. Biblical narratives frequently echo one another, repeating words, ideas, motifs, themes, etc. These repetitions are not mere redundancies; rather, they invite comparison, enabling readers to observe how different protagonists encounter similar circumstances and make decisions that reveal character, spiritual insight, or moral failure. Through this comparison lens, typology uncovers subtle nuances and theological insights that might remain hidden in isolated readings of a single story. In typological exegesis, the Old Testament shadow or prefigurement of someone or something is referred to as the type. Its fulfillment in a person or event of the New Testament is referred to as antitype, meaning reality.[9] Typological interpretation, what I'm practicing in this book, operates by recognizing recurring patterns that appear multiple times across Scripture, with the biblical authors themselves providing signals that readers should connect earlier and later instances.

The test of legitimate typology is straightforward:

7. Foster, *How to Read Literature*, 29.

8. Pentiuc, *Studies in Orthodox*, 30.

9. Stylianopoulos, *New Testament*, 116.

1. Does the pattern appear multiple times and ultimately point to Christ, his saving economy, and the life of the church?
2. Does the typological correspondence cohere with the church's received understanding of Christ and salvation?
3. Is the pattern or correspondence generative? (Does it explain *why* certain narratives unfold the way they do, not just that they're similar?)

If the answer to these three questions is yes, we're not imposing meaning; we're recognizing the structure the biblical authors built into the text.

## THREE LEVELS OF TYPOLOGICAL ANALYSIS

The Bible can use typological analysis across three distinct levels, each offering unique insights into Scripture's interconnected nature:

- Direct typology: Occurs when the New Testament explicitly references the Old Testament, often quoting it word-for-word. These clear citations are typically accompanied by a narrative explanation that identifies the type-antitype relationship. For example, in the Gospel of Matthew, Isaiah is quoted directly in reference to John the Baptist's ministry of "preparing the way" (Isa 40:3, Matt 3:1–3). Such direct parallels provide immediate recognition of continuity between the Old and New Testaments, reinforcing the theological argument of fulfillment while anchoring interpretation in historical-textual evidence. These direct connections establish the clearest foundation for typological interpretation, as the biblical authors themselves draw explicit connections between Old Testament promises and their New Testament fulfillment. The Gospels particularly demonstrate this approach, showing how Jesus fulfills specific prophetic utterances and embodies the roles prefigured by Old Testament institutions and figures by directly quoting the Old Testament.
- Indirect typology: Indirect typology, commonly called an "allusion," is more nuanced and interpretively demanding. It resembles navigating a mansion with many rooms, where each symbolic key unlocks another space, revealing connections that are implied rather than explicitly stated. In this form, scattered references, allusions, or symbolic motifs across different biblical passages are linked by shared language, narrative patterns, or thematic resonance. Unlike direct typology, indirect

typology often appears disjointed or fragmentary at first, but careful analysis uncovers the interconnectedness of Scripture. The interpretive challenge of indirect typology lies in distinguishing legitimate patterns from forced connections. The key lies in identifying multiple points of correspondence that illuminate consistent theological principles rather than superficial similarities.

- Divine principles (logoi): Having a principle from the foundation of the world (Gen 1–4) allows an initial story to provide a lens through which the entirety of Scripture may be interpreted. This approach relies on identifying foundational stories as paradigms for human-divine interaction. These patterns have multiple confirming instances, not just one-to-one correspondence. In literary terms, such stories function as frame narratives, enclosing later stories within a broader thematic or moral structure. This approach recognizes that certain biblical narratives serve as constitutional, foundational stories, establishing the fundamental principles that showcase how God interacts with humanity across all subsequent stories. This approach makes one's principle reading falsifiable since it can be tested. For example, find a biblical story where a leader heeds a subordinate voice over divine command and receives blessing instead of judgment. There isn't one.

Most biblical interpretations of the Old Testament through a Christological lens uncover numerous profound indirect connections between Christ and Old Testament figures. However, these connections are often explored through comparison, which can sometimes obscure their larger significance or the overarching principle or theme they are meant to highlight. Recognizing patterns across multiple stories to identify commonalities is only the beginning. To grasp their greater significance, one must delve into the overarching principles behind those patterns. Among all biblical narratives, the Adam and Eve story serves as the foundational story since it is the first story of mankind, giving us what we can term the "Adam and Eve type-scene," a foundational pattern that scales across different realities within biblical narrative.

Type-scenes are recurring narrative patterns that highlight significant, often pivotal, moments in characters' lives. Alter explains, "Since biblical narrative characteristically captures its protagonists only at critical and revealing points in their lives, the biblical type-scene occurs not in the routines of daily existence but at crucial junctures in the lives of the heroes, from conception and birth to betrothal to deathbed."[10] A classic example is the type-scene of a protagonist meeting a woman at a well, leading to betrothal, a pattern seen in the stories of Isaac, Jacob, Moses, and even hinted at with Jesus. As Alter emphasizes, the Bible "requires some detailed awareness of the grid of conventions upon which, and against which, the individual work operates."[11] This is Adamic typology, where you find an Adam figure and an Eve figure in each story, looking for whether one is acting in obedience or disobedience in their role. As Adam and Eve's failure to obey God led to the fall, we need to review who is receiving wisdom from God, who is passing it to their followers, and if this dynamic is maintained or reversed. Questions like "Is the Eve figure listening to the Adam figure?" have real implications one should see. Likewise, the question is whether the Adam figure is listening to the Eve figure in a manner that goes against God's command. This makes the type-scene so useful. Alter notes, "The type-scene is a way of formally recognizing a particular kind of narrative moment; it is also a means of attaching that moment to a larger pattern of historical and theological meaning."[12] This narrative moment examines whether the characters in the Bible are performing their roles correctly and are being obedient to God's will.

The spiritual meaning of Adam and Eve carries real power because it offers a worldview and interpretive lens that guided Christ, the apostles, and the ancient Israelites. Genesis 1–3, and the lessons and instructions one can draw from these narratives, functions much like a frame narrative in literature. A frame narrative is a literary technique in which an initial story sets the stage and context for all the stories that follow, allowing the reader to see a story within a story. For example, in Mary Shelley's *Frankenstein*, the narrative begins with letters written by the protagonist, establishing his circumstances, conflicts, and the experiences that led him to that point. These letters create context, build tension, and prepare the reader to understand the unfolding events of the main story. Likewise, Gen 1 is supposed to be used to inform Gen 2, and so on, so that earlier stories, especially the Adam and Eve story, can provide instruction and the interpretive grammar for understanding later stories. Reading the Bible forward in this way allows meaning to accumulate as the narrative unfolds.

10. Alter, *Art of Biblical Narrative*, 60.

11. Alter, *Art of Biblical Narrative*, 55.

12. Alter, *Art of Biblical Narrative*, 72.

While some scholars have argued that the chapters are disjointed or contradictory, one can see the continuity of ordering and life in each. Genesis 2 continues these themes, now with a focus on human responsibility and further flourishing through man and woman performing established roles. Adam is tasked with cultivating the garden, acting as God's steward. Eve expands this responsibility into a relational partnership, being a counterpart and extension of her husband who ultimately will bring forth life, highlighting the harmony and unity inherent in creation. The frame narrative approach also illuminates why the Old Testament remains Christian Scripture rather than merely a historical background. These stories aren't simply chronological preparation for Christ but structural preparation—they establish the patterns that make Christ's work intelligible as the ultimate resolution of humanity's fundamental problem.

Many readers treat biblical characters as moral examples—follow Abraham's faith, avoid David's adultery. But frame narrative interpretation reveals something more sophisticated. These figures aren't primarily moral examples but structural positions within the foundational pattern. Abraham succeeds as an "Adam figure" when he trusts divine promise over human understanding (Isaac's birth) but fails when he yields to corrupted "Eve figure" pressure (Hagar incident). The pattern, not the personality, drives the narrative. With the Adam and Eve story being just two chapters of the Bible, we don't remain long with these characters, but the lessons one should learn from their story should stay and be used for the rest of the Bible, as I will explain and demonstrate when I apply principles from Adam and Eve across the rest of the Bible. Genesis 1–4 equips us to read Scripture as a unified narrative. Next, we'll see how the Adam and Eve principle recurs throughout biblical history.

# 2

# The Adam and Eve Principle and Scaling the Principle

Having established Genesis as a foundational lens for biblical interpretation, we now turn to the first of three principles that this book proposes: the Adam and Eve principle. This principle reveals how the dynamics established in Gen 2–3—divine authority, human responsibility, proper ordering, and the consequences of obedience or disobedience—recur throughout Scripture at every scale of reality. A question I have is: Does the story of Adam and Eve provide truths and instructions for just a couple, meaning the story is only helpful for a marriage? I think not; the principles we can draw are scalable and apply also to a family, community, or nation; obedience to God is necessary over earthly or fleshly persuasion.

When Adam "heeded the voice" of Eve (Gen 3:17) rather than maintaining obedience to God's direct command, he established a pattern that would echo through biblical history: leaders yielding to pressure from those they're meant to guide, resulting in the breakdown of divine order. Let's begin by reviewing this authority dynamic step-by-step in Gen 2 and 3:

## BREAKDOWN OF THE ADAM AND EVE PRINCIPLE

Step 1 The original setup: Adam as the authority figure (Gen 2:15–17)

God places Adam in the garden and gives him direct commands—to tend the garden and not eat from the tree of knowledge of good and evil. Adam's role: receive divine instruction, steward creation, and transmit God's wisdom. The command: "Of every tree of the garden you may freely eat; but of the tree of the knowledge of good and evil you shall not eat, for in the day that you eat of it you shall surely die" (vv. 16–17).

Step 2 Eve's creation and role as helper

Created as Adam's "helper comparable to him," his counterpart (Gen 2:18). Her position in this instance was to receive God's command as mediated by Adam. Proper dynamic: Adam provides divine wisdom; Eve provides earthly insight and partnership.

Step 3 The temptation (Gen 3:1–6)

The serpent's strategy: Bypasses Adam and approaches Eve directly, questioning God's command. Eve's response: she engages with an alternative interpretation of divine instruction. The critical moment: Eve "took of its fruit and ate. She also gave to her husband with her, and he ate" (v. 6).

Step 4 The authority breakdown

Adam's failure: Instead of maintaining God's command, he "heeded the voice" of Eve (Gen 3:17). Role reversal: the Eve figure (receiver of mediated wisdom) becomes the source of instruction. The pattern established: when the Adam figure yields to pressure from those he's meant to guide, divine order collapses.

Step 5 The consequences (Gen 3:8–24)

Immediate: Shame, fear, broken communion with God. Relational: Blame, conflict between the couple. Cosmic: Curse on creation, expulsion from Eden, death enters the world.

This principle scales from individual relationships to corporate bodies, like a group, a nation, or a church. Paul himself demonstrates this scaling in Eph 5:30–32, where he directly quotes Gen 2:24: "For we are members of His body, of His flesh and of His bones. 'For this reason a man shall leave his father and mother and be joined to his wife, and the two shall become one flesh.' This is a great mystery, but I speak concerning Christ and the church." Paul is using the Adam and Eve story and the scale of a marriage to provide instruction on the proper dynamics of Christ and a corporate body, the church. If Paul reads Genesis marriage as a fractal template revealing how authority and union function at multiple levels, the same methodology applies to Gen 3:17.

When Adam "heeded the voice of his wife" rather than God's command, that authority breakdown pattern operates wherever such structures exist—individual, marital, tribal, national, cosmic. We're following the apostolic method, not imposing external frameworks. Understanding this principle transforms isolated biblical episodes into interconnected demonstrations of a single, recurring truth about authority, responsibility, and the human response to divine order, highlighting that the Adam and Eve story has universal application.

## UNDERSTANDING "HEAD" AND SCALING THE PRINCIPLE

To understand this scaling principle, it's essential to clarify the term "head." The Ignatius Catholic Study Bible notes that "head" can refer to the physical head of a man (Matt 5:36) but also, more broadly, to a ruler or leader. This flexibility in how the head is used in the Bible allows us to grasp how it relates to our principle. "In the Old Testament, the individual (male) person may be viewed as extending beyond himself to include those who 'belong' to him. Thus, the husband (at the family level) and the king (at the national level) both possess an individual and corporate existence, encompassing, respectively, the household and the nation."[1] The concept of headship implies not domination but stewardship—the responsibility to order reality according to divine wisdom while remaining accountable to God for the well-being of those under one's care. Paul uses "head" in 1 Cor 11:3—"But I want you to know that the head of every man is Christ, the head of woman is man, and the head of Christ is God"—thereby revealing a hierarchical structure embedded in reality itself.

The Adam figure: the mediator between heaven and earth—serving as husband, priest, leader, or head at the relevant scale. This figure bears primary responsibility for:

1. Ellis, *Old Testament in Early*, 110.

- Receiving and interpreting divine instruction
- Ordering earthly reality according to heavenly wisdom
- Protecting and providing for those under his care
- Maintaining communion between God and his sphere of responsibility

The Eve figure: the helpmate, observer, and respondent who possesses specialized knowledge of earthly realities. This figure's legitimate functions include:

- Observing ground-level conditions and reporting to the Adam figure
- Refining and expressing the Adam figure's vision through practical application
- Posing necessary questions to understand the command, which tests the integrity of the ordering
- Preserving sacred space through faithful response to proper authority

Many notice that as you work your way through the Bible, the scale of reality increases, as seen below:

Individual → couple → family → tribe/community → nation → kingdom → church

This principle also illuminates the distinct, complementary roles of man and woman, or more broadly, the Adam and Eve figures at all scales. The Adam figure is called to order the world by providing wisdom from above, enabling followers to understand and abide by it. The Eve figure, in turn, refines this ordering by expressing the Adam figure's vision, informing on the ground realities, and posing questions when necessary to ensure they both work to preserve this sacred space. Critically, the inappropriate performance of these roles can lead to detrimental consequences.

The book of Hosea provides the most explicit biblical evidence for scaling between individual and corporate realities. God commands Hosea to marry Gomer, a promiscuous woman, specifically because "the land has committed great harlotry by departing from the Lord" (Hosea 1:2). This isn't a metaphor added later—God deliberately structures Hosea's personal marriage to embody Israel's corporate unfaithfulness. Throughout the book, the text moves fluidly between scales without explanation: "She is not My wife, nor am I her Husband" (2:2) applies simultaneously to both Gomer and Israel. The prophet never pauses to explain this correspondence because his audience already understood that individual marital dynamics revealed corporate covenant dynamics. When Hosea redeems his unfaithful wife (3:1–3), it simultaneously portrays God's redemption of unfaithful Israel. The prophetic message assumes—rather than argues for—the principle that patterns at one scale of reality illuminate patterns at another, demonstrating that scaling was native to Israelite thought rather than a later interpretive imposition.

This principle provides the coherence to biblical narratives by highlighting relational conflicts of authority. Every interaction involves a head (God or his mediator) and a body (the people). The story's outcomes make sense because they are directly tied to whether this divine structure is maintained or inverted. Blessing flows from proper order; chaos and judgment result from its breakdown. The tension arises from the conflict over sovereignty—Who is the rightful authority? Whose voice will be heeded? For example, Saul's downfall comes from violating this structural rule: "Saul said, 'I have sinned, for I have transgressed the commandment of the Lord and your words, because I feared the people and obeyed their voice'" (1 Sam 15:24). Authority is inverted, and the structure collapses.

## GRUMBLING ACROSS SCALES OF REALITY

Below are examples from the Bible from each scale of reality and how one can see commonality of the "grumbling" of each of the Eve figures in the story. We see this commonality in the stories of crisis, whether real or perceived by the Eve figure, leading to submission to their complaints. In each of these narratives, the pressure point is framed as death, creating urgency. It is under the shadow of death that order collapses. Their grumbling is a direct challenge to the authority God vested in their leaders, trying to overturn the hierarchy—highlighting how principles, being fractal patterns, work at all scales of reality.

### Person Scale of Reality

"Now Jacob cooked a stew; and Esau came in from the field, and he was weary. And Esau said to Jacob, 'Please feed me with that same red stew, for I am weary.' Therefore, his name was called Edom. But Jacob said, 'Sell me your birthright as of this day.' And Esau said, 'Look, I am about to die; so what is this birthright to me?'" (Gen 25:29–32). Esau allowed the grumbling of his body to convince him that the sustenance of the red stew was worth forgoing his birthright.

### Marital/Couple Scale of Reality

Samson and Delilah: "And it came to pass, when she pestered him daily with her words and pressed him, so that his soul was vexed to death, that he told her all his heart" (Judg 16:16–17).

The grumbling of Samson's wife, Delilah, persuaded Samson to share the secret of his strength, which led to his downfall.

### Corporate Scale of Reality

Moses and Aaron and Israel: "And all the children of Israel complained against Moses and Aaron, and the whole congregation said to them, 'If only we had died in the land of Egypt! Or if only we had died in this wilderness!'" (Num 14:2). The grumbling of the people of Israel led them to want to find a leader to return them to Egypt, which angers the Lord so much that he wants to send plagues upon Israel and dispossess them. Moses must intercede on their behalf to stop this and restore communion.

## DYNAMICS OF CORRUPTION: THE EVE FIGURE AND GRUMBLING

A recurring motif that we discussed earlier is that corruption spreads when the persistent "grumbling" leads the Adam figure to submit to earthly demands. These instances reflect an earthly instinct: when faced with a perceived crisis, the Eve figure seeks immediate solutions, often bypassing God's command. The Adam figure, if lacking discernment or spiritual vigilance, is vulnerable to yielding, especially when there is a crisis when one may seek to compromise to "fix" the situation.

Sarai and Rachel both illustrate this dynamic. Their barrenness produces frustration, and they attempt to resolve what only God can accomplish by directing Abraham and Jacob to act contrary to divine timing and instruction. Sarai directs Abraham to produce an heir through her maidservant Hagar; Rachel similarly instructs Jacob to father children through her maidservant Bilhah. The narratives emphasize the importance of prayer, patience, and reliance on God. Psalm 55:22 reminds us, "Cast your burden on the Lord, and He shall sustain you," and Phil 4:6–7 exhorts believers to present requests to God in supplication and thanksgiving. Failure to do so, as Sarai and Rachel demonstrate, leads to human schemes with lasting consequences. Likewise, the Adam figure is called to resist yielding to temporal or relational pressure, safeguarding sacred order and preventing further complications in family dynamics in the case of Sarai and Rachel.

## THE PROMISE OF BLESSING THROUGH OBEDIENCE

In *The Lost World of Adam and Eve*, John Walton emphasizes Adam's mediating priestly function as described in Genesis. He writes, "Adam's role must then be understood in light of the role of the priests in the ancient world. When we read the Bible, we often think of priests as ritual experts and as instructing the people in the ways of the Lord and the law. That is true, but those tasks fit into a larger picture. The main task of the priest was the preservation of sacred space."[2] Sacred space is the condition where divine presence and human communion align, characterized by order, stability, and life maintained through obedience. But how was this preservation to be accomplished? Through comprehending and faithfully applying the wisdom provided by God through obedience to divine commands. Adam was positioned as a gardener tending plants, but as a king and priest called to govern the earth and guide creation toward divine harmony and order. The scope of this calling becomes clear when we consider St. Gregory of Nyssa's insight: "But man's form is upright, and extends aloft towards heaven, and looks upwards: and these are marks of sovereignty which show his royal dignity."[3] This divine guidance for ordering the world in Gen 2 directly parallels the cosmic ordering in Gen 1, where God brought order out of chaos through his speech (Gen 1:3). The parallel is striking; God's act of ordering continues, but now it operates through human mediation.

Central to maintaining this sacred space was strict obedience to God's commands: "And the Lord God commanded the man, saying, 'Of every tree of the garden thou mayest freely eat: But of the tree of the knowledge of good and evil, thou shalt not eat of it: for in the day that thou eatest thereof thou shalt surely die'" (Gen 2:16–17). This command was not arbitrary but fundamental to Adam's mediatorial function—it required trust in divine

2. Walton, *Lost World*, 108.

3. Gregory of Nyssa, *St. Gregory of Nyssa*, 542.

wisdom that transcended human understanding. The test would reveal whether Adam would operate through faith in God's guidance or through reliance on his own finite perception.

The blessings one receives when maintaining obedience to God are consistently reinforced throughout the Bible. The clearest statement of this principle appears in Deuteronomy: "Now it shall come to pass, if you diligently obey the voice of the Lord your God, to observe carefully all His commandments which I command you today, that the Lord your God will set you high above all the nations of the earth. And all these blessings shall come upon you and overtake you, because you obey the voice of the Lord your God" (Deut 28:1–2). For the blessing to occur, we can now see how to apply this instruction to the particular scale of reality, giving these stories profound meaning. This passage allowed the Israelites then—and allows us now—to have a lens through which to understand the stories of the Old Testament, offering clear guidance on how God interacts with humanity at all scales of reality (individual, relationship, group) and how one should respond with freedom. The Deuteronomic principle reveals that blessing is not arbitrary divine favoritism, but the natural result of aligning human will with God's.

When Adam figures faithfully steward their responsibilities and Eve figures faithfully fulfill their supportive roles, the result is flourishing at every level—personal wholeness, relational harmony, social justice, and national prosperity. Disobedience to God leads to disordered relationships at all scales of reality. These consequences follow naturally from the disruption of proper ordering, just as health follows from proper bodily function and sickness from dysfunction. At every scale of reality depicted in the Bible, we encounter distinct masculine and feminine characters or archetypes, each endowed with specific roles within their relational dynamics. These roles are not arbitrary; they fundamentally shape how these figures are meant to act within the narrative and significantly contribute to the story's greater theological and relational themes, all reflecting aspects of the original divine design. For Christians today our goal is to enter God's kingdom. "Thus, the kingdom of God is the content of the Christian faith—the goal, the meaning and the content of the Christian life."[4] To understand why the Adam figure is so vulnerable to this pressure in the first place, we must go deeper than the structural pattern and ask what was damaged in Adam himself when the breakdown occurred.

4. Schmemann, *Eucharist*, 40.

## THE BREATH, THE NOUS, AND THE FALL

When God formed Adam from the dust of the ground, he did not leave him as mere clay. "The Lord God formed man of dust from the ground, and breathed into his nostrils the breath of life; and man became a living soul" (Gen 2:7). This divine breath was not only biological animation but spiritual illumination: it integrated the human nous with divine life, enabling Adam to perceive God's will beyond his initial generic commands of "tend and keep " the garden (Gen 2:15) and "be fruitful and multiply" (Gen 1:28), Adam can now mediate between Creator and creation, ordering his setting accordingly. The nous, when functioning properly, served as the faculty of spiritual perception through which Adam aligned with God's will, ordered creation, and transmitted divine wisdom into the world. Thus, Adam began as a faithful mediator. He named the animals, exercised stewardship, and dwelt in harmony with Eve and with the garden sanctuary. His nous was clear, receptive, and oriented toward God's voice. The divine breath animated not only his body but also his highest faculty, enabling heart-centered perception of truth.

But when Adam and Eve turned from divine command to the serpent's counsel, "heeding to the voice" of that which is lower in the hierarchy and eating the fruit, this breath-illumined faculty became darkened. The nous, once attuned to divine initiative, was displaced to autonomous reasoning and sensory judgment. In *Patristic Theology*, Romanides writes, "The Fathers teach that with the Fall, the human nous became darkened. Adam's nous became darkened. The Fathers are not concerned with Adam per se, but with Adam's nous and the sickness that followed from the darkening of his nous. The Fathers speak about a nous void of understanding. Throughout Patristic literature, the whole issue of the Fall centers on this darkening of the human nous."[5] Deceived by appearances and seduced by serpent logic, they ceased to receive knowledge through faith and sought it through disordered desire and one's own reasoning. The result was corruption: separation from God, disintegration of relationships, and eventual exile from sacred space. From this moment forward, humanity's great tragedy has been the darkening of the nous. The very faculty meant to perceive God became clouded, leaving man vulnerable to serpent-like reduction, reduced from mediator to deceived, from steward to exile, from participant in divine life to mortal dust.

5. Romanides, *Patristic Theology*, 32.

## APPLICATION—BIBLE STUDY

Every biblical story becomes an exploration of the same fundamental dynamics:

- Who serves as the Adam figure (authority/leadership role)?
- Who serves as the Eve figure (supportive/responsive role)?
- Is divine wisdom being transmitted faithfully downward?
- Are ground-level realities being communicated faithfully upward?
- Where do role reversals or authority breakdowns occur?
- What are the consequences of proper or improper ordering?
- Is this a personal failure only or also a failure of office?

## CONCLUSION

Having established how the Adam and Eve principle operates across different scales of reality, we can now understand what happens when this divine ordering fails. The same pattern that produced consequences in Eden—leaders yielding to pressure from those they're meant to guide—appears consistently throughout biblical history with equally devastating results. This fractal nature reveals a deeper unity within Scripture: the same relational dynamics appear across countless stories. True biblical authority exists to serve God's purposes, not personal agendas, and leaders who demand obedience to their preferences rather than divine commands have themselves become corrupted "Adam figures." Subordinates have both the right and responsibility to challenge authority that contradicts Scripture, following the pattern of Nathan confronting David or Paul opposing Peter. A healthy application requires discerning the difference between pressure that moves us away from God's revealed will and correction that calls us back to it. Leaders who understand this distinction welcome accountability that supports their faithfulness to God rather than their comfort or convenience. To see this principle in action, we now turn to Abraham, whose journey from failure to faith reveals how proper ordering restores communion with God.

# 3

# Abraham as an Adam Figure

ABRAHAM, AS THE PATRIARCH, is known for his faithfulness to God by leaving his homeland at an advanced age. "Abraham's abandonment of Mesopotamia for the Land of Canaan marks the beginning of the history of the chosen people."[1] He acts as an example of the beginning of a "return to the garden" in the sense that he is the first protagonist in the Bible to move westward towards the promised land, rather than eastward, where Adam and Eve, Cain, and others will be exiled, highlighting Abraham as an Adam figure. Yet Abraham's path to faithful mediation began with failure, making his eventual success all the more instructive for readers.

Abraham did not always perform his mediatorial role correctly. When Sarah remained barren despite God's promise of descendants, she pressured her husband toward an earthly solution: "So Sarai said to Abram, 'See now, the Lord has restrained me from bearing children. Please, go in to my maid; perhaps I shall obtain children by her.' And Abram heeded the voice of Sarai" (Gen 16:2). The phrase "heeded the voice" deliberately echoes Adam's failure in Gen 3:17: "Because you have heeded the voice of your wife, and have eaten from the tree of which I commanded you." Abraham yielded to Sarah's impatient scheme rather than trusting God's timing. The result was Ishmael's birth through Hagar the Egyptian, creating lasting conflict between Isaac's and Ishmael's descendants that continues to this

1. Adar, *Biblical Narrative*, 109.

day. What seemed like a practical solution to an earthly problem actually represented distrust in divine promise and abandonment of the mediator's responsibility to maintain faith when human understanding falters.

When God later commanded Abraham to send Hagar and Ishmael away at Sarah's insistence (Gen 21:12), Abraham initially resisted, since "the matter was very displeasing in Abraham's sight because of his son" (Gen 21:11). But God's direct intervention taught Abraham a crucial distinction: Sarah's earlier pressure to take Hagar violated divine wisdom, while her later insistence on protecting Isaac's covenant inheritance aligned with it. Abraham learned through costly experience to discern which wifely counsel reflected heavenly wisdom and which reflected earthly expediency.

## ABRAHAM'S FEAST: SACRED SPACE AND DIVINE BLESSING

We see that when three mysterious visitors appeared at Mamre, Abraham had always strived to maintain faithful mediation. His actions serve as a model for how divine messengers should be honored and treated. "Then the Lord appeared to Abraham by the terebinth trees of Mamre, where he sat at the entrance of his tent in the heat of the day. When Abraham looked up, he saw three men standing nearby. He quickly ran from the tent entrance to meet them, bowed low to the ground, and said, 'My Lord, if I have found favor in Your sight, please do not pass by Your servant. Let a little water be brought so that you may wash your feet and rest under the tree. I will bring a morsel of bread to refresh your hearts. Afterward, you may continue on your way, since you have come to your servant.' And they replied, 'Do as you have said'" (Gen 18:1–5). Abraham treats the divine messengers as honored guests, showing respect and hospitality.

Importantly, he maintains his mediatorial authority throughout the encounter. He directs Sarah's preparation for the communion: "So Abraham hurried into the tent to Sarah and said, 'Quickly, make ready three measures of fine meal; knead it and make cakes'" (Gen 18:6). He does not allow his wife to decide how they will treat these visitors but ensures that her actions align with his direction—a stark contrast to his earlier failure with Hagar. Sarah, who had learned alongside her husband through their shared failures and divine corrections, faithfully listens to Abraham and fulfills her role as his helpmate, helping to create a sacred space of communion with God.

The yield due to this proper ordering came swiftly. "And He said, 'I will certainly return to you according to the time of life, and behold, Sarah your wife shall have a son'" (Gen 18:10). Abraham's faith, combined with Sarah's obedience in this moment, produced the covenant child who would carry God's promises to all nations. The feast that honored divine presence became the occasion for new life—the very promise they had once tried to secure through their own schemes with Hagar now arriving through patient faithfulness and proper ordering. When Abraham's understanding faltered—questioning how Sarah, being elderly, could bear a child—he relied on faith. This alignment of proper authority structure with faith in divine promise exemplifies what the Adam figure is called to perform.

## HEROD'S WICKED FEAST: CORRUPTED SPACE AND DIVINE JUDGMENT

The wicked feast of Herod, which resulted in the murder of God's divine messenger, John the Baptist, starkly contrasts with the feast hosted by Abraham. As a mediator and prophet in Israel, John serves as the divine messenger of heavenly wisdom, fulfilling the prophecy: "As it is written in the Prophets: 'Behold, I send My messenger before Your face, Who will prepare Your way before You'" (Mark 1:2). This verse emphasizes that it is God who sends his messenger to Israel, which highlights the title given to John in the church: the "Heavenly Messenger."

John's ministry concludes with his imprisonment and martyrdom at the hands of Herod Antipas. In the story of John's murder, we encounter another Adam and Eve type-scene. Herod, a tetrarch and leader, represents an Adam figure—one who was meant to faithfully guide Israel, as he was a practicing Jew. Instead, Herod imprisons John for rebuking him, treating God's heavenly messenger in a way that is unbefitting anyone who seeks to remain in God's favor.

Interestingly, Herod initially feared John and refused to allow harm to come to him, even though his wife, Herodias, wanted him killed for rebuking Herod's marriage to her—since she had originally been married to Herod's brother. "Therefore, Herodias held it against him [John] and wanted to kill him, but she could not; for Herod feared John, knowing that he was a just and holy man, and he protected him. And when he heard him, he did many things, and heard him gladly" (Mark 6:19–20). Like Abraham, who knew God's promise yet wavered under Sarah's pressure with Hagar, and like Adam, who knew God's command yet wavered under Eve's influence, Herod understood righteousness yet remained vulnerable to his wife's corrupted counsel. Herod allowed himself to play the role of a flawed Adam figure by yielding to his wife, Herodias, letting her dictate his actions during the feast with the leaders of Galilee. "Then, on an opportune day, Herod held a feast for his nobles, the high officers, and the chief men of Galilee to celebrate his birthday. When Herodias' daughter entered and danced, pleasing both Herod and those who reclined with him, the king said to the girl, 'Ask me for whatever you want, and I will give it to you.' He also swore to her, 'Whatever you ask, I will give you, up to half my kingdom'" (Mark 6:21–23).

Herod acted foolishly when he allowed himself to be seduced by Herodias' daughter, granting her the power to ask for anything. So she went out and asked her mother, "What shall I ask for?" Her mother replied, "The head of John the Baptist!" Immediately, she returned to the king in haste and requested, "I want you to give me at once the head of John the Baptist on a platter." The king was deeply distressed; yet, because of his oaths and the presence of those who sat with him, he did not want to refuse her. Without hesitation, the king sent an executioner to behead John in prison. The executioner brought his head on a platter and gave it to the girl (Mark 6:24–28).

Despite it being against his wishes, Herod complied with the request, had John killed, and cruelly brought his head to the feast, presenting it to his stepdaughter and in front of all the "nobles, the high officers, and the chief men of Galilee" (Mark 6:21), highlighting how all those that make up the head of Galilee were corrupt. Unlike Abraham, who learned from his failure with Hagar and eventually discerned which wifely counsel served God's purposes, Herod never progressed beyond that moment of yielding. He remained stuck in the pattern of the first Adam, yielding to the wrong voice and reaping death rather than life.

## THE PATTERN REVEALED THROUGH CONTRAST

The Abraham-Herod comparison provides us with contrasting models for how Adam figures respond when tested through hospitality and the influence of their wives.

Abraham's feast:

- Ran to greet the divine messenger with reverence
- Directed wife's preparation of the meal
- Created sacred space for communion with God
- Received blessing: Isaac's promised birth

Herod's feast:

- Imprisoned a divine messenger despite recognizing his holiness
- Yielded to wife's manipulation through her daughter
- Desecrated celebration with murder
- Received judgment: military defeat as divine punishment

Abraham's journey demonstrates that the Adam figure can fail, learn through consequences, and eventually succeed in proper mediation. In the next chapter, we will see how different failures have different levels of severity. By the time heavenly visitors arrived at Mamre, he had learned to maintain proper authority structure while receiving and properly weighing counsel. He welcomed the visitors and instructed Sarah, she obeyed, and God blessed their household with the covenant child they had been promised.

Herod's tragedy lies in allowing an authority breakdown, which got an innocent man murdered. Despite knowing John was "a just and holy man," despite hearing him gladly and protecting him from Herodias initially, Herod ultimately inverted the proper structure when pressure intensified. Herodias determined the outcome through her daughter's manipulative request; Herod obeyed despite his conscience to save face before his assembled nobles, and judgment followed. The historian Josephus records that "some of the Jews thought that the destruction of Herod's army came from God, and that very justly, as punishment of what Herod did against John, that was called the Baptist."[2] This stands in stark contrast to how one should treat a divine messenger: as a guest, with respect, and through proper ordering of household relationships that honor God's authority structure.

The Adam and Eve principle operates through proper ordering: when the head maintains divine wisdom and directs the body faithfully—even after learning through earlier failures, like Abraham—sacred space emerges

2. Josephus, *Complete Works*, 581.

and communion with God happens. When the head repeatedly abdicates authority to corrupted influence without ever developing discernment, like Herod, death enters even festive occasions meant for celebration.

## FOREIGN INFLUENCE AND COVENANT LOYALTY

Both narratives involve foreign women whose allegiances proved significant for the outcomes. Hagar the Egyptian became the instrument of Abraham and Sarah's impatient scheme, producing Ishmael and lasting conflict between his descendants and Isaac's. Yet when Sarah later insisted that "the son of this bondwoman shall not be heir with my son, namely with Isaac" (Gen 21:10), God validated her mature discernment: "In all that Sarah has said to you, listen to her voice; for in Isaac your seed shall be called" (Gen 21:12). Sarah's earlier mistake with the foreign woman Hagar had taught her vigilance against foreign influence that could compromise Isaac's covenant inheritance. This is a rare instance of God's direct intervention between husband and wife, and many have wondered why God would agree with Sarah's seemingly harsh request. But Sarah's actions were aimed at ensuring Abraham's destiny was fulfilled, even in a way that Abraham initially struggled to follow. Therefore, God intervened appropriately and providentially.

Herod's marriage to Herodias highlights a recurring biblical theme: leaders marrying foreign women to the detriment of themselves and Israel. Herodias, a foreigner from Idumea, was not a practicing Jew. In obliging her request, Herod ordered the execution of John, the divine messenger to Israel, further exposing the backwardness of his rule. Throughout the Bible, obeying the desires of foreign wives—such as seen with Samson and Delilah, King Solomon and his foreign wives, King Ahab and Jezebel—leads to ruin. This pattern is evident, as a foreign wife may hold allegiances that do not align with her husband's or his people's. A foreign wife who does not share your faith in God will not comply with the commands a husband has received from God.

## BIBLICAL EXAMPLES OF ADAM FIGURES YIELDING TO CORRUPTED EVE FIGURES

1. Aaron and the people (Exod 32:1): When the Israelites demand a golden calf, Aaron yields, creating an idol and defiling the covenant. The Adam figure's role as priest is to mediate God's will, maintain sacred order, and resist corrupting influences. By failing in this responsibility, Aaron allows the collective Eve figure—the people's impatience—to dictate actions contrary to divine command.
2. Samson and Delilah (Judg 16:16–17): Delilah's repeated persuasion eventually compels Samson to disclose the secret of his strength. Samson, despite his role as God's chosen judge, yields to personal desire and relational pressure, demonstrating how the Adam figure can be led astray by corrupted human influence.
3. Jacob and Rachel (Gen 25:29–32; 30:1–2): Rachel's barrenness and her plea to Jacob demonstrate the recurring dynamic of a corrupted Eve figure pressing the Adam figure to intervene in divine matters. When she exclaims, "Give me children, or else I die!" Jacob responds, "Am I in the place of God?" (Gen 30:2). Rachel then instructs Jacob to father children with her maid Bilhah, echoing Sarai's earlier action.
4. Saul and the people (1 Sam 15:24): Saul explicitly acknowledges that he sinned because he "feared the people and obeyed their voice." As an Adam figure, Saul's role as king and mediator of God's covenant required him to uphold divine instruction over popular demand. His failure underscores the principle that fear of human judgment can easily usurp reverence for God, a pattern repeated throughout biblical history.
5. Solomon and his wives (1 Kgs 11:4): Even Solomon, endowed with divine wisdom, succumbs to the influence of his wives, turning his heart toward other gods. The narrative illustrates how spiritual vulnerability is amplified when relational attachment overrides obedience.
6. Esther and King Xerxes (Esth 5:3): "And the king said to her, 'What do you wish, Queen Esther? What is your request? It shall be given to you—up to half the kingdom!'" Esther, in contrast, exemplifies the use of this pattern for the benefit of Israel. She engages the king strategically, aligned with God's plan to save Israel.

These failures demonstrate that the Adam and Eve principle functions as both explanation and prediction. When we see leaders abandoning divine instruction under pressure from their followers—whether Aaron with the people, Saul with popular opinion, or Solomon with his wives' religious influences—we can anticipate the same pattern of consequences that began in Eden. Understanding this pattern helps identify when biblical narratives are building toward breakdown and judgment, revealing the consistent principles governing God's interaction with humanity across all scales of reality, giving rigor and predictability to these stories. Yet it also points toward the appearance of the one Adam figure who will succeed completely where all previous Adam figures have failed or succeeded only partially, maintaining obedience, restoring communion with God. This prepares us to see how Christ emerges as the perfect Second Adam. These Genesis patterns provide the essential background of the temptations he faced.

## CONCLUSION

The Adam and Eve principle appears dozens of times throughout Scripture, highlighting how the Bible highlights the roles every character embodies. Likewise, we today should understand the roles and relationships we participate in and ensure we remain faithful to God. This approach helped transform my Bible reading from mere information gathering into pattern recognition across all stories, which enables both understanding and application.

# 4

# Ordering Through Naming

## The Adam Figure's Discernment

THE EARLY CHAPTERS OF Genesis offer profound insights into the nature of humanity and its relationship with the divine. A key theme that emerges is the concept of "ordering" through speech. Adam, as both the first man and a mediator between God and creation, exemplifies this in his setting, using his voice like God. This pattern is first established in God's own ordering of the cosmos through speech in Gen 1. "God called the light Day, and the darkness he called Night. And the evening and the morning were the first day" (Gen 1:5). Adam's task, then, is presented as an extension of this divine ordering in Gen 2:18–20: "Out of the ground the Lord God formed every beast of the field and every bird of the air, and brought them to Adam to see what he would call them. And whatever Adam called each living creature, that was its name. So Adam gave names to all cattle, to the birds of the air, and to every beast of the field. But for Adam there was not found a helper comparable to him" (Gen 2:18–20). The text deliberately highlights this parallel between God and Adam. In Gen 2:19, when God brings the animals to Adam, the Septuagint uses the Greek word *καleo* for "called," precisely the same word used for God's naming actions in Gen 1.

Adam's primary role as a mediator was to bring divine order to creation. This is demonstrated most clearly in his God-given task of naming the animals. This was not a simple act of labeling but an exercise of discernment: "That was its name." This establishes Adam's discerning capabilities before the fall, making his later failure more potent. This act is far more than a simple cataloging; it is an exercise of wisdom and discernment that mirrors God's own creative declarations.

The ancient world, and the biblical narrative, understood naming as an act that revealed the very essence and character of a thing. As the *Holman Illustrated Bible Dictionary* explains, "The biblical concept of naming was rooted in the ancient world's understanding that a name expressed essence. To know the name of a person was to know that person's total character and nature."[1] Adam's subsequent naming of the animals was not just creating a unique sound for each animal but a demonstration of his innate ability to perceive and articulate the unique character and identity of each creature, participating in ordering reality. Fr. Alexander Schmemann aptly emphasizes in *For the Life of the World*, "In the Bible, a name is infinitely more than a means of distinguishing one thing from another. It reveals the very essence of a thing, or rather its essence as God's gift. To name a thing is to manifest the meaning and value God gave it, to know it as coming from God, and to know its place and function within the cosmos created by God."[2] This act of naming, intrinsically linked to speech, projects wisdom and understanding into the world, aligning human agency with divine precedent.

The principle of naming operates directionally: you receive your name from what is above you in the hierarchy; you give names to what is below you. Adam received his identity from God. Adam named the animals beneath him. Adam named Eve as his counterpart. When this direction inverts—when creatures name themselves or demand to name what is above them—authority collapses.

This is why "let us make a name for ourselves" (Gen 11:4) captures Babel's character. They weren't just building a tower; they were claiming the prerogative that belongs only to God. Self-naming is self-determination. Every time God renames someone in Scripture (Abram to Abraham, Jacob to Israel, Simon to Peter), he is restoring proper authority flow: identity received from above, not claimed from below.

1. Brand et al., *Holman Illustrated Bible Dictionary*, 1145.

2. Schmemann, *For the Life*, 15.

## ADAM ACQUIRES A WIFE AND NAMES HER "WOMAN" (GEN 2:23)

Adam's ordering authority was not limited to the animal kingdom; it extended to his divinely appointed wife. God, recognizing Adam's need for a truly comparable helper, created a woman: "And the Lord God caused a deep sleep to fall on Adam, and he slept; and He took one of his ribs and closed up the flesh in its place. Then the rib which the Lord God had taken from man He made into a woman, and He brought her to the man" (Gen 2:22). Eve's creation from Adam's side powerfully symbolizes their intrinsic unity and mutual dependence. It highlights their shared, yet bifurcated, nature as humanity's progenitors—the masculine and feminine aspects, each with distinct inclinations, roles, and functions within the world.

Next, Adam declares, "This is now bone of my bones and flesh of my flesh; she shall be called Woman because she was taken out of Man" (Gen 2:23). Again, the Septuagint text uses *καleo* for "called," highlighting how Adam not only named the animals but his wife as well. Together, Adam and Eve are tasked with fulfilling God's initial command to "be fruitful and multiply; fill the earth and subdue it" (Gen 1:28). As inheritors of God's image, they are to continue his ordering and stewardship responsibly, a command that inherently carried an evangelistic aspect within creation, extending God's presence and order.

As Adam's wife and helpmate, Eve was to understand the profound significance of her name in preserving and maintaining the sacred space of the garden. She was the rightful counterpart, a role the animals could not fulfill precisely because they were incapable of providing the nuanced feedback Adam needed as he carried out the ordering process.

This feedback from Eve was crucial for refreshing the sacred space, aligning their stewardship more closely with God's command to "tend and keep" the garden (Gen 2:15). Eve would help Adam by offering insight and feedback, ensuring his work remained aligned with God's instructions while responding to new circumstances.

This pattern applies to the church today: members must communicate challenges to their leaders, while leaders must provide wise guidance. Simultaneously, the church must listen to and obey the guidance of these leaders to be refreshed and maintain communion with God. The woman, as the helpmate, actively assists her husband in addressing the dynamic challenges within their sacred domain. The command "to tend and keep" implies a continuous striving for perfection and improvement, rather than a static maintenance. Eve's initial name, "Woman," thus signifies her foundational role as a helpmate, sustainer, and essential counterpart to man.

## THE REESTABLISHING OF AUTHORITY: EVE'S RENAMING

Once Eve ate the forbidden fruit, she effectively severed her union with both God and Adam. By disobeying the commands—both God's original one and Adam's transmitted instruction—she compromised Adam's authority over her. This breach necessitated God's reestablishment of that authority. When God confronted Adam and Eve regarding their disobedience, part of Eve's curse was the declaration "Your desire shall be for your husband, and he shall rule over you" (Gen 3:16). This pronouncement directly reasserted Adam's headship.

Following this, in Gen 3:20, Adam renames his wife: "And Adam called his wife's name Eve because she was the mother of all living." The *IVP Bible Background Commentary* highlights the profound significance of this renaming: "Here his naming of Eve suggests Adam's position of rule, as referred to in verse 16. In the ancient world, when one king placed a vassal king on the throne, a new name would often be given to demonstrate the overlord's dominion."[3] Eve's initial role as an ideal helpmate, providing discerning feedback for the "tending and keeping" of the garden, was diminished by the fall. Her new desire for her husband, coupled with his reaffirmed rule over her, became a defining characteristic of her post-fall existence, and her new name, "Eve," underscored her primary function as the "mother of all living."

Renaming is throughout the Old Testament, signifying a shift in status, identity, or authority. For instance, God renamed Abram to Abraham (Gen 17:5) and Sarai to Sarah (Gen 17:15) as he established his covenant and authority over them, commanding Abraham to "keep my covenant, you and your descendants after you throughout their generations" (Gen 17:9). Similarly, Pharaoh renamed Joseph "Zaphnath-Paaneah" when appointing him over Egypt, signifying Joseph's new authority and position within the kingdom (Gen 41:45). When Daniel and his companions were taken to Babylon, they were given new Babylonian names—Belteshazzar, Shadrach, Meshach, and Abed-Nego—by the chief of the eunuchs, a symbolic act of authority and assimilation (Dan 1:6–7). In these instances, the renamed

3. Walton and Matthews, *IVP Bible Background Commentary*, 22.

individuals, like Joseph and Daniel, faithfully served their new authorities, gaining favor and proving instrumental in their respective kingdoms.

In the context of Adam and Eve, the renaming of "Woman" to "Eve" symbolizes a similar shift in their relational dynamic post-fall. While Eve's role as helpmate remained, its character was altered, now framed within a reestablished hierarchy. The biblical narrative frequently illustrates women providing feedback to male mediators. This feedback often leads to a change in the mediator's approach, allowing the Adam figure to gain a better understanding of the earthly situation and to perform his ordering more effectively. However, the tragedy of the fall is that this dynamic, which was intended to be harmonious and aligned with God's will, became complicated by sin, leading to the reassertion of hierarchical rule that characterizes the fallen world.

## THE SERPENT: NAMED, KNOWN, AND CUNNING IN CHARACTER

As Adam named all the animals, this ordering he performed gave him insight into their character and dominion over them (Gen 1:26–28). Many assume Adam did not name or exercise dominion over the serpent. However, the Scriptures clearly indicate otherwise. Genesis 2:20 states, "So Adam gave names to all cattle, to the birds of the air, and to every beast of the field." Genesis 3:1 then introduces the serpent by stating, "Now the serpent was more cunning than any beast of the field which the Lord God had made." The repetition of "beast of the field" strongly reinforces that the serpent was among the creatures Adam named and, crucially, that Adam understood its character.

Adam, therefore, named the serpent in a way that revealed its very essence, its deceptive nature. The *NKJV Cultural Backgrounds Study Bible* adds that "the giving of a name is an act of discernment in which the name is determined by the circumstances."[4] These insights confirm that Adam named the serpent with profound discernment, recognizing its deceptive nature.

The Bible frequently uses serpent imagery to depict venomous treachery. "Their wine is the poison of serpents, And the cruel venom of cobras" (Deut 32:33) and "The wicked are estranged from the womb; They go astray as soon as they are born, speaking lies. Their poison is like the poison of a

4. Keener and Walton, *NKJV Cultural Backgrounds*, 11.

serpent" (Ps 58:3–4) illustrate how the physical poison of serpents symbolizes the destructive nature of lies and false teachings. Genesis emphasizes the serpent's cunning, and Adam's naming reflected this inherent truth, a fact implicitly acknowledged by God. The identification of the serpent as a symbol of deception and evil is a recurring motif throughout the Bible, culminating in the book of Revelation, where it is explicitly named as Satan, the devil: "And the great dragon was cast out, that old serpent, called the Devil, and Satan, which deceiveth the whole world" (Rev 12:9). This verse powerfully links the deceiver from Genesis to the ultimate antagonist in the final drama of salvation history, underscoring his consistent role. Satan is also known as the accuser, one who seeks to sow division and separation among God's people.

This naming was valid because God brought the animals to Adam, and "whatever Adam called each living creature, that was its name" (Gen 2:19). The serpent's subsequent lie to Eve, "You shall not die" (Gen 3:4), which was proven false by Eve's eventual death, confirms the accuracy of Adam's naming. This suggests that God trusted Adam's discernment, confident that the properly named serpent would not deceive him directly in the garden. God had already equipped Adam with the command and the capacity to name. Adam possessed both the law (Don't eat) and the definition (This is a deceiver). He needed no further warning; he needed only to stand his ground. Nikolai Velimirović, in *The Universe as Symbols and Signs*, states, "For sinless Adam in Paradise was perfectly able to comprehend the sense and significance of all creation. He possessed the capacity to give every animal the very name which represented it symbolically."[5]

Adam's earlier naming of the serpent, as he named all animals, established an order that he himself violated when he ate the fruit. This context explains why God's question later of "Where are you?" (Gen 3:9) carries such weight. It's not asking for location but for accountability: Why aren't you at your post? Why aren't you maintaining the tending and keeping I commanded you? Adam has abandoned his priestly role, allowing chaos (the serpent) to corrupt order (Eve and the garden). His failure isn't passive but a failure of performance.

A parallel can be seen when the Israelites in Exod 32. When Moses goes up to the mountain to be with God, the people are left in Aaron's care, but after forty days, they and Aaron decide to make the golden calf. When Moses returns, he immediately asks Aaron a priestly question—"And Moses

5. Velimirović, *Universe as Symbols*, 13.

said to Aaron, "What did this people do to you that you have brought so great a sin upon them?" (Exod 32:2)—meaning Aaron had failed in his duty. Next, the text called the people unrestrained (Exod 32:25), highlighting this failure of Aaron to maintain the order, to guard the people (Eve figure) from chaos and disorder. Aaron's response to Israel's demand for a golden calf exemplifies this breakdown at the corporate scale. When the people pressured him, saying, "Come, make us gods who will go before us" (Exod 32:1), Aaron faced the same choice Adam encountered: maintain divine instruction or yield to those he was meant to lead.

Like Adam, Aaron chose to "heed the voice" of his followers rather than God's clear commands. The consequences mirrored Eden—broken communion with God, divine anger, and death entering the community. Saul's confession in 1 Sam 15:24 reveals the same dynamic: "I have sinned, for I have transgressed the commandment of the Lord . . . because I feared the people and obeyed their voice." The king, serving as Israel's Adam figure, prioritized popular pressure over divine command, resulting in his rejection and the kingdom's eventual division.

A law, like the naming Adam performed, is only as good as the righteous people who follow it. So, Adam betrayed himself as well as God, which is hypocrisy and self-destructive. This knowledge transforms Adam's sin from a simple act of disobedience into a profound failure of his priestly office—a failure to protect the sacred space and the person entrusted to his care from a threat he had already identified. Paul makes this explicit when he writes, "And Adam was not deceived, but the woman being deceived, fell into transgression" (1 Tim 2:14). This Adamic role of discerning essence and naming reality did not end in Genesis. It established a pattern that finds its ultimate fulfillment in the New Testament, where Christ, the Second Adam, and his forerunner, John the Baptist, perform this same sacred act of ordering. The serpent's deception succeeded not through force but through perceptual manipulation—making the forbidden fruit "good for food, pleasing to the eye, and desirable for wisdom" (Gen 3:6). This sequence—seeing, judging, taking—establishes a pattern of temptation that recurs throughout Scripture, where disordered perception leads to disordered action.

## THE SIGNIFICANCE OF SIGHT AND THE SEARCH FOR A HELPER

A crucial detail in the narrative is that God brought the animals to Adam to see (Gen 2:19), meaning to inspect or perceive. Adam's perceptive abilities in the garden were unblemished, and God affirmed the names he bestowed, suggesting a perfect alignment between Adam's discernment and divine truth. This passage also emphasizes that while all animals were created to assist Adam, none were "comparable" to him. They could not provide the intellectual and relational feedback necessary to complete him, which God reinforced when he said it was not good when Adam was alone (Gen 2:18). They could not, for instance, offer a discerning perspective on his naming or actions.

This theme of "seeing" and its connection to discernment introduces a critical pattern. Throughout biblical narratives, characters often "see" something that appears good or pleasant in their own eyes, needing them to discern whether it is good. This underscores that faith is paramount when our limited perception cannot fully grasp a situation, acting as our greatest defense against deception. Our sense of sight, therefore, plays a unique and powerful role in our journey of understanding and discernment. The recurring motif of protagonists using their sight to make critical decisions is not an arbitrary coincidence. It serves as a narrative instruction: in moments where our understanding presents something as pleasant or good but it contradicts God's will, we must overcome the temptation to rely solely on our own perception and remain faithful to God.

The profound consequences of Eve's lack of deeper understanding concerning the "pleasant" looking fruit serve as a timeless warning. These narratives instruct believers to exercise faith over sight when facing temptation. If Adam possessed the discernment to recognize that no animal qualified as a suitable helper (Gen 3:20), requiring God to create Eve, then his capacity for accurate perception was well-established before the fall. This makes his encounter with the serpent more significant: Adam had demonstrated the ability to discern truth, yet failed to exercise this capacity when it mattered most.

## SEEING, JUDGING, AND TAKING: A BIBLICAL PATTERN OF TEMPTATION AND FAITH

A recurring theme in the Bible is how humans are drawn into sin through a familiar sequence: first seeing, then judging it good in their own eyes, and finally taking. This pattern illustrates a fundamental tension between human desire and God's will. What may appear desirable or advantageous to us is not always pleasing to God. Understanding this dynamic helps illuminate the moral lessons threaded throughout Scripture.

The story of Eve provides the earliest and most striking example: "So when the woman saw that the tree was good for food, that it was pleasant to the eyes, and a tree desirable to make one wise, she took of its fruit and ate. She also gave it to her husband with her, and he ate" (Gen 3:6). Eve's choice demonstrates the threefold pattern of temptation: she saw the fruit, decided it was good, and took it, ultimately disobeying God. Her lapse sets a paradigm for all human temptation. Patrick Reardon notes, "Her temptation serves as a kind of paradigm of all temptation; Eve stands as the Bible's first negative model of the moral life; her lapse provides the initial description of how the demons deal with the human soul."[6]

The Scriptures consistently reinforce the principle that human perception is fallible, and faith must guide action: "Trust in the Lord with all your heart, and lean not on your own understanding; in all your ways acknowledge Him, and He shall direct your paths. Do not be wise in your own eyes; fear the Lord and depart from evil" (Prov 3:5–7). And as Paul states, "For we walk by faith, not by sight" (2 Cor 5:7). Walking by faith, rather than by sight, allows humans to overcome temptation. Jesus exemplifies this principle perfectly, resisting all worldly enticements through obedience to God. Across Scripture, this same sequence—seeing, judging by human standards, and taking—recurs in numerous narratives, demonstrating both human vulnerability and the need for divine guidance.

## EXAMPLES FROM SCRIPTURE OF THOSE WHO SAW, THOUGHT GOOD IN THEIR EYES, AND TOOK

- Lot choosing Sodom (Gen 13:10–11): "And Lot lifted up his eyes and saw all the plain of Jordan, that it was well watered everywhere (before the Lord destroyed Sodom and Gomorrah) like the garden of the

6. Reardon, *Creation*, 41.

Lord, like the land of Egypt as you go toward Zoar. Then Lot chose for himself all the plain of Jordan, and Lot journeyed east."

- Abram and Sarai: "'See now, the Lord has restrained me from bearing children. Please, go into my maid; perhaps I shall obtain children by her.' And Abram heeded the voice of Sarai" (Gen 16:2).
- Rachel and the mandrakes (Gen 30:14–16): "Now Reuben went in the days of wheat harvest and found mandrakes in the field, and brought them to his mother Leah. Then Rachel said to Leah, 'Please give me some of your son's mandrakes.' But she said to her, 'Is it a small matter that you have taken away my husband? Would you take away my son's mandrakes also?' And Rachel said, 'Therefore he will lie with you tonight for your son's mandrakes.'"
- Judah: "Then he turned to her by the way, and said, 'Please let me come in to you;' for he did not know that she was his daughter-in-law. . . . 'What will you give me, that you may come in to me?'" (Gen 38:15–16).
- Shechem: Impulsively acting on desire, Shechem seizes Dinah, violating her: "And when Shechem . . . saw her [Dinah], he took her and lay with her, and violated her" (Gen 34:2).
- Achan's confession of taking the plunder: "When I saw among the plunder a beautiful robe . . . and two hundred shekels of silver and a bar of gold . . . I coveted them and took them" (Josh 7:21).
- Samson: Samson's attraction to a harlot leads him astray: "Now Samson went to Gaza and saw a harlot there, and went in to her" (Judg 16:1).
- Saul: The first king of Israel misjudges what is valuable, sparing what he deems good but disobeying God's command: "But Saul and the people spared Agag and the best of the sheep, the oxen. . . . But everything despised and worthless, that they utterly destroyed" (1 Sam 15:9).
- David: David's desire for Bathsheba begins with merely seeing her, escalating to sin through action: "Then it happened one evening that David . . . saw a woman bathing. . . . David sent messengers, and took her" (2 Sam 11:2–5).
- Esther: "When the king saw Queen Esther standing in the court, . . . she found favor in his sight . . . Then Esther went near and touched

the top of the scepter" (Esth 5:2). Esther demonstrates that awareness, combined with wisdom and faith in God, can transform human desire into a tool for salvation and protection. She emerges as one of the Bible's most strategic and faithful figures, showing that the human faculties of perception and judgment can serve God's people.

## CONCLUSION: THE ADAMIC CALLING TO ORDER REALITY

Adam's ordering through naming established the pattern for all mediatorial authority. This wasn't arbitrary labeling but discernment of essence, perceiving spiritual reality beneath physical appearance, bringing divine order to earthly chaos. The serpent's corruption targeted precisely this capacity—darkening human discernment so we can no longer distinguish truth from deception, essence from appearance. Throughout Scripture, faithful Adam figures demonstrate this ordering capacity: Abraham discerning divine messengers, David perceiving Goliath's spiritual weakness beneath physical might, Jesus renaming Simon as Peter to reveal his essence. Each demonstrates that authentic authority operates through Spirit-illumined discernment rather than autonomous human wisdom.

The pattern of seeing, judging good, and taking reveals humanity's recurring temptation: trusting sight apart from faith, autonomous assessment apart from divine wisdom. Eve saw, judged, took—establishing the pattern that echoes throughout Scripture. Only when sight serves faith rather than replaces it does discernment function properly. For Christians today, this principle proves urgent. We constantly face the serpent's question: "Has God indeed said?" Will we trust divine wisdom mediated through Scripture and church tradition or rely on our own discernment? The ordering capacity Adam received—and corrupted—is restored in Christ, who discerned spiritual reality and orders his church through Spirit-illumined wisdom. Our calling remains Adamic: perceiving essence, naming truthfully, ordering reality according to divine wisdom rather than corrupted human sight.

# 5

# David as an Adam Figure

Having seen how the Adamic calling involves ordering creation through discernment and naming, we now turn to David, a complex and pivotal Adam figure. David embodies this calling not by naming animals in a garden, but by perceiving the true, spiritual nature of the enemies of Israel. His encounter with Goliath reveals a profound capacity to see beyond terrifying outward appearances to the spiritual reality beneath. Next, the Adam and Eve principle provides the key to solving one of the Old Testament's most perplexing questions: Why does God preserve David's kingship after his great personal sins, yet reject King Saul for what appears to be a lesser offense? By examining David's life through this lens, we will distinguish between a leader's personal failure and a corporate failure, revealing that God's judgment is not based on the severity of the sin alone, but on whether the mediator has fundamentally abandoned their God-given role.

## WHAT DAVID SAW

Beyond the naming Adam performed in Genesis, the Bible presents another "Adam figure" who exhibits a similar capacity for discernment—the ability to perceive the true nature of individuals, often likening them to animals. This echoes Adam's initial task of understanding the character and identity of creatures. One striking example is the story of David and Goliath, when

David, functioning as an Adam figure, perceives a crucial reality that eludes everyone else.

What did David see that no one else saw? While the Israelite army and King Saul are paralyzed by what they saw of Goliath, an imposing stature and a formidable appearance, David recognizes him not as an unbeatable human foe, but as another wild beast like those he, as a shepherd, had already conquered. Fokkelman, in *Reading Biblical Narrative: An Introductory Guide*, notes, "Whereas the Israelites let themselves be intimidated by the appearance of the giant and place their faith in weapons as ardently as their enemies do, David stands apart with a metaphoric view of reality."[1] David's confidence stems from his past experiences. He boldly declares to Saul, "Your servant has killed both lion and bear; and this uncircumcised Philistine will be like one of them, for he has defied the armies of the living God." Moreover, David declared, "The Lord, who delivered me from the paw of the lion and from the paw of the bear, will deliver me from the hand of this Philistine" (1 Sam 17:36–37). David's comparison is rhetorical; it is a profound insight into Goliath's essential character. Goliath, enraged by David's youthful appearance and lack of traditional weaponry, unwittingly confirms David's assessment by asking, "Am I a dog, that you come to me with sticks?" (1 Sam 17:43).

Fokkelman dissects this: "Goliath thinks he is asking a rhetorical question to which everyone knows the answer: of course, he is not a dog. David and his audience (Saul and we, the readers) know better. We take this question seriously and discover: yes, Goliath is a dog. If only he knew he was now facing someone with experience in eliminating lions and bears!"[2] David, through his discernment, identifies Goliath, stripping him of his perceived invincibility and reducing him to a manageable "beast." As we know, David, with his sling and a stone, kills Goliath, succeeding where all others saw only impossibility.

David's exceptional ability to perceive the deeper, animalistic reality of Goliath, when no one else could, powerfully embodies the spirit of an "Adam figure." He performed boundary awareness that Adam lacked. He acted to ensure Israel remained free from Philistine rule. This unique sight of David's allowed him to demonstrate his ability to bring order back to Israel in a manner that echoes the dominion and rule Adam was given.

1. Fokkelman, *Reading Biblical Narrative*, 32.

2. Fokkelman, *Reading Biblical Narrative*, 31.

## CORPORATE VS. PERSONAL FAILURE

Next, one of the most perplexing questions in biblical narrative is why some leaders survive catastrophic moral failures while others lose everything for seemingly lesser offenses. Why does David retain his throne after adultery and murder, while Saul forfeits his kingdom for incomplete obedience? Why does Moses remain Israel's mediator after striking the rock in anger, while Aaron's golden calf nearly costs him the priesthood? The Adam and Eve principle provides a systematic answer: the critical distinction lies not in the severity of the sin but in whether the failure occurs within the mediatorial role/office itself.

Biblical narrative reveals two distinct types of failure among those occupying Adam-figure roles: corporate-scale failures occur when leaders yield to pressure from those they're meant to guide, inverting the proper flow of divine authority. The failure happens in the performance of the mediatorial function—the leader abandons divine instruction specifically because the corporate body (the Eve figure) demands it. Personal-scale failures occur when leaders sin as individuals while maintaining the proper authority structure. The failure happens despite rather than within the mediatorial role—the leader commits personal wickedness but doesn't yield his responsibility to transmit divine wisdom to subordinate pressure. Saul is the example of corporate failure. Saul's rejection as king demonstrates the first category with devastating clarity. When commanded to utterly destroy the Amalekites and all their possessions, Saul instead spares King Agag and the best livestock by taking matters into his own hands, making himself the authority over Samuel and implicitly God. His confession to Samuel reveals the precise nature of his failure: "I have sinned, for I have transgressed the commandment of the Lord and your words, because I feared the people and *obeyed their voice*" (1 Sam 15:24, emphasis added). Considering Saul confessed his sins openly but didn't change his actions, he wasn't fit for office. Saul's sin is disobedience—it is role abandonment. As Israel's king, his function was to ensure the nation obeyed God's voice. Instead, he reversed the proper ordering: the head heeded the voice of the body, inverting the whole structure. The corporate Adam figure yielded to the corporate Eve figure's demand, exactly mirroring Adam's original failure when he "heeded the voice" of Eve rather than God's direct command. Samuel's response confirms that this represents a categorical failure of kingship: "Because you have rejected the word of the Lord, He also has rejected you from being king" (1 Sam 15:23). The mediatorial role is forfeited because the essential function of that role—maintaining divine ordering against contrary pressure—has been abandoned.

David is an example of personal sin without structural breakdown: David's adultery with Bathsheba and murder of Uriah represent far more severe moral violations than Saul's incomplete obedience. Yet David retains his throne, and God's covenant with his dynasty continues. The key difference lies in the nature of the failure. When Nathan confronts David, the prophet's rebuke focuses entirely on abuse of power and personal wickedness: "Why have you despised the commandment of the Lord, to do evil in His sight? You have killed Uriah the Hittite with the sword; you have taken his wife to be your wife" (2 Sam 12:9). Notably absent is any suggestion that David committed these sins because he yielded to popular pressure or allowed subordinates to redirect his authority. David's response is immediate and personal: "I have sinned against the Lord" (2 Sam 12:13). There is no deflection to circumstances, no claim that others pressured him into sin. His confession in Ps 51 maintains this entirely personal focus: "Against You, You only, have I sinned, and done this evil in Your sight" (Ps 51:4). David failed as a man, but he did not fail as mediator by yielding his God-given authority to those he was meant to guide. The consequences David faces are devastating but remain largely personal and familial: his child dies, his family descends into violence and betrayal, his son Absalom rebels. Yet the kingdom continues, the dynasty persists, and David's role as Israel's mediator is not forfeited. He sinned grievously, but he did not commit the structural sin of inverting divine authority.

This distinction between corporate and personal failure clarifies numerous biblical narratives: Jonah resists God's command and attempts to flee from his prophetic calling, revealing profound personal failure. Yet his prophetic office remains intact, and God continues to work through him as a mediator to Nineveh. The principle reveals that God's concern is not only with moral perfection but with maintaining the proper flow of divine authority through human mediators. Leaders can be personally flawed—even grievously sinful—and still function as mediators in their office as long as they maintain the structural integrity of their role. But when they invert the authority structure by yielding to those they're meant to guide, they forfeit the mediatorial function regardless of whether the specific act seems severe. This explains the apparent harshness of Saul's rejection and the apparent mercy toward David. God is not capricious or inconsistent. Rather, different categories of failure carry different consequences precisely because they represent different kinds of disorder. Personal sin disorders the individual and brings personal/familial consequences but can be repaired through repentance.

Structural sin disorders the mediatorial relationship itself and forfeits the role, because the role's essential function has been abandoned. This distinction provides predictive power for reading biblical narrative. When a text emphasizes that a leader acted because they "feared the people," "heeded the voice" of subordinates, or yielded to pressure from those they should guide, the reader can anticipate role forfeiture. The pattern signals corporate-scale failure. When a text describes a leader's personal moral failure without this structural element, restoration remains possible. The narrative arc may include devastating personal consequences, but the mediatorial role can survive genuine repentance. This is not about the severity of sin in abstract moral terms—it's about the location of failure within the divinely-established authority structure. Understanding this distinction prevents misreading biblical judgment as arbitrary or disproportionate. It also clarifies that the Adam and Eve principle concerns authority structures ordained for transmitting divine wisdom, not a ranking of personal worth or a license for leaders to abuse their position—as Nathan challenged David, precisely because David's sin was personal abuse of power rather than proper exercise of his mediatorial role. The Adam and Eve principle is the key that unlocks the seemingly inconsistent judgments of God throughout the Old Testament.

Unlike Saul, whose authority breakdown occurred corporately when he "feared the people and obeyed their voice," David's failure with Bathsheba was personal. This distinction explains God's different responses to seemingly disparate sin severities. When David "saw" Bathsheba and took her despite knowing she was Uriah's wife, he committed what appears more serious than Saul's incomplete obedience. Yet God removed Saul's kingdom while preserving David's. The principle explains this: Saul's sin inverted authority at the structural level, corrupting his mediatorial office. David's sin, though morally grievous, remained personal—he failed individually while his office stayed intact. God judges differently based on whether failure occurs personally or in one's mediatorial office. When authority structures themselves corrupt—when mediators heed voices below rather than maintaining divine wisdom—consequences extend beyond the individual to everyone under that authority. Saul's corporate failure meant Israel couldn't maintain proper communion through his mediation. David's personal failure required serious consequences (the child's death, family turmoil, Absalom's rebellion) but didn't corrupt his office.

The Levitical system reinforces this priority. On the Day of Atonement, the high priest must first offer a sacrifice for his own sins before mediating for the people (Lev 16:11). God builds personal imperfection into the mediatorial system, establishing that the office functions validly despite the officeholder's need for atonement. Jesus teaches this principle directly: "The scribes and the Pharisees sit in Moses' seat. Therefore, whatever they tell you to observe, that observe and do, but do not do according to their works" (Matt 23:2–3). Their teaching authority remains valid despite personal hypocrisy—office and person are distinguishable. Even Caiaphas, plotting Jesus' murder, prophesied truly, "being high priest that year" (John 11:51). The mediatorial office transmitted divine truth through a corrupt vessel. This is not a license for wickedness but recognition of how God works: maintaining channels of divine authority even through flawed human mediators, because covenant continuity depends on structural integrity, not personal perfection.

## THE SAUL-SOLOMON COMPARISON: VALIDATING THE PRINCIPLE

There are many similarities between Saul and Solomon. Both kings experienced corporate failures that resulted in kingdom loss. Saul "feared the people and obeyed their voice" rather than God's command through Samuel (1 Sam 15:24), while Solomon's wives "turned away his heart" after foreign gods (1 Kgs 11:4). Both built unauthorized worship sites—Saul offered sacrifices, usurping the priestly role; Solomon constructed high places for Chemosh and Molech. Both failures occurred within their mediating offices as Israel's representatives before God.

Yet their judgments differed dramatically. God told Saul, "The Lord has torn the kingdom of Israel from you today" (1 Sam 15:28)—immediate removal.

Likewise, God explicitly acknowledges Solomon has failed and his kingdom will be torn as well. God told Solomon, "I will surely tear the kingdom away from you and give it to your servant. Nevertheless I will not do it in your days, for the sake of your father David; I will tear it out of the hand of your son" (1 Kgs 11:11–12). This distinction validates the framework's sophistication by revealing corporate failure. Corporate violation occurs when both failed as king. Such violations receive immediate judgment regardless of mitigating factors because the constitutional order itself is corrupted. Solomon remained king only due to God's mercy. God's explicit statement—"for the sake of David your father"—reveals the second crucial factor: covenant protection. The Davidic covenant promised, "When he commits iniquity, I will discipline him . . . but my steadfast love will not depart from him, as I took it from Saul" (2 Sam 7:14–15). Saul possessed no such covenant; Solomon inherited David's promises.

The biblical text's explicit distinction between these cases—delayed judgment "for the sake of David"—confirms that the framework captures a genuine distinction of violations rather than imposing artificial categories. The comparison between Saul and Solomon provides critical validation of the corporate versus personal failure distinction—while simultaneously revealing important nuance within corporate failure itself.

## WHEN AUTHORITIES CONFLICT: ABIGAIL

The story of Abigail (1 Sam 25) presents another apparent challenge: a wife directly disobeys her husband yet receives divine approval. Understanding this through scaled authority reveals not contradiction but clarification—higher authority supersedes lower authority when they conflict.

Nabal's name means "fool," matching his character. When David's men—who had protected Nabal's shepherds—request provisions, Nabal responds with contempt: "Who is David? And who is the son of Jesse?" (1 Sam 25:10). His refusal reveals corrupted mediation at the household scale: failure to recognize higher authority (David as God's anointed), failure in basic hospitality despite obligation, and purely earthly calculation ("my bread and my water and my meat").[3]

The Eve figure is supposed to be the counterpart and sustainer of their Adam figure, creating or giving body to his head. Nabal and his material riches are supposed to be correctly oriented toward ensuring the preservation of one's space. If David and his men cannot be sustained and can no longer protect Nabal's flocks, then Nabal will lose his flocks anyway. Even his servants recognize his darkened nous: "he is such a scoundrel that one cannot speak to him" (1 Sam 25:17). The nous is our spiritual perception—the part of you designed to perceive God's will and truth. When Abigail learns David plans to destroy the household, "she made haste" (1 Sam

3. 1 Sam 25:11.

25:18)—acting without Nabal's knowledge. Her actions demonstrate understanding of scaled authority:

- She recognizes David's higher authority: "Please, let not my lord regard this scoundrel Nabal" (1 Sam 25:25).
- She bypasses household authority to appeal to kingdom authority.
- She preserves life by preventing both David's vengeance and household destruction.

David validates her action: "Blessed is the Lord God of Israel, who sent you this day to meet me! And blessed is your advice" (1 Sam 25:32–33). Abigail didn't rebel against hierarchy—she appealed to higher hierarchy. Lastly, the pattern completes when God strikes Nabal dead (1 Sam 25:38)—not arbitrary judgment but divine removal of a corrupted mediator who refused to honor higher authority. David explicitly states, "For the Lord has returned the wickedness of Nabal on his own head" (1 Sam 25:39). And David later marries Abigail (1 Sam 25:39–42), restoring proper hierarchical ordering at both household and kingdom scales.

## The scales in conflict

- God's purposes (highest)
- David as anointed king (kingdom scale)
- Nabal as household head (family scale)
- Individual family members (lowest)

When lower-scale authority contradicts higher-scale authority, proper ordering requires the higher to prevail. When wickedness in authority threatens imminent destruction, appeal to a legitimate higher authority while maintaining a submissive posture, then trust God's providence to establish justice. This pattern appears throughout Scripture: Hebrew midwives disobeying Pharaoh's infanticide command (Exod 1:15–21), apostles refusing the Sanhedrin's prohibition on preaching (Acts 5:29), Daniel continuing prayer despite royal decree (Dan 6).

Critical limitations—this isn't license for autonomous rebellion:

- Objective corruption must be evident (Nabal's foolishness recognized by all).
- Higher authority must be clear (David's anointed status established).
- Imminent danger must exist (household facing destruction).
- The goal is preservation, not power (saving lives, not seizing authority).
- Accountability is maintained (Abigail informed Nabal afterward).

Abigail's case enriches the hierarchical framework: authority operates through multiple scales simultaneously, with God as the ultimate source. Faithfulness sometimes requires bypassing corrupted lower authority to honor higher authority—not as rebellion but as proper recognition of vertical ordering through all scales of reality. The Abigail episode demonstrates further complexity. When David determined to destroy Nabal's household contrary to God's justice, Abigail's intervention created an apparent authority conflict. The framework clarifies: Abigail wasn't pressuring David to violate divine command but calling him back to it. She represented true wisdom, correcting corrupted judgment, distinguishing legitimate accountability from dangerous heeding of corrupting voices. David's response reveals spiritual maturity: he recognized her correction as aligned with divine wisdom and thanked God. This demonstrates a healthy authority structure—leaders welcoming correction that brings them back to God's will rather than defending autonomy.

## CONCLUSION

David's story reveals the authority principle operating at the individual scale with crucial nuance. Unlike Saul, whose authority breakdown occurred corporately when he "feared the people and obeyed their voice," David's failure with Bathsheba was personal. This distinction explains God's different responses to seemingly disparate sin severities. When David "saw" Bathsheba and took her despite knowing she was Uriah's wife, he committed what appears more serious than Saul's incomplete obedience. Yet God removed Saul's kingdom while preserving David's. The framework explains this: Saul's sin inverted authority at the structural level, corrupting his mediatorial office. David's sin, though morally grievous, remained personal—he failed individually while his office stayed intact.

When authority structures themselves corrupt—when mediators heed voices below rather than maintaining divine wisdom—consequences extend beyond the individual to everyone under that authority. Saul's corporate failure meant Israel couldn't maintain proper communion through his mediation. David's personal failure required serious consequences (the child's death, family turmoil, Absalom's rebellion), but didn't corrupt his office.

David's response reveals spiritual maturity: he recognized her correction as aligned with divine wisdom and thanked God. This demonstrates a healthy authority structure—leaders welcoming correction that brings them back to God's will rather than defending autonomy. David's story teaches us to distinguish personal failures (which we all experience) from structural inversions corrupting our mediating roles. Personal sin requires deep repentance, but needn't mean abandoning our callings. Authority inversions prove more dangerous than personal moral failure. Next, we will see how these Adamic qualities can be seen in the New Testament.

6

# Ordering in the New Testament

The early chapters of the New Testament introduce two pivotal figures: John the Baptist and Jesus. Their miraculous births, divine naming given from above, and subsequent ministries establish a profound narrative that mirrors other Adam figures. This section will explore how their stories, and especially the concept of naming, illuminate the nature of mediators sent by God and the ongoing spiritual battle against deception.

## THE BIRTH NARRATIVES

The birth narratives of both Jesus and John the Baptist are marked by divine intervention, beginning with the announcement of their names by angels. Just as God initially named Adam and Eve "Man," placing them in the garden of Eden, entrusting them with its care, the names John and Jesus are delivered directly from God. This signifies that this mediator role continues, being divinely appointed. For Jesus, in the announcement to Joseph we see this pattern again: "An angel of the Lord appeared to him in a dream, saying, 'Joseph, son of David, do not be afraid to take to you Mary your wife, for that which is conceived in her is of the Holy Spirit. And she will bring forth a Son, and you shall call His name Jesus" (Matt 1:21–23). "Then the angel said to her, "Do not be afraid, Mary, for you have found favor with

God. And behold, you will conceive in your womb and bring forth a Son, and shall call His name Jesus" (Luke 1:30).

Similarly, John's birth is foretold with a specific name and purpose: "But the angel said to him, 'Do not be afraid, Zacharias, for your prayer is heard; and your wife Elizabeth will bear you a son, and you shall call his name John'" (Luke 1:13). The name John (meaning "God is gracious") foreshadows his role as the herald of God's grace, preparing the way for the Messiah. After John's miraculous birth and the public confirmation of his name by his father, a sense of awe and expectation spread throughout Judea: "Fear came on all who dwelt around them; and all these sayings were discussed throughout Judea's hill country. And all those who heard them kept them in their hearts, saying, 'What kind of child will this be?' And the hand of the Lord was with him" (Luke 1:65–66)." For thirty years, the people of Israel were curious of John, anticipating the unfolding of his divinely appointed destiny.

## JOHN THE BAPTIST: A VOICE IN THE WILDERNESS

John began his ministry in the desert, a place of spiritual solitude and purification. His reputation, stemming from his miraculous birth and the prophetic pronouncements made by his father, drew large crowds from across Israel. Filled with the Holy Spirit from birth (Luke 1:15), John preached a powerful message of repentance and renewal, urging Israel to prepare for the coming Messiah. Even the religious leaders of the day, the Pharisees and Sadducees, were drawn to his baptism. When John saw them approaching, he confronted them with a sharp rebuke, revealing their true spiritual condition. "But when he [John] saw many of the Pharisees and Sadducees coming to his baptism, he said to them, 'Brood of vipers! Who warned you to flee from the wrath to come? Therefore bear fruits worthy of repentance'" (Matt 3:7–8).

This bold identification of the Pharisees as "serpents" or a "brood of vipers" is significant. Both John the Baptist and later Jesus (Matt 12:34; 23:33) used this imagery, drawing a direct parallel to the deceptive serpent in the garden of Eden. This reflects their shared "Adamic work," to discern and expose the true nature of those who oppose God's truth. Jesus further elaborates on this, connecting their inner corruption to their outward speech: "Brood of vipers! How can you, being evil, speak good things? For out of the abundance of the heart the mouth speaks" (Matt 12:34). Here,

Jesus emphasizes that an evil heart cannot produce good words, implying that the Pharisees' deceptive speech mirrored the serpent's lies in Genesis.

As discussed, the act of naming by Jesus and John serves to reveal the true nature of individuals to their followers. Among these creatures, believers are called to become followers of Christ, often symbolized as sheep, signifying their faithful adherence to his shepherd leadership.

## JESUS CALLS HIS BRIDE AND NAMES HIS FOLLOWERS

John the Baptist's ministry of repentance effectively drew a multitude of followers, indicating a spiritual awakening in Israel and establishing John as a significant mediator. "Then Jerusalem, all Judea, and all the region around the Jordan went out to him and were baptized by him in the Jordan, confessing their sins" (Matt 3:5–6). Following John's preparatory work, Jesus' ministry begins with a similar call to repentance but then moves to the direct "calling" of his disciples to follow him. This "calling" parallels Adam's naming of Eve.

> And Jesus, walking by the Sea of Galilee, saw two brothers, Simon called Peter, and Andrew his brother, casting a net into the sea; for they were fishermen. Then He said to them, "Follow Me, and I will make you fishers of men." They immediately left their nets and followed Him. Going on from there, He saw two other brothers, James the son of Zebedee, and John his brother, in the boat with Zebedee their father, mending their nets. He called [*καleo*] them, and immediately they left the boat and their father, and followed Him. (Matt 4:18–22)

This "calling" mirrors Adam's declaration in Gen 2:23: "And Adam said: 'This is now bone of my bones and flesh of my flesh; she shall be called Woman.'" The detail of James and John leaving their father also alludes to Gen 2:24—"Therefore a man shall leave his father and mother and be joined to his wife, and they shall become one flesh"—emphasizing a new covenantal relationship. Just as Eve was formed from Adam's side to be his helpmate, the disciples are "called out" from their old lives to form the body of Christ. They leave their natural fathers to cleave to the New Man, fulfilling the bride/groom pattern of Gen 2.

## MARY THE THEOTOKOS

The birth narratives reveal divine ordering at work, but Mary's unique role as Theotokos (God-bearer) deserves particular attention. Her receptivity to God's word—"Let it be to me according to your word" (Luke 1:38)—demonstrates the proper ordering response that contrasts with Eve's grasp for unauthorized knowledge. Mary is also seen as a new Eve, which is deeply rooted in the church fathers' writings. While Eve failed in her role by disobeying God and eating the fruit, she then offered it to Adam, causing him to transgress as well. Mary fulfills her role as "mother" and "woman." At the Annunciation (Luke 1:26–38), the mystery of divine obedience meets human freedom. The angel Gabriel's greeting—"Rejoice, highly favored one, the Lord is with you; blessed are you among women!" (v. 28)—invites Mary into a dialogue of faith that reverses the tragedy of Eden. Whereas Eve's conversation with the serpent ends in disbelief and self-assertion, Mary's conversation with the angel culminates in faith and self-surrender. Eve questions and grasps out of desire, whereas Mary trusts and yields to God's will. The two dialogues mirror each other, yet their outcomes couldn't be more opposite: one opens the way to exile, the other to incarnation, becoming the mother of all spiritually living.

Next, at the wedding of Cana, when they were out of wine, instead of commanding her "head" (Jesus), she informs him on a problem of the earthly realities in her setting: "The mother of Jesus said to Him, 'They have no wine'" (John 2:3). In response, Jesus immediately "calls" (names) Mary "Woman" in John 2:4. Jesus is not distancing himself. He is citing Genesis. He is identifying her as the "woman" of Gen 3:15—the one whose seed will crush the serpent. He is confirming that the Adamic naming is still in effect. In this act, Mary is receiving a recovered name that Eve lost in Gen 2, the title of "Woman" (Gen 2:23)—a title Eve lost through her disobedience and corruption by the serpent. Eve's initial name of Woman highlighted her role as counterpart, informer, and extension of Man in the garden. Mary's purity and obedience allow Christ to be born into the world, thereby delivering humanity from the curse initiated by Eve.

Christ's poignant address from the cross further highlights Mary's dual aspect as mother and woman: "When Jesus therefore saw His mother, and the disciple whom He loved standing by, He said to His mother, "Woman, behold your son!" By calling her "Woman," Jesus recalls the first "woman" of Genesis, Eve, whose disobedience initiated humanity's fall, highlighting that Jesus is the seed of the woman that has come to crush the serpent's head (Gen 3:15). It is like saying, "Behold your seed."

Then he said to the disciple, "Behold your mother!" (John 19:26–27), highlighting that this is the mother of the living, the spiritually living, as Eve was the mother of all living (Gen 3:20). Mary stands as the new Eve. As the Festal Menaion states, "The Theotokos [Mary], who is to deliver Eve from her pains in travail and Adam from the curse."[1] This parallel is further underscored by the fact that Jesus, through his incarnation, becomes bone of her bone and flesh of her flesh, echoing Adam's declaration to Eve.

## PETER, PAUL, AND THE CHURCH AS BRIDE

Finally, Jesus' naming of Simon as Peter ("Rock") in Matt 16:18—"You are Simon, the son of Jonah. You shall be called Cephas"—establishes the foundation of his church. Peter and Mary act in unique ways since they are the Eve figure. The relationship between Christ and the church, seen in Mary and Peter, is profoundly compared to that of a husband and wife (Eph 5:30–32). Later we will show the distinct ways Mary and Peter fulfill this role—and how the truth of their participation is revealed through their relationship with Christ and his response to them in their role.

Just as the church is called to obey and manifest the order given by Christ, the wife is called to be a counterpart and life-giver, bearing spiritual fruit within her union. These two relationships demonstrate how unity and multiplicity converge. Through this husband-and-wife analogy, the spiritual unity in Christ empowers the diverse gifts and expressions of the church to radically manifest Christ's love in the world. Jesus' ministry in Israel can thus be understood as the perfect enactment of mankind's unique mediating role, employing the faculties of his voice—speech, praise, and naming—as essential tools for preserving sacred space and providing divine guidance to his followers. Critically, the efficacy of speech emanates from the heart: "For out of the abundance of the heart the mouth speaks. A good man, out of the good treasure of his heart, brings forth good things, and an evil man, out of the evil treasure, brings forth evil things" (Matt 12:34–35). Jesus sowed the word of God (the seed) on the "tilled ground" of Israel, delivered through his authoritative voice—a unique characteristic of humanity. Through this divine speech, Jesus preaches the words of God, healing the sick and forgiving the sinful of their sins, bringing spiritual

1. Orthodox Eastern Church, *Festal Menaion*, canticle 6, second canon.

renewal to Israel. Bishop Nikolai Velimirović comments: "You [Jesus] cured the sick with words and raised the dead with words, for You recognized the mystery of love. And the mystery of love is a mystery of words. Through all creatures, as through piercing and blaring trumpets, words pour forth—and through words, the love of Heaven."[2]

Paul, as the apostle to the gentiles, appears to be one of the first, outside of Christ's immediate followers, to recognize Jesus as the Messiah and the fulfillment of the Old Testament. Many of the patterns discussed also impacted Paul. The Bible highlights his "renaming" from Saul to Paul (Acts 13:9), emphasizing his distinct role as the apostle to the Gentile world.

Paul's journey to Christ can be seen in his temporary loss of sight—"And he was three days without sight, and neither ate nor drank" (Acts 9:9)—which he later regained. This period of blindness serves as a powerful metaphor for a protagonist who can no longer rely on physical sight for understanding. Paul was undergoing a spiritual crisis, beginning to grasp Christ's message and how it fundamentally disrupted his worldview as a Pharisee.

## CONCLUSION

The New Testament presents Christ as the fulfillment of the Adamic calling, uniting and perfecting the roles of naming, discerning, and mediating that first appeared in Genesis. From the angelic announcements of John and Jesus' names, we see that divine purpose originates not in human will but in God's sovereign choice. John, the forerunner, embodies this calling by exposing deception and preparing Israel through repentance, while Jesus, the true Mediator, embodies salvation itself as "the Lord saves" and "God with us." His ministry reveals the heart as the source of truth, speech, and order, restoring humanity's voice to its sacred purpose.

Mary, as the new Eve, and the disciples, who are called and renamed, further demonstrate how Christ forms a new covenantal community that mirrors the creation order yet transcends its corruption. Paul extends this vision by identifying Christ as the Last Adam, whose obedience inaugurates a new humanity and whose headship over the church orders creation in righteousness. Thus, the themes of naming, authority, and mediation converge in Christ, who redeems the failures of Adam and establishes a restored creation. In him, the church discovers its true identity and vocation: to manifest divine order and embody the unity of the new humanity.

2. Velimirović, *Prayers by the Lake*, 73.

# 7

# Jesus and Peter

We now turn to how Jesus himself faced temptation to abandon God's appointed path. In each case, Jesus demonstrates what the Second Adam accomplishes—perfect resistance to corrupted counsel, whether it comes from beloved friends, foes, or enthusiastic crowds. Jesus, as a perfect mediator, knew that yielding to earthly pressures would represent the same failure Adam committed—allowing the body (followers, religious establishment) to dictate to the head (divine mediator).

## THE WILDERNESS TEMPTATIONS

After Jesus' baptism and before his public ministry, "Jesus was led up by the Spirit into the wilderness to be tempted by the devil" (Matt 4:1). Following forty days of fasting, Satan approached him with three temptations, each offering legitimate goods through illegitimate means.

First, Satan attacks Jesus' alignment with God the Father's provision: "If you are the Son of God, command that these stones become bread" (Matt 4:3). It's an invitation to self-provision, life apart from the Father. Jesus refuses: "Man shall not live by bread alone, but by every word that proceeds from the mouth of God" (Matt 4:4). The Second Adam, though starving, commanded his flesh to submit to his spirit. He refused to let the "lower" need override the "higher."

Second, Satan attacks God the Father's authority: "If you are the Son of God, throw yourself down" (Matt 4:6). Here the tempter misuses Scripture, urging the Son to test the Father. Jesus answers, "You shall not tempt the Lord your God" (Matt 4:7), refusing to test God the Father. This mirrors when the serpent in the garden made Eve doubt God's love when he questioned her about the commands they were given: "Has God indeed said . . .?" (Gen 3:1).

The third temptation particularly illuminates Satan's trickery: "Again, the devil took Him up on an exceedingly high mountain, and showed Him all the kingdoms of the world and their glory. And he said to Him, 'All these things I will give You if You will fall down and worship me'" (Matt 4:8–9). Jesus' response was swift: "Away with you, Satan! For it is written, 'You shall worship the Lord your God, and Him only you shall serve'" (Matt 4:10). Jesus refused to act on Satan's time but ensured he aligned with the Father's will. He maintained proper orientation and relied on the Father's timing.

## PETER'S REBUKE

The test escalated when pressure came not from questioners outside Jesus' inner circle but from his closest disciple. Jesus introduced a troubling reality: "From that time Jesus began to show to His disciples that He must go to Jerusalem, and suffer many things from the elders and chief priests and scribes, and be killed, and be raised the third day" (Matt 16:21). The disciples' messianic expectations centered on a conquering king who would overthrow Roman occupation and restore Israel's glory. Jesus' announcement of suffering and death shattered this vision. Peter, who moments earlier received divine revelation, now reacted from purely human understanding. Matthew records his response: "Then Peter took Him aside and began to rebuke Him, saying, 'Far be it from You, Lord; this shall not happen to You!'" (Matt 16:22).

Peter's rebuke emerged from genuine love and concern. He cannot fathom his Master suffering and dying. From Peter's earthly perspective, the proposed path represents disaster—the end of their movement, the destruction of their hopes, the senseless waste of Jesus' life. In this moment, Peter functions as a corrupted Eve figure not through malice but through incomplete spiritual understanding.

The parallel to Genesis becomes clear when we examine Peter's actual words. By saying "Far be it from You, Lord; this shall not happen to

You," Peter attempts to convince Jesus that God's announced plan should not come to pass. This echoes the serpent's strategy with Eve: questioning what God has clearly stated and offering an alternative understanding that appears more reasonable to human wisdom. The serpent told Eve, "You will not surely die" (Gen 3:4), denying the consequence God had warned about. Peter essentially tells Jesus the same thing—"You shall not suffer and die"—denying the necessity that Jesus had just announced from God.

Jesus' response is swift and startling in its severity: "But He turned and said to Peter, 'Get behind Me, Satan! You are an offense to Me, for you are not mindful of the things of God, but the things of men'" (Matt 16:23). At first glance, Jesus' rebuke may appear unduly harsh, even shocking. He just blessed Peter as the rock of the church, and now he calls him Satan? Yet a careful reading within the pattern reveals the profound necessity of this response. Jesus doesn't suggest Peter is possessed or is himself evil. Rather, Jesus identifies that Peter's counsel, however well-intentioned, serves Satan's purposes by attempting to derail God's redemptive plan.

The phrase "Get behind Me" restores proper ordering. Peter had "taken Him aside" to rebuke him privately, positioning himself as advisor and Jesus as one who needed correction. This inverts the proper authority structure—the body attempting to direct the head, the Eve figure attempting to redirect the Adam figure. Jesus' command reestablishes the hierarchy: Peter must follow behind, not attempt to lead from ahead or alongside. The mediator between heaven and earth does not receive direction from earthly concerns, no matter how loving or reasonable they appear.

Jesus makes the issue explicit: "You are not mindful of the things of God, but the things of men." This diagnosis reveals the fundamental problem with Peter's counsel. Peter's human mind, operating from human understanding, cannot comprehend the divine necessity of the cross, of a seed needing to first die to produce (John 12:24). What appears disastrous from earth's perspective accomplishes redemption from heaven's perspective. Peter sees with earthly eyes and speaks earthly wisdom, exactly as the serpent did in Eden—offering what appears good and reasonable while actually opposing God's stated plan. This moment demonstrates what successful resistance to corrupted Eve-figure counsel looks like. Unlike Adam, who remained silent and complied with Eve's offer of forbidden fruit, Jesus immediately names the source of the temptation (Satan working through human intermediaries), identifies the fundamental error (prioritizing earthly thinking over divine wisdom), and reestablishes proper authority structure: "Get behind me," resume your role as follower rather than leader.

Peter's rebuke essentially repeated Satan's wilderness temptation in more sympathetic form. Where Satan explicitly offered earthly authority through worship of evil, Peter implicitly offered preserved earthly ministry through avoiding suffering. Both temptations would abort the true mission. Both prioritized earthly outcomes over obedience to God's specific plan. Both represented attempts to redirect the mediator from the appointed path through appeal to legitimate earthly concerns—whether desire for authority or desire to avoid pain.

When direct temptation through his own voice failed in the wilderness, Satan worked indirectly through the voice of Jesus' closest disciple. The temptation clothed itself in love, concern, and loyalty rather than appearing as obvious evil. This demonstrates why Jesus' response called Peter "Satan"—not because Peter was possessed, but because Peter's loving counsel functioned exactly as Satan's earlier temptation had, attempting to redirect Jesus from the cross through appeal to self-preservation and earthly wisdom.

Brandon Crowe observes the magnitude of what Jesus accomplished: "Jesus had to overcome temptation in the wake of thousands of years of rebellion, whereas Adam's failure came in the prelapsarian world."[1] Jesus faced temptation in a world already corrupted by countless failures of mediation. The very disciples he was training to continue his mission offered counsel that would abort that mission. The weight of human expectation, the pull of human affection, and the apparent reasonableness of avoiding suffering—all pressed against Jesus' commitment to divine wisdom.

Yet Jesus maintained perfect ordering. He did not deliberate about Peter's suggestion or weigh its merits against God's plan. He recognized immediately that any counsel directing him away from the cross, regardless of its source or motivation, opposed God's purposes and served the enemy's agenda. This is what the Second Adam accomplishes—immediate recognition of corrupted counsel and unwavering maintenance of divine ordering even when the pressure comes from those he loves most.

1. Crowe, *Last Adam*, 30.

### THE CROWD'S DEMAND

Lastly, at the corporate scale, this temptation appears after Jesus feeds five thousand men (plus women and children) with five loaves and two fish. The miracle demonstrated Jesus' power to provide abundant resources from minimal means. John records the crowd's response: "Then those men, when they had seen the sign that Jesus did, said, 'This is truly the Prophet who is to come into the world.' Therefore when Jesus perceived that they were about to come and take Him by force to make Him king, He departed again to the mountain by Himself alone" (John 6:14–15). The crowd wanted to crown Jesus immediately. They had just witnessed his power to multiply bread and fish. In their minds, such a leader could overthrow Roman occupation, restore Israel's independence, and ensure endless prosperity. They saw Jesus as the political and military messiah they expected, and they moved to "take Him by force"—not to harm him but to compel him to accept the kingship they believed he deserved and Israel needed.

This represents the Eve figure operating on the national scale. The entire corporate body of Israel, represented by this enthusiastic crowd, attempts to redirect the Adam figure (Jesus as Messiah-King) toward an earthly understanding of his mission. They offer him exactly what he came to establish—the kingdom of God—but according to their earthly vision rather than God's heavenly plan. From their perspective, Jesus should seize this moment of popular support and leverage it into a political revolution. Now, an entire multitude moves to physically force him into their understanding of messiahship. Whether the pressure comes from religious questioners, beloved disciples, or enthusiastic crowds, Jesus maintains the same response: refuse to yield to earthly expectations and preserve the divinely appointed mission. The number of people offering corrupted counsel (crowd) doesn't make it correct. The sincerity of their love doesn't make their understanding align with God's purposes. The apparent righteousness of their desires—wanting Jesus to be king—doesn't make their timing or method appropriate.

## Corruption, Time, and the Darkened Nous

The repeated yielding to corrupted Eve figures also connects to broader themes of time, space, and spiritual perception. As discussed in earlier sections, Adam and Eve's disobedience introduced humanity into temporal inconsistency—time as the realm of mortality, uncertainty, and temptation. The Adam figure, when yielding to a corrupted Eve figure, effectively abandons sacred space, allowing temporal concerns, anxiety, and relational pressures to dictate action rather than divine command. The corruption of time that is supposed to be purposed for eternal communion with God, became wandering, insecurity, and confusion. Thus, the darkened nous experiences time as decay, not communion. Obedience reorients time toward eternity. Each act of faithful submission restores the nous to the rhythm of divine constancy.

This darkening of one's nous, as discussed, means the Adam figure loses the capacity to discern God's will clearly, rendering him susceptible to corrupted influence. Every narrative of Adam figures yielding to an Eve figure reflects this principle: the leader's spiritual perception is compromised, and human schemes replace divine wisdom. The darkened nous specifically leads to failures in authority (can't discern God's voice), cooperation (relies on self-effort, misunderstands synergy), and orientation (defaults to pride/self-reliance).

After both Adam and Eve had eaten the fruit, they hid from God under the trees: "And they heard the sound of the Lord God walking in the garden in the cool of the day, and Adam and his wife hid themselves from the presence of the Lord God among the trees of the garden" (Gen 3:8). They believed the knowledge they had gained—intellectual understanding divorced from faith—would be sufficient to protect them from God's presence.

## Corruption and Human Faculties

The darkening of the nous illustrates a broader spiritual truth: corruption affects discernment, righteousness, and the capacity for spiritual perception. When the highest human faculties are clouded, the soul struggles to receive and apply heavenly wisdom, making it more susceptible to bodily temptations and self-interest. This aligns with the Orthodox understanding that humanity, while wounded by the fall, retains the capacity for good. The divine image is obscured but not obliterated, and the intellect, will, and heart remain capable of transformation and participation in divine life through repentance, obedience, and communion with God. Having traced the inner mechanics of corruption, Scripture next reveals how divine initiative restores the darkened nous through living examples.

Jesus' withdrawal to the mountain, "by Himself alone" (John 6:15), overcomes this temptation. He doesn't debate the crowd about political messiahship versus suffering servant. He simply removes himself from their attempt to force an earthly solution to spiritual problems. The following day, when the crowds find Jesus again, he confronts their motivations directly: "Most assuredly, I say to you, you seek Me, not because you saw the signs, but because you ate of the loaves and were filled. Do not labor for the food which perishes, but for the food which endures to everlasting life, which the Son of Man will give you" (John 6:26–27). Jesus exposes their earthly orientation—they want an earthly king who will supply physical needs, not the Bread of Life who supplies spiritual sustenance through his sacrificial death.

## PETER AND THE RESTORATION OF FAITH-ACTIVATED NOUS

Peter's faith provides a clear and compelling example of the human nous restored to proper function, illustrating how divine initiative, heart-centered reception, and obedience converge in a faithful mediator. Scripture presents multiple moments that reveal the same principle repeatedly: divine illumination received through faith transforms perception, decision, and action.

### Peter's Confession at Caesarea Philippi (Matt 16:16–18)

When Christ asked, "Who do you say that I am?" Simon Peter answered boldly: "You are the Christ, the Son of the living God" (Matt 16:16). Jesus' response underscores the operative dynamic of faith-activated nous: "Blessed are you, Simon Bar-Jonah, for flesh and blood has not revealed this to you, but My Father who is in heaven" (Matt 16:17). Here, Jesus explicitly contrasts two sources of knowledge. "Flesh and blood" represents human faculties operating autonomously—intellect, observation, reasoning, and accumulated testimony. In contrast, "My Father in heaven" represents direct divine illumination, apprehended through the properly functioning nous activated by faith. Peter's confession demonstrates that when the highest human faculty operates under divine initiative and faith, spiritual truth becomes immediately recognizable, surpassing the limitations of human reasoning.

The significance extends beyond Peter himself. Jesus immediately declares, "And I tell you that you are Peter, and on this rock I will build my church" (Matt 16:18). In Orthodox understanding, the "rock" is not Peter as a person, but the revelation itself—the capacity for direct spiritual illumination through faith. The church is founded upon this principle: knowledge received through divine grace, not autonomous intellect. Peter's nous demonstrates the restoration of humanity's original calling. Where Adam, placed as mediator between God and creation, yielded to deception, Peter now perceives truth directly and acts obediently. Thus, Peter's faith does affirm Christ's identity; it restores the original modes of spiritual perception lost in Eden—knowledge through faith.

## Peter Walking on Water (Matt 14:22–33)

The episode of Peter walking on water illustrates the dynamics of faith-activated nous in action. When Jesus calls, "Come" (Matt 14:29), Peter steps onto the water, responding not to natural observation but to divine command. For a brief moment, his faith directs his nous, and he participates in a reality beyond human capacity. Yet when Peter notices the wind and the waves, fear overtakes him, and he begins to sink (Matt 14:30). The narrative emphasizes the influence between faith and one's perception: when faith wavers, spiritual discernment is clouded. Jesus immediately reaches out, saying, "You of little faith, why did you doubt?" (Matt 14:31). Peter's nous, momentarily clouded by fear and sensory distraction, is restored through divine initiative, showing that even wavering faith can be recovered and realigned with God's purpose.

## Peter's Post-Resurrection Recognition (John 21:7)

The post-resurrection appearance at the Sea of Galilee demonstrates the maturation of Peter's faith and the stability of a restored nous. When John recognizes the risen Christ through the miraculous catch of fish—"It is the Lord!" (John 21:7)—Peter responds immediately, wrapping his outer garment and jumping into the water to reach him. Here, perception and action are aligned: Peter apprehends the divine reality directly through faith, without hesitation or distraction. His obedience is instantaneous and wholehearted, illustrating the full restoration of the human mediating faculty. Where Adam once failed to mediate divine presence faithfully, Peter now perceives, acts, and participates in the pronouncing the good news of Christ. The narrative underscores the transformative power of faith-activated perception, showing that God restores and elevates human faculties for divine service.

## Peter and John at the Temple Gate: Heeding the Correct Voice

Peter and John's encounter at the Beautiful Gate in Acts 3–4 demonstrates the Adam and Eve principle operating at the apostolic level. When confronted with conflicting authorities—human commands versus divine commission—the apostles maintained proper ordering, producing remarkable yield. The pattern begins with obedience to divine instruction. Peter commands the lame beggar: "In the name of Jesus Christ of Nazareth, rise up and walk" (Acts 3:6). The healing produces immediate yield—the man, "leaping up, stood and walked and entered the temple with them—walking, leaping, and praising God" (Acts 3:8). This single act of faithfulness generated crowds in Solomon's Portico, providing Peter opportunity to preach Christ. The yield was extraordinary: "Many of those who heard the word believed; and the number of the men came to be about five thousand" (Acts 4:4). Five thousand souls—the fruit of faithful obedience to divine commission.

Then came the test that threatened this harvest. The priests, captain of the temple, and Sadducees arrested them, bringing them before "Annas the high priest, Caiaphas, John, and Alexander, and as many as were of the family of the high priest" (Acts 4:6)—the highest earthly religious authority in Israel. These leaders—functioning as a corrupted corporate Eve figure—directly commanded: "They commanded them not to speak at all nor teach in the name of Jesus" (Acts 4:18). This was the critical Gen 3 moment. Would these Adam figures "heed the voice" of Israel's religious establishment over God's direct commission, potentially forfeiting the harvest of five thousand believers? Peter's response demonstrates faithful mediation: "Whether it is right in the sight of God to listen to you more than to God, you judge. For we cannot but speak the things which we have seen and heard" (Acts 4:19–20). Unlike Adam, who heeded Eve's voice rather than God's command, Peter refuses to let even the high priest redirect his divine mission.

The yield multiplied beyond the initial five thousand. After release, believers prayed for boldness, and "they were all filled with the Holy Spirit, and they spoke the word of God with boldness" (Acts 4:31). Peter and John's refusal to yield to corrupted pressure—their maintenance of proper divine ordering—transformed five thousand believers into the foundation of a church that would fill the earth. When Adam figures resist the voice of earthly authority to maintain divine commission, the yield extends exponentially through generations.

## CONCLUSION

These confrontations reveal Jesus' consistent pattern: he resists corrupted counsel, aligning with God's will. He also exposes the earthly reasoning behind these temptations and calls people to reorient toward heavenly wisdom. Whether with the devil's temptations in the desert, the Pharisees, who constantly tried to control or undermine his ministry, the crowd wanting to make him a king, or Peter, Jesus overcomes. With Peter, he identified the source of temptation and commanded proper positioning. With the crowd, he reveals their earthly motivations and offers a heavenly perspective. Unlike Abraham, who learned discernment through the costly failure with Hagar, or David, whose great personal sins brought chaos to his own family, Jesus demonstrates perfect and preemptive discernment. His success is absolute, not corrective, setting him apart as the one true Mediator who never falters. As believers, we can have greater clarity of obedience from Jesus' example and teachings to resist temptation, rely on God's word, and remain steadfast in our commitment to God's kingdom. The temptations of Jesus remind us of the spiritual battles we face and encourage us to emulate Christ in our pursuit of righteousness and obedience to God's will. Having examined how authority operates through proper ordering and mediation, we now turn to the second principle: cooperation. While authority establishes the structure through which communion flows, cooperation provides the process—the dynamic interaction between divine provision and human response. No matter how properly ordered authority may be, without faithful cooperation, no fruit results. The tilling/rain/yield principle reveals how divine-human partnership produces blessing when both parties contribute according to their distinct roles.

# 8

# Tilling/Rain/Yield Principle

Having spent the last several chapters exploring the principle of mediation, authority, and hierarchy, we now turn to another principle established in Genesis: the process of divine-human cooperation. While the Adam/Eve principle describes the structure of God's order, the tilling/rain/yield principle describes the process of how fruitfulness occurs within that structure. While the last chapter explained the Adam/Eve principle, revealing authority breakdowns in hierarchical structures in the Bible, the tilling/rain/yield principle of this chapter shows what proper divine-human cooperation looks like when it succeeds.

The significance of Adam's role is underscored by the state of creation prior to his creation: "In the day that the Lord God made the earth and the heavens, before any plant of the field was in the earth and before any herb of the field had grown . . . the Lord God had not caused it to rain on the earth, and there was no man to till the ground" (Gen 2:4–5). This conveys that before Adam's creation, the earth remained barren and unproductive, emphasizing divine-human cooperation for life to flourish. Adam's participation in priestly stewardship is necessary to cultivate the earth's potential and facilitate its flourishing. Adam, therefore, was essential to connecting heavenly wisdom (symbolized often as divine "rain") with prepared earthly matter (the "tilled ground"), enabling creation to "bring forth and bud" its intended spiritual and physical fruit (Isa 55:10). Adam's job to till the ground was humanity's participation in the divine-human cooperation needed to produce a yield.

The symbolism of rain is that of the life-giving word of God and divine grace that descends to humanity for spiritual nourishment and life. As stated in Deut 32:2, "Let my teaching drop as the rain, My speech distill as the dew, As raindrops on the tender herb, And as showers on the grass." Isaiah also proclaims, "The rain comes down, and the snow from heaven, And do not return there, But water the earth, And make it bring forth and bud" (Isa 55:10). Adam, positioned as a bridge between the spiritual and material, was created to participate actively in creation's ordering and flourishing. Man's obedience is what God required: "If you walk in My statutes and keep My commandments, and perform them, then I will give you rain in its season, the land shall yield its produce, and the trees of the field shall yield their fruit" (Lev 26:3–4).

This is reinforced in Hosea 10:12: "Sow for yourselves righteousness; Reap in mercy; Break up your fallow ground, For it is time to seek the Lord, Till He comes and rains righteousness on you." This passage connects the three elements—breaking up fallow ground (tilling/preparation), divine rain (God's blessing), and reaping righteousness (spiritual yield). He was to prepare the ground for the heavenly "rain" so that it might "bring forth" life, mirroring God's own creative acts in Gen 1:12.

Adam's identity transcends that of merely the progenitor of humanity; he is archetypally understood as a mediator between heaven, the dwelling place of God (Deut 26:15; Ps 115:3), and the physical earth, the ground. Matthieu Pageau highlights this by stating, "In the Bible, the union of heaven and earth is often defined in terms of wisdom and understanding."[1] The wisdom imparted to Adam in his "head"—symbolized by the divine breath entering his nostrils—is only truly effective when it descends into his heart, enabling it to work both internally within his being and externally in fulfilling God's will. This principle is a consequence of the fall but a constitutional law of human purpose established in Eden. When God placed Adam in the garden, he commanded him to both "work it and keep it" (Gen 2:15). The Hebrew root used for "to work" is "to serve" or "to minister." This reveals that the act of tilling—the human input—was created as a sacred, joyful responsibility; it was humanity's eternal, intended form of ministry and preparation, existing in perfect communion with God's grace (rain). The curse did not create the principle; it merely corrupted the process, turning

1. Pageau, *Language of Creation*, 43.

the joyful service ('avad) into painful toil and sweat, but the law of tilling/rain/yield remains the fundamental pattern for spiritual growth and flourishing.

This divine-human cooperation that Genesis reveals finds theological expression in what Orthodox theology calls "synergy"—the working together of divine grace and human response. "The Orthodox refer to this cooperation with God as 'synergy.' Synergy is the process of salvation in which Christians cooperate with the Holy Spirit in conforming their will to God's will in Jesus Christ."[2] Rather than God acting alone or humans receiving blessings through works, the tilling/rain/yield pattern shows both elements working in harmony, particularly in the context of salvation and spiritual growth. The term "synergy" comes from the Greek word *synergeia*, meaning "working together." Within Orthodoxy, this describes the cooperative relationship between divine grace and human freedom. It rejects both extremes of complete divine determinism and absolute human autonomy. Instead, Orthodox synergy asserts that salvation is neither achieved solely by God without human response nor earned entirely by human effort apart from God's grace.

## THE PRINCIPLE

Human preparation (tilling) → divine blessing (rain) → fruitfulness (yield).

- Tilling (preparation): Human action involving spiritual preparation, repentance, faithful obedience, character formation, or readiness to receive divine blessing. This includes breaking up "fallow ground" of the heart, purification (katharsis), removing obstacles to spiritual growth, and positioning oneself to receive divine intervention.
- Rain (divine blessing): God's response to proper preparation through the impartation of wisdom, blessing, empowerment, revelation, or grace. This divine bestowal of illumination (theoria) is often described using metaphors of water, breath, spirit, or light descending from heaven.
- Yield (fruitfulness): The resulting spiritual, physical, or communal blessing that emerges from the cooperation between human preparation and divine intervention. This includes personal transformation

2. Tibbs, *Basic Guide*, 29.

(theosis), community flourishing, national restoration, or the reproduction of spiritual life in others, depending on the scale of reality.

This synergy and pattern are prevalent throughout the Bible and highlight another instance of a fractal pattern, seen below.

## Abraham's Call (Gen 12–22)

- Tilling: Abraham left his country and kindred when God called him (Gen 12:1–4). He believed God's promise despite his advanced age and Sarah's barrenness (Rom 4:18–20). He was willing to sacrifice Isaac when God tested him (Gen 22:2–3).
- Rain: God appeared to Abraham and confirmed his covenant promises multiple times (Gen 12:7; 15:1; 17:1). God provided a ram in place of Isaac at the crucial moment (Gen 22:13). God swore by himself to bless Abraham because of his obedience (Gen 22:16–17).
- Yield: Abraham became the father of many nations as promised (Gen 17:4–5). All nations of the earth are blessed through his seed (Gen 22:18). He received the covenant promises for his descendants (Gen 17:7–8).

## Jacob's Transformation (Gen 28–35)

- Tilling: Jacob wrestled with God all night and would not let him go without a blessing (Gen 32:24–26). He served Laban faithfully for fourteen years despite being deceived (Gen 29:20–30).
- Rain: God appeared to Jacob in a dream at Bethel, promising to be with him (Gen 28:12–15). God changed Jacob's name to Israel after the wrestling match (Gen 32:28).
- Yield: Jacob became the father of the twelve tribes of Israel (Gen 35:23–26). He established altars and worship centers (Gen 35:1–7). His descendants inherited the covenant promises (Gen 35:11–12).

### God's Creation and Provision (Psalm 104)

- Tilling: People go out to their work, to their labor (Ps 104:23).
- Rain: He waters the mountains (Ps 104:13).
- Yield: "That he may bring forth food from the earth" (Ps 104:14); "the earth is satisfied with the fruit of Your works" (Ps 104:13).

Having established the three-part pattern of human preparation, divine intervention, and spiritual fruit, we can now examine the middle element more closely. Divine "rain" represents the crucial mystery of God's timing and action—when and how heaven responds to faithful human "tilling." This principle provides the procedural coherence of the narrative. It explains the "how" of spiritual life—the consistent process through which God's blessing is enacted in the world. A story's outcome is logical because it follows a predictable sequence: human action and preparation (tilling) create the condition for divine intervention (rain), which produces a spiritual result (yield). The tension comes from the uncertainty of the process. Will the tilling be faithful? Will the rain come as expected? The parable of the sower illustrates this: "Some fell by the wayside . . . some on stony places . . . some among thorns . . . but others fell on good ground and yielded a crop" (Matt 13:3–8). The same rain (God's word) produces different yields depending on the soil (the heart).

## DAVID'S PREPARATION IN THE WILDERNESS

David's path to kingship demonstrates the tilling/rain/yield principle operating at the national scale. Samuel anointed David as a shepherd boy: "The Spirit of the Lord came upon David from that day forward" (1 Sam 16:13). Yet between divine anointing and earthly throne lay years of preparation that constituted the tilling phase. Saul pursued David through the wilderness of Judah. David hid in the cave of Adullam with "everyone who was in distress, everyone who was in debt, and everyone who was discontented" (1 Sam 22:2)—four hundred men representing Israel's marginalized. Twice Saul fell into David's power. His men urged action: "This is the day of which the Lord said to you, 'Behold, I will deliver your enemy into your hand, that you may do to him as it seems good to you'" (1 Sam 24:4). Circumstances, political justification, and military capacity all aligned to support seizing the throne. Yet David's tilling consisted of submission rather than conquest. At En Gedi, David cut Saul's robe but "his heart struck him" (1 Sam 24:5). He declared, "The Lord forbid that I should do this thing to my master, the Lord's anointed, to stretch out my hand against him, seeing he is the anointed of the Lord" (1 Sam 24:6). The preparation involved learning that divine appointment does not authorize human usurpation. David was cultivating restraint, patience, and dependence on God's timing—character formation that would prove essential for faithful kingship.

## DIVINE INTERVENTION: WHEN HEAVEN MOVES

God intervened decisively. "Now the Philistines fought against Israel; and the men of Israel fled from before the Philistines, and fell slain on Mount Gilboa. Then the Philistines followed hard after Saul and his sons. And the Philistines killed Jonathan, Abinadab, and Malchishua, Saul's sons. . . . So Saul took a sword and fell on it" (1 Sam 31:1–4). David had not acted. Divine sovereignty removed the obstacle David had refused to remove. David's response validated his wilderness preparation. When an Amalekite arrived claiming to have killed Saul and presenting the crown, expecting reward, David executed him: "How was it you were not afraid to put forth your hand to destroy the Lord's anointed?" (2 Sam 1:14). Even with Saul dead, David maintained the authority structure God had established. He composed a genuine lament: "The beauty of Israel is slain on your high places! How the mighty have fallen!" (2 Sam 1:19). The preparation had transformed his character—he mourned his pursuer's death.

The divine rain continued. "It happened after this that David inquired of the Lord, saying, 'Shall I go up to any of the cities of Judah?' And the Lord said to him, 'Go up.' David said, 'Where shall I go up?' And He said, 'To Hebron'" (2 Sam 2:1). Notice the pattern: with Saul dead and the path clear, David still inquires. He waits and moves when directed. Years of preparation had established this pattern of dependence on divine initiative.

## THE YIELD: A KINGDOM THAT ENDURES

At Hebron, "the men of Judah came, and there they anointed David king over the house of Judah" (2 Sam 2:4). The yield remained incomplete—Israel divided, with Ish-bosheth claiming the northern tribes under Abner's backing. Seven more years of partial rule followed. When Ish-bosheth's commanders assassinated him and brought his head to David, expecting reward, David's response mirrored his treatment of Saul's killer: "'When wicked men have killed a righteous person in his own house on his bed, should I not now require his blood at your hand and remove you from the earth?' So David commanded his young men, and they executed them" (2 Sam 4:11–12). He refused to build his kingdom on unauthorized bloodshed. Approximately fourteen years after Samuel's anointing, the full yield arrived: "Then all the tribes of Israel came to David at Hebron and spoke, saying, 'Indeed we are your bone and your flesh. . . . You shall be shepherd over Israel, and you shall be ruler over My people Israel.' Therefore all the elders of Israel came to the king at Hebron, and King David made a covenant with them at Hebron before the Lord. And they anointed David king over Israel" (2 Sam 5:1–3). The cooperation was complete. David had tilled through years of restraint. God sent rain through sovereign intervention. The yield was a unified kingdom under "a man after God's own heart" (1 Sam 13:14)—not through military prowess or political maneuvering, but through patient dependence on divine timing. David's fourteen-year gap between anointing and complete authority reveals that divine timing operates differently than human expectation. The tilling must be thorough. Only when human faithfulness aligns with divine sovereignty does lasting yield emerge. David's reign demonstrates that human preparation without divine initiative produces nothing enduring, while divine blessing without human readiness finds no prepared ground. When a leader cultivates faithfulness through obscurity, refusing shortcuts that violate God's order, then God provides rain that produces a kingdom without end.

These examples demonstrate how to read Scripture as a unified whole rather than isolated passages and how coherent this pattern is. We can also see that when Adam figures properly prepare their spheres of responsibility (tilling), they create conditions for divine blessing (rain) that produces corporate flourishing (yield). This pattern of divine-human cooperation echoes throughout Israel's history. Yet all these smaller cycles were themselves a preparation for the ultimate act of "tilling": the ministry of John the Baptist, the prophet tasked with breaking the hardened soil of an entire nation to prepare it for the coming of Christ.

## JOHN THE BAPTIST: TILLING THE GROUND OF ISRAEL. THE FOUR-HUNDRED-YEAR DROUGHT

Like other prophets, God spoke directly to John the Baptist in the wilderness: "The word of God came to John the son of Zacharias in the wilderness" (Luke 3:2), breaking a four-hundred-year drought from the last biblical prophet, Malachi. This four-hundred-year silence from God parallels Israel's 400 years in Egypt—both involve periods of preparation where God's people await deliverance through a mediator (Moses, then Christ).

The typological parallel suggests God works in these extended cycles, using periods of apparent absence to create readiness for dramatic intervention. Spiritually, Israel at this time resembled the barren earth described in Gen 2:4–5, lacking true spiritual fruit because no adequate mediator had "tilled the ground" and there had been no "rain" of God's word upon the land. The prophet Jeremiah had prophetically described Israel's condition in terms that perfectly paralleled John's situation: "I looked on the earth, and behold, it was without form and void; and to the heavens, and they had no light" (Jer 4:23). This verse deliberately echoes the primordial chaos of Gen 1:2, suggesting that Israel's spiritual condition had regressed to a pre-creation state of formlessness and darkness. The covenant people had become spiritually "without form and void"—lacking the divine structure and order that gave meaning to their existence. The "heavens" that should have provided light and guidance had grown dark, symbolizing the absence of prophetic revelation and divine communication.

By John's time, this prophetic vision had become a literal reality: Israel existed in chaos, being under subjugation by the Romans, with religious leaders harassed by installed governmental leaders and a people wandering in moral and spiritual confusion. The very institutions that should have maintained order and provided divine illumination had become sources of darkness and disorder. John's wilderness ministry represented God's intervention to bring form out of chaos, light out of darkness—recreating spiritual order from the primordial confusion that Israel had become through centuries of covenant unfaithfulness and divine silence. This prolonged silence had created a spiritual wasteland. Like fallow ground that becomes compacted and hard when left unworked, Israel's heart had grown to expect a messianic figure who would unyoke them from the Romans, not understanding the spiritual transformation that should occur. The nation desperately needed someone to break up this hardened soil and prepare it for the divine rain. John emerges as the first mediator we encounter in the

New Testament narratives, uniquely positioned to restore order to Israel's chaotic spiritual state. As a descendant of the priestly line of Aaron (Luke 1:5), he inherited Israel's mediatorial tradition while receiving a prophetic calling that would bridge the old and new covenants.

His mission, as the angel Gabriel had prophesied, was "to make ready a people prepared for the Lord" (Luke 1:17), underscoring his role as mediator, forerunner, and the final prophet of the old covenant. John's ascetic lifestyle served as a visible "tilling"—his very existence demonstrated the radical preparation he preached. His clothing of camel's hair and leather belt (Matt 3:4) deliberately echoed Elijah's appearance (2 Kgs 1:8), signaling prophetic continuity while rejecting worldly comfort. His diet of locusts and wild honey represented complete reliance on God's provision rather than human systems of security. By dwelling in the wilderness rather than Jerusalem's religious centers, John demonstrated necessary separation from the corrupt religious establishment. The wilderness itself carried profound theological significance—it was where Israel had been formed as a nation, where they learned dependence on God, and where divine encounters occurred.

This austere living authenticated his message that true preparation requires abandoning worldly securities to make room for divine intervention. John modeled the repentance he called others to embrace, breaking up the fallow ground of spiritual complacency through radical simplicity. His personal discipline demonstrated that effective tilling begins with the mediator himself—before John could prepare Israel's heart, his own heart had to be thoroughly prepared through years of wilderness discipline and direct communion with God. The wilderness years represented John's personal tilling/rain/yield cycle: his tilling through ascetic discipline, God's rain through direct revelation (Luke 3:2), and the yield of a powerful ministry that would prepare an entire nation.

## JOHN'S TILLING MINISTRY: BREAKING UP HARDENED GROUND

John's central message was repentance (metanoia), which functions as essential tilling that prepares human hearts for divine blessing. The Greek word means "change of mind" or "turning around"—a fundamental reorientation from self-directed living toward God-directed living. Like a farmer breaking up hardened soil, repentance breaks up the compacted ground of human pride, self-sufficiency, and spiritual complacency that prevents divine grace from taking root. Baptism itself symbolized this tilling process—immersion representing death to the old self and emergence representing readiness for new life (Rom 6:4). The Jordan River location deliberately recalled Israel's crossing into the promised land, suggesting that John's baptism prepared people for entrance into God's kingdom. Unlike ritual purifications that addressed external cleanliness, John's baptism demanded internal transformation, making it a powerful tool for spiritual cultivation.

John's ministry revealed different types of ground through the varied responses he received. Tax collectors and soldiers exemplified successful tilling. These marginalized groups recognized their spiritual bankruptcy and asked, "What shall we do?" (Luke 3:10–14). This question demonstrated the broken ground of genuine conviction. John provided immediate, practical guidance for righteous living—his inspired teaching served as preliminary "rain" that began producing immediate "yield" in transformed behavior. They became examples of genuine repentance, demonstrating that preparation could happen across social boundaries and that even the most unlikely people could become fertile ground for God's work. The general crowds showed mixed preparation. Messianic expectation was stirred as people wondered if John himself was the Christ (Luke 3:15–16), indicating their hearts were being cultivated.

However, John's role was to direct this expectation beyond himself to "the Coming One" (Matt 11:3), demonstrating that successful tilling points away from the human mediator toward the divine source of blessing. The revival stirring throughout the region demonstrated divine rain taking effect as crowds flocked from Jerusalem, Judea, and the Jordan region (Matt 3:5) seeking baptism. In stark contrast, the Pharisees and Sadducees exemplified failed tilling. They approached John without genuine repentance, relying instead on Abrahamic heritage—their ground remained hard and unprepared. John refused to baptize them, calling them a "brood of vipers" and warning that "God is able to raise up children to Abraham from these stones" (Matt 3:7–9).

Their rejection of John's preparatory work meant they were unprepared to receive the coming blessing, creating a leadership crisis that would have national consequences. Luke later confirms this devastating reality: "All the people, even the tax collectors, when they heard Jesus' words, acknowledged that God's way was right, because they had been baptized by John. But the Pharisees and the experts in the law rejected God's purpose for themselves because they had not been baptized by John" (Luke 7:29–30). This failure of Israel's religious leadership highlighted a crucial principle: when those responsible for tilling neglect their duty, the entire community suffers. The Pharisees' hardened hearts prevented them from preparing the nation they were supposed to lead, creating the division and opposition that would later characterize Israel's response to the Messiah.

## DIVINE RAIN AND THE YIELD OF PREPARED HEARTS

John's ministry represented the return of divine communication after centuries of silence. The word of God coming to John (Luke 3:2) broke the prophetic drought, and through his preaching, God's voice once again addressed Israel directly. John's inspired teaching—whether calling for repentance, providing practical guidance to tax collectors and soldiers, or confronting religious hypocrisy—served as immediate "rain" watering the ground his ministry had tilled. The immediate yield of John's ministry appeared in the transformed lives of those who received his baptism. Tax collectors began acting honestly, soldiers showed mercy and contentment with their wages, and ordinary people developed genuine spiritual hunger.

These individual transformations demonstrated that the tilling/rain/yield principle was operating successfully at the personal level, producing concrete ethical and spiritual fruit. On a larger scale, John's ministry created a movement of spiritual renewal that swept through Israel. The widespread baptisms represented unprecedented acknowledgment of spiritual need and desire for divine intervention. This national stirring created the conditions necessary for the next phase of God's redemptive plan. John's disciples would become the core of the early Christian movement, his baptismal practice provided the foundation for Christian baptism, and his message of repentance and kingdom preparation became central themes in apostolic preaching. The success of John's preparatory work received divine validation through multiple confirmatory signs. The return of prophetic revelation after four hundred years of silence demonstrated God's approval of John's ministry. The mass response from all levels of society—except the religious establishment—showed that his tilling had successfully broken up Israel's hardened spiritual ground. Most significantly, the spiritual awakening John initiated continued to bear fruit long after his imprisonment and death, indicating that his work had created a lasting transformation rather than a temporary emotional response.

John's recognition that he must "decrease" so that the ultimate blessing could "increase" (John 3:30) showed that successful mediators understand their role as preparers rather than ultimate sources of blessing. This humility enabled the smooth transition from preparatory ministry to fulfilling ministry, ensuring that the yield of his work continued to multiply. The readiness John cultivated established a pattern that continues today, as believers are called to maintain constant preparedness for divine intervention. The Bible consistently emphasizes this necessity for preparedness: "Therefore you also be ready, for the Son of Man is coming at an hour you do not expect" (Matt 24:44), and "those who were ready went in with him to the wedding; and the door was shut" (Matt 25:10). This call for readiness applies equally to Christians today, who are called to make themselves "ready" for the marriage of the Lamb (Rev 19:7).

John the Baptist's ministry exemplifies the tilling/rain/yield principle operating at multiple levels simultaneously. Through personal discipline and prophetic calling, he prepared himself as a mediator. Through baptism and preaching, he tilled the hardened ground of Israel's heart. Through inspired teaching and spiritual guidance, he channeled divine rain to those ready to receive it. Through transformed lives and prepared hearts, his ministry yielded fruit that established the foundation for the next phase of redemptive history. Understanding John's role through this framework reveals the essential nature of preparation in receiving divine blessing. It demonstrates that spiritual fruitfulness requires both human preparation and divine intervention working in harmony.

## CONCLUSION

From Genesis through Revelation, this pattern governs how God interacts with individuals, families, and nations. Unlike approaches that emphasize either human effort or divine sovereignty exclusively, this principle shows their necessary cooperation. As we'll explore in the next chapter, Jesus emerges as the perfect example of this principle, being both the perfect mediator and the ultimate "rain" of divine blessing that produces eternal fruit.

# 9

# Jesus, the Sower of Heavenly Wisdom

Having established how the tilling/rain/yield principle governs divine-human cooperation throughout Scripture, we now turn to its ultimate fulfillment in Jesus Christ. Where Adam failed as the first mediator between heaven and earth, and where subsequent biblical figures achieved only partial success in their mediatorial roles, Christ emerges as the perfect embodiment of what the tilling/rain/yield pattern was always meant to accomplish. This chapter will demonstrate how Christ's identity as the perfect mediator transforms our understanding of the tilling/rain/yield principle. Rather than being merely a pattern that biblical figures either succeed or fail in completing, in Jesus, we see the pattern's intended purpose.

Jesus' ministry clearly built upon and continued the work John had begun. N. T. Wright notes, "It is clear that Jesus regarded John as an important fixed point at the beginning of his own ministry."[1] This continuity is strikingly evident in Christ's own initial message, which precisely echoed John's summons to Israel: "Repent, for the kingdom of heaven is at hand" (Matt 3:2; 4:17). Bishop Kallistos Ware profoundly observes, "St. John the Baptist and our Lord Jesus Christ both begin their preaching with the same words: 'Repent, for the kingdom of heaven is at hand' (Matt 3:2; 4:17). Such

1. Wright, *Jesus and the Victory*, 161.

is the starting point of the Good News—repentance. Without repentance, there can be no new life, no salvation, no entry into the Kingdom."[2]

Jesus highlights rain imagery: "He makes His sun rise on the evil and on the good, and sends rain on the just and on the unjust" (Matt 5:45). Jesus identifies the Father as the source of both physical and spiritual rain, positioning himself as the mediator who brings this divine blessing to prepared hearts. John's priestly ministry of repentance, therefore, served as the essential preparatory act for the coming Messiah that had come down from heaven. Paul declares Jesus as the singular and perfect Mediator of the new covenant: "But now He has obtained a more excellent ministry, inasmuch as He is also Mediator of a better covenant, which was established on better promises" (Heb 8:6); "And for this reason He is the Mediator of the new covenant, by means of death, for the redemption of the transgressions under the first covenant, that those who are called may receive the promise of the eternal inheritance" (Heb 9:15). Every previous mediator in Scripture was himself a recipient of divine rain before he could till for others—Moses needed the burning bush, Elijah needed the still small voice, the priests needed atonement for their own sin before Israel's. Christ alone required no preparation because he was himself the source of the rain he brought. He did not receive divine wisdom and transmit it; he was divine wisdom incarnate, which is why his yield—the church, the resurrection, eternal life—is of a categorically different order than anything that preceded it.

The preparation of those in Israel for a Messiah was successful since when Jesus called the fishermen to come and follow him, they "immediately left their nets and followed Him" (Mark 1:18). This response highlights that these men lived in regions where John's ministry had prepared hearts for the Messiah's arrival and ministry, immediately leaving their former occupations and following Christ. The disciples who received both John's preparation and Jesus' divine rain would themselves become participants of the tilling/rain/yield principle. Jesus commissioned them: "Go therefore and make disciples of all the nations, baptizing them in the name of the Father and of the Son and of the Holy Spirit, teaching them to observe all things that I have commanded you" (Matt 28:19–20). Notice the progression: they would prepare hearts through teaching (tilling), baptize as a sign of divine grace (rain), and produce new disciples who would repeat the cycle (yield).

Peter's Pentecost sermon and the crowd's response highlight this principle. Peter called the crowd to "repent, and let every one of you be baptized

2. Ware, *Inner Kingdom*, 43.

in the name of Jesus Christ for the remission of sins; and you shall receive the gift of the Holy Spirit" (Acts 2:38). The result was immediate fruitfulness: "Then those who gladly received his word were baptized; and that day about three thousand souls were added to them" (Acts 2:41). The disciples had become mediators themselves, facilitating the same divine-human cooperation they had experienced. This demonstrates how the tilling/rain/yield principle scales—what began with John preparing hearts expanded through Jesus to prepared followers, who then prepared thousands in and out of Israel, establishing the church as the ultimate yield of this divine-human cooperation. All highlight the human-divine cooperation at work in Israel. Below are how Peter and Paul align with this principle.

## Peter: The Miraculous Catch (Luke 5:1–11)

- Tilling: The "tilling" is the complete exhaustion of human effort and expertise, shown in Peter's admission of failure: "Master, we have toiled all night and caught nothing!" (Luke 5:5).
- Rain: The divine "rain" is Christ's command, which supersedes earthly experience: "Launch out into the deep and let down your nets for a catch" (Luke 5:4). This is met with Peter's faithful obedience: "Nevertheless at Your word I will let down the net" (Luke 5:5).
- Yield: The result is a threefold "yield," moving from the physical to the spiritual and vocational: a miraculous physical harvest, so that "they caught a great number of fish, and their net was breaking. . . . And they came and filled both the boats, so that they began to sink" (Luke 5:6–7).

## Paul's Conversion (Acts 9:1–22)

- Tilling: For three days he was without sight, and neither did eat nor drink (Acts 9:9). His fasting and blindness signify the humbling of pride, the breaking of self-reliance, and the inward preparation for divine encounter.
- Rain: Ananias entered the house and laid his hands on him, saying, "Brother Saul, the Lord Jesus . . . hath sent me, that thou mightest receive thy sight, and be filled with the Holy Spirit" (Acts 9:17).

Immediately there fell from his eyes as it were scales, and he received sight and arose, and was baptized (Acts 9:18).

- Yield: "Immediately he preached the Christ in the synagogues, that He is the Son of God" (Acts 9:20). The persecutor became the apostle, bearing witness before gentiles, kings, and the children of Israel (Acts 9:15, 22).

Notably, Christ didn't perform miracles in the towns where the people lacked faith. The human cooperation was missing and so the divine response wasn't made. Matthew 13:57-58: "So they were offended at Him. But Jesus said to them, 'A prophet is not without honor except in his own country and in his own house.' Now He did not do many mighty works there because of their unbelief." Faith is a human act of cooperation in the principle of synergy, the cooperative movement of human will and divine grace in which neither replaces the other. Christ does not override human freedom to produce yield; he requires the ground of a willing heart. Nazareth's unbelief was not a power failure on Christ's part but a cooperation failure on theirs. The principle cannot be forced; it can only be fulfilled.

## JESUS AS DIVINE RAIN IN THE SERMON ON THE MOUNT

The Beatitudes as divine rain patterns: the Beatitudes (Matt 5:3–12) illustrate the tilling/rain/yield principle. Each beatitude follows the same structure:

"Blessed are the poor in spirit, for theirs is the kingdom of heaven" (Matt 5:3):

- Tilling: recognizing spiritual poverty and need for God (humility)
- Rain: Jesus declaring divine blessing upon this condition
- Yield: receiving the kingdom of heaven

"Blessed are those who mourn, for they shall be comforted" (Matt 5:4):

- Tilling: genuine mourning over sin and brokenness
- Rain: divine comfort flowing from heaven
- Yield: consolation and healing

"Blessed are those who hunger and thirst for righteousness, for they shall be filled" (Matt 5:6):

- Tilling: intense spiritual hunger and seeking
- Rain: God's righteousness descending to meet that hunger
- Yield: spiritual satisfaction and fulfillment

## PRACTICAL APPLICATIONS:

Jesus makes the dynamic explicit: "Ask, and it will be given to you; seek, and you will find; knock, and it will be opened to you" (Matt 7:7). This teaching reveals the tilling/rain dynamic—proper spiritual preparation (asking, seeking, knocking) enables divine response. The pattern is obvious—proper spiritual posture enables divine response. Those who ask receive; those who seek find. The Sermon on the Mount is itself divine rain falling on the prepared crowds, and Jesus tells them how to continue receiving: maintain the posture, and heaven remains open.

Salt and light (Matt 5:13–16): Jesus describes his followers as those who have received divine rain and now produce a yield that benefits others. The salt preserves and the light illuminates—both representing the fruitfulness that flows from receiving heavenly wisdom.

The Golden Rule (Matt 7:12): this represents the yield phase—those who have received divine rain (mercy, forgiveness, love) now extend the same to others, completing the cycle of divine-human cooperation. This connects Jesus' teaching directly to your established pattern while showing how his words themselves function as the divine rain that produces transformation in prepared hearts.

## THE PARABLES

Importantly, Christ communicates how the ground is understood on multiple scales. In the parable of the sower (Matt 13, Mark 4, Luke 8), the "soil" is clearly identified as the human heart—some hearts are hard, rocky, thorny, or good, and the word takes root or withers depending on that interior condition. The parable is not merely an agricultural metaphor; it discloses how preparation and receptivity to God determine the yield within the human heart. Since the human person is a microcosm of creation, the same spiritual realities unfold both inwardly and cosmically. But in the parable of the weeds (Matt 13:24–30, 36–43), the "field" is explicitly called the world, where the good seed are the "sons of the kingdom" and the weeds are "sons of the evil," highlighting how like the fractal nature of the frameworks discussed, we can see how Christ and the Bible see unity among the scales.

When disciples ask why he speaks in parables (Matt 13:10), Jesus responds, "To you it has been given to know the mysteries of the kingdom . . . but to them it has not been given." This sounds like an arbitrary divine choice until you read the next verse: "For whoever has, to him more will be given . . . but whoever does not have, even what he has will be taken away." That's the tilling principle. Those who prepared their hearts to receive ("whoever has") receive more revelation. Those with hardened hearts ("whoever does not have") can't receive even what's offered. Same seed, different soil preparation.

## THE PARABLES: JESUS AS MASTER INTERPRETER OF GENESIS PATTERNS

Jesus' teaching ministry reveals him as a moral teacher but also as the authority on the kingdom of heaven and the total corpus of the Old Testament. He is the perfect mediator, bringing heavenly rain to a now tilled, prepared earth. One example of this can be in his role, revealing the kingdom of heaven to his followers in the preaching of the parables. Matthew reveals the profound significance of Christ's parabolic teaching: "That it might be fulfilled which was spoken by the prophet [Isaiah], saying: 'I will open my mouth in parables; I will utter things kept secret from the foundation of the world'" (Matt 13:35). These are not arbitrary moral lessons but revelations of the fundamental cosmology established in Genesis.

While the text doesn't specify which secrets Jesus reveals, his consistent reference to Genesis themes—seeds, soil and fruit, serpents, new wine, the bridegroom's presence—suggests he's unveiling the foundational patterns of divine-human relationship established in creation. The mysteries kept secret include how God's kingdom operates according to principles established "from the foundation"—the very principles we see in Gen 1–4. Christ provides the keys to unlock the foundational stories of the Old Testament, revealing what was hidden to those who did not understand the spiritual meaning of the Genesis patterns.

Isaiah highlights that these parables reveal truths "from the foundation of the world"—truths on how the kingdom of heaven comes to enter and dwell on earth, precisely the cosmology established in the Adam and Eve narrative. When Jesus declares "He who has ears to hear, let him hear!" (Matt 13:9), he is calling his audience to use their spiritual faculties to perceive these foundational patterns. Specifically, one can see much commonality with the parable of the sower: "But he who received seed on the good ground is he who hears the word and understands it, who indeed bears fruit and produces: some a hundredfold, some sixty, some thirty" (Matt 13:23).

We know that good ground are those prepared, tilled, and who come with a repentant, humble heart ready to receive the words of God and flourish, producing a yield in multitudes. When someone properly fulfills the Adam roles (receiving and transmitting divine wisdom), they create conditions for others to develop their own communion with God. The "hundredfold" return represents successful spiritual reproduction—one person properly fulfilling their authority role enables many others to do the same.

Jesus often urges his audience, "Let those with ears hear, and those with eyes see," underscoring the necessity of using one's faculties with spiritual discernment to truly receive and understand the words of God. He laments, "For seeing they do not see, and hearing they do not hear, nor do they understand. Indeed, in their case, the prophecy of Isaiah is fulfilled, which says: 'You will indeed hear but never understand, and you will indeed see but never perceive. For this people's heart has grown dull; with their ears they can barely hear, and their eyes they have closed, lest they should see with their eyes, hear with their ears, understand with their heart, and turn, and I would heal them" (Matt 13:10–15). This passage highlights the spiritual blindness and deafness of those who refuse to prepare their hearts, hindering the reception of heavenly wisdom.

## The Mustard Seed (Matt 13:31–32)

"The kingdom of heaven is like a mustard seed, which a man took and sowed in his field, which indeed is the least of all the seeds; but when it is grown it is greater than the herbs and becomes a tree, so that the birds of the air come and nest in its branches." This parable shows how proper Adam-Eve ordering begins small (individual/family scale) but grows to provide shelter and blessing for "all the birds of the air" (corporate/national scale). The pattern of divine wisdom properly received and applied scales upward to bless entire communities.

### The Leaven (Matt 13:33)

"The kingdom of heaven is like leaven, which a woman took and hid in three measures of meal till it was all leavened." This demonstrates how divine wisdom, properly received by faithful mediators, transforms entire communities from within. The woman in this parable represents the positive Eve function—taking what has been provided and working it throughout the entire household until transformation is complete. These parables contrast sharply with the first Adam, who possessed the ultimate treasure in his relationship with God but traded it for immediate earthly satisfaction. The perfect response these parables illustrate shows what Adam's reaction should have been when offered alternative wisdom.

### The Wedding Banquet (Matt 22:1–14)

"The kingdom of heaven is like a certain king who arranged a marriage for his son" (v. 2). This parable presents the invitation to the ultimate Adam-Eve relationship—Christ and his church. The original invited guests who refuse to come represent Israel's religious leaders who rejected their calling as mediators. The servants who go into the highways represent faithful mediators who gather anyone willing to come. The man without wedding garments represents those who attempt to participate in the divine union without proper preparation (righteousness), demonstrating that even participation in the final Adam-Eve relationship requires appropriate spiritual clothing.

## THE PARABOLIC REVELATION OF GENESIS PATTERNS

Through this comprehensive parabolic teaching, Jesus reveals himself as the master interpreter of the Genesis patterns we have established. Every parable illuminates different aspects of the fundamental truths of reality:

- Receptivity: The varying soils show different levels of openness to divine wisdom.
- Growth: The mustard seed and leaven show how proper ordering scales upward.
- Priority: The treasure and pearl show the supreme value of divine wisdom.

- Obedience: The two sons and wicked tenants show faithful versus unfaithful mediation.
- Preparation: The virgins show the necessity of maintaining spiritual readiness.
- Judgment: The dragnet and talents show the ultimate consequences of mediatorial success or failure.
- Consummation: The wedding feast shows the ultimate Adam-Eve union between Christ and his church.

Jesus doesn't tell random moral stories but reveals how the Genesis creation order finds its fulfillment in the kingdom of heaven. He positions himself as the Second Adam who succeeds where the first Adam failed, perfectly receiving divine wisdom, maintaining obedience under temptation, and producing the ultimate yield—the church as his bride.

## The Disciples' Privilege: "Blessed Are Your Eyes"

When Jesus declared to his disciples, "But blessed are your eyes because they see, and your ears because they hear. For truly I tell you, many prophets and righteous people longed to see what you see but did not see it, and to hear what you hear but did not hear it" (Matt 13:16–17), he was revealing far more than their privilege of witnessing his earthly ministry. These words, spoken immediately after explaining the parable of the sower, point to a profound privilege—the disciples were receiving interpretive and ontological keys that others in the past were not privy to.

The timing of this declaration proves crucial. Jesus had just explained why he spoke in parables: "The knowledge of the secrets of the kingdom of heaven has been given to you, but not to them" (Matt 13:11). The "secrets" were not just doctrinal truths but also interpretive principles that would enable the disciples to understand how all Scripture coheres around the fundamental Adam-Eve patterns established in Genesis. Through his parables, Jesus was providing the missing hermeneutical pattern and ontological insights that even the greatest Old Testament figures lacked.

This interpretive privilege explains why the apostles could later write with such confidence about how Old Testament narratives prefigured Christ. Paul's ability to see Adam as a "type of the one who was to come" (Rom 5:14), his insight that Abraham's two sons constituted an allegory (Gal 4:24), and his recognition that Israel's wilderness experiences "happened to them as examples" (1 Cor 10:11) all flow from the foundation Jesus established through his parabolic method. The phrase "many prophets and righteous people longed to see" carries profound implications for contemporary biblical interpretation. Daniel may have received visions of future kingdoms, but he could not fully comprehend their meaning—the parabolic keys that would unlock his prophecies had not yet been revealed. While Jesus established the new method of teaching through parables, he also had to establish his new authority by closing the era of the old. This transition is most visibly marked in the fate of his forerunner, John the Baptist.

## JOHN THE BAPTIST: ISRAEL'S PROPHETIC HEAD

From the beginning, the head has cosmological significance. God breathed life into Adam through his nostrils (Gen 2:7), making the head the entry point for the divine Spirit. Yet by opening his mouth to the forbidden fruit, Adam made the head—the place designed for life—the channel of death: "For in the day that you eat of it you shall surely die" (Gen 2:17). From Eden onward, Scripture reveals this pattern: whenever the head is overtaken—whether nostrils, mouth, or crown—life gives way to judgment.

The prophetic office in Israel culminated in John the Baptist. Jesus himself confirmed John's significance: "For all the prophets and the law prophesied until John" (Matt 11:13). With John's death, the prophetic head of Israel was removed. As Heb 1:1–2 explains, "God, who . . . spoke in time past to the fathers by the prophets, has in these last days spoken to us by His Son." Israel, having killed John and rejecting Jesus Christ, lost its prophetic head. He was Israel's prophetic head, bridging law and promise, declaring Christ as "the Lamb of God who takes away the sin of the world" (John 1:29). At Jesus' baptism, John bore witness to his divine identity and role as Savior, fulfilling his mission to prepare Israel for the Messiah. Like Nathan before David or Elijah before Ahab, John rebuked Herod's sin—and for this, his head was literally cut off. John's beheading is the physical act signifying Israel's prophetic end, being cut off.

John was the son of Zechariah, a priest, symbolizing a priestly lineage that had come to an end. By humbly surrendering his authority and followers to Christ, John acted as one of the few inheritors who embraced his office and faithfully fulfilled his role. His death, therefore, marks the violent end not only of a prophet but also of the priesthood of the old covenant. This paves the way for Christ to establish the priesthood of the new covenant (of Melchizedek), which transcends earthly lineage and national borders. The beheading thus signifies that the ancient earthly system of mediation through bloodline is complete and has been replaced by the final act of mediation through the cross. Yet in Christ, the pattern of the breath of life entering a body continues—Christ breathes life into his disciples, and they receive the Holy Spirit. (John 20:22).

## ISRAEL WITHOUT A HEAD: THE WITNESS AFTER PENTECOST

The following text from the apocryphal Secret Book of James describes a conversation between Jesus and his disciple James, said to take place after Pentecost: "Then I asked Him, 'Master, can we prophesy to those who ask us to prophesy to them?' . . . The Master answered and said, 'Do you not know that the head of prophecy was cut off with John?'"[3]

In this text, the disciples appear concerned about their ministry and their ability to prophesy to Israel still. Yet Israel repeatedly hardened their hearts and denied Christ as their Messiah, crucifying him. The "head of prophecy" being cut off applies to Israel, which rejected Jesus and the witness that John bore about him. As a result, Israel will no longer receive prophets to intercede on their behalf. James emphasizes the existential reality of this severance: "The body without the spirit is dead" (Jas 2:26). St. Ephrem writes, "The daughter of Sara [Israel] beheld the King's Son; she saw that He was chaste, and she became downcast. She saw that He was pure, and so she pretended to be sick, for she was accustomed to adulterers. She accused Him so that she might not herself be accused."[4] St. Ephrem suggests that Israel, in its spiritual blindness, took on the role of the accuser, mirroring Satan's character. This resonates with John the Baptist's sweeping indictment of "all Israel" as a "brood of vipers" in Luke 3:7–8, implying a pervasive influence of deception and spiritual corruption. This broader application suggests a widespread spiritual malaise within Israel, not confined to the religious elite. John's message challenges the assumption that lineage alone guarantees salvation, calling for genuine repentance and transformed lives for all of Israel.

3. Meyer, *Nag Hammadi Scriptures*, 26.

4. Brock, *Luminous Eye*, 119.

When Christ breathes on the disciples—"Receive the Holy Spirit" (John 20:22)—he restores what John's beheading severed. The prophetic breath that entered Adam through his nostrils, which was cut off when John's head was taken, now flows again through the risen Head of the church. At Pentecost, tongues of fire rest upon each head (Acts 2:3), demonstrating that prophecy no longer depends on a single national head but is distributed through Christ to his entire body. What Israel lost through rejection, the church receives through faith—not as replacement but as expansion of divine purposes beyond national boundaries into "all nations" (Matt 28:19). Speaking to the Jews, "Paul and Barnabas grew bold and said, "It was necessary that the word of God should be spoken to you first; but since you reject it, and judge yourselves unworthy of everlasting life, behold, we turn to the Gentiles" (Act 13:46).

## THE FLOATING HEAD: VINDICATION AND ASCENT

Yet John's story does not end in silence. Apocryphal tradition records a startling vision at that wicked feast of Herod's: "Suddenly the head of the blessed John let the locks of its hair loose from the plate, spread them, and flew to the center of the room in front of the king and high officials. At that very moment, the roof of the building opened and John's head flew high into the air."[5] John is the representative of the faithful remnant of Israel, separate from the corrupt generation. Here, the martyr's decapitated head, lifted beyond earthly confines, highlights his faithfulness. This theme of floating or rising recurs throughout Scripture. In 2 Kgs 6:5–6, Elisha causes a sunken axe-head to rise: "So he cut off a stick, and threw it in there; and he made the iron float." The axe-head, like John's head, is lifted from chaotic waters, emblematic of divine preservation: the purified element of God's people is not submerged in worldly turbulence but rescued and elevated. Likewise, Noah's ark was lifted "high above the earth" (Gen 7:17). Genesis recounts, "The waters increased and lifted up the ark, and it rose high above the earth. The waters prevailed and greatly increased on the earth, and the ark moved about on the surface of the waters" (Gen 7:17–18). John's floating head belongs to the same pattern: the faithful remnant, though severed, is lifted above chaos. In all these cases—John's head, the floating axe, the ark—the underlying principle is the triumph of the faithful remnant. Whether through martyrdom, miraculous preservation, or divinely

5. Burke and Landau. *New Testament Apocrypha*, 289.

orchestrated ascent, the motif of "floating" signifies participation in God's salvific plan. John does not simply die; he is lifted, elevated, and foreshadows the vindication of those who remain true to God.

## HEAD COSMOLOGY FROM GENESIS TO CHRIST

Christ as Head of his church now aligns proper authority with God, overcoming the fallen headship of Adam.

- The fall: Adam, the first head, fails in his role of headship.
- The promise: God immediately promises that the serpent's head—the source of the rebellion—will be crushed.
- The curse reversed: Christ, the new Head, takes the curse of the ground ("thorns and thistles") directly onto his own head.
- The old order ends: The prophetic head of old-covenant Israel, John the Baptist, is literally severed, signifying the end of that era's authority. Christ becomes the new Head of the church, his body. Yet Christ, the true Head, reverses the pattern. In baptism, heads go under the waters not to drown but to rise. In the Eucharist, mouths are filled not with judgment but with the Bread of Life. And in the church, prophecy flows anew—not through a single national head, but through Christ to his whole body. Paul captures the climax: God "put all things under His feet, and gave Him to be head over all things to the church, which is His body, the fullness of Him who fills all in all" (Eph 1:22–23).

## CONCLUSION

This analysis reveals Jesus as the perfect fulfillment of the tilling/rain/yield principle established in Genesis and demonstrated throughout Scripture. Where John's ministry provided essential tilling through repentance, preparing Israel's hardened ground, Jesus emerges as the ultimate divine rain—heavenly wisdom descending to prepared hearts, ultimately raining down the Holy Spirit upon his disciples. The ultimate yield of Jesus' perfect mediation is the church itself—disciples who become agents of the same tilling/rain/yield cycle, preparing hearts through teaching, channeling divine grace through baptism, and producing spiritual multiplication across generations. What began with Adam's failed mediation finds its consummation in Christ's perfect success, establishing the pattern for all subsequent divine-human cooperation in the church age.

His Sermon on the Mount shows how proper spiritual postures (poverty of spirit, mourning, hungering for righteousness) create receptivity for divine blessing. His parables reveal how Genesis patterns find their ultimate expression in the kingdom of heaven, from individual heart conditions (parable of the sower) to cosmic realities (wheat and tares). The disciples' privilege in receiving these interpretive keys extends to contemporary Christians who can now read Scripture with the hermeneutical tools Jesus provided.

# 10

# Inheritor-Versus-Renewer Principle

ANOTHER PRINCIPLE SEEMS TO be established with Cain and Abel in Gen 4, what I call the "inheritor-versus-renewer principle"—a pattern that reveals why God consistently chooses the younger over the elder, the unexpected over the obvious, the renewer over the inheritor, throughout Scripture. This pattern centers on the story of two brothers, Cain and Abel, but encompasses the fundamental dynamics of how God works to preserve his chosen people, reorienting their hearts back to him. This pattern can most commonly be seen in two brothers. While this may not be strictly accurate for all the characters we will review, in the Bible, the term "brother" is often used loosely to indicate relationships that reflect this same principle. As this pattern seems to apply to those who aren't strictly siblings, such as Jonathan (the older) and David (the younger), or Abraham and Lot, we see that the biblical authors understood something deeper at work. David refers to Jonathan as his brother (2 Sam 1:26), and Abraham calls Lot his brother (Gen 14:14). This shows that even within the Bible, the term "brother" isn't used rigidly but points to a relationship between those who inherit earthly problems and those called to renewal. If the use of "brother" seems unconvincing, we can refer to it more precisely as the pattern of the "inheritor" versus the "renewer."

This pattern aligns with the Jewish custom and its implications, where the elder brother, possessing the birthright, inherited the majority of the family property, while the younger brother was often overlooked.

"The birthright consists of the material inheritance. The firstborn usually received a greater share from the father because he was expected to become the paterfamilias, having ultimate responsibility for all members of the extended family. . . . With greater responsibility came greater resources."[1] You might think the elder would always be the ideal figure to follow, given their inherited advantages and responsibilities, but that is often not the case in the stories we read. As Robert Alter observes, "The firstborn often seems to be the loser in Genesis, simply due to the very condition of their birth."[2] This seeming paradox reveals something profound about how God's order operates—it challenges human assumptions about power, inheritance, and worthiness.

To understand this pattern and its implications, we must recognize that it reflects the fundamental tension between center and periphery, between divine wisdom and earthly concerns, that we have traced throughout Scripture. The elder brother typically inherits not just material possessions but the consequences of the fall—the cursed ground, the thorns and thistles, the burden of maintaining order in a disordered world. The elder inherits the land and, more importantly, the problems of the land. John 3:31 illuminates this principle: "He who is of the earth is earthly and speaks of the earth. He who comes from heaven is above all." Being so close to the earthly problems, the elder often relies on earthly solutions—solutions that may be "too low" within the role as mediator. The elder's closeness to the world and all its thorns, combined with expectations for leadership and management of inherited problems, usually makes him trapped at the periphery, focused on managing chaos rather than moving toward divine order.

Meanwhile, the younger brother, neglected by worldly standards and freed from the burden of inheritance, often finds himself in a position to prioritize communion with God over earthly concerns. Within this symbolic geography, the elder, bound to the periphery or lower earthly realities by inheritance or exile, has a harder time overcoming these temptations and having a proper orientation toward God. While the younger is free to move toward the center or look to heaven—this explains the consistent pattern we see throughout Scripture. The inheritance represents attachment to the material realm and its limitations, while the divine represents the possibility of transcending those limitations through participation in heavenly order. The elder brother becomes symbolic of humanity's natural tendency

1. Keener and Walton, *NKJV Cultural Backgrounds*, 64.

2. Alter, *Art of Biblical Narrative*, 5.

to trust in inherited structures and earthly solutions, while the younger represents the possibility of renewal through divine intervention that transcends natural expectations. As discussed previously, Cain, as an inheritor, needed to restore communion with God, putting faith in God to provide.

## CAIN AND ABEL: THE ORIGIN OF THE PATTERN

After Adam and Eve's fall from the garden—their exile from center to periphery—they had two sons, Cain and Abel. Their primary responsibility was to restore their relationship with God and create a sacred space that would restore communion with divine presence, bringing stability to the land through proper mediation. Understanding their story within the pattern illuminates why their different approaches led to such dramatically different outcomes. Cain, as the older brother, inherited the world and its burdens—specifically, the cursed ground mentioned in Gen 3:17—from his parents. This inheritance placed him at the periphery, dealing directly with the consequences of the fall, in exile. Like his father, he became a tiller of the ground (Gen 4:2), continuing the family tradition and believing this inherited approach would help them survive in their harsh environment. His occupation connected him directly to the cursed earth and its resistance to human efforts.

Yet Cain, like his father, Adam, remained a mediator—a "Son of Man" figure—since he communicated directly with God. Cain's conversations with God in Gen 4:6 and 4:9 highlight the role inherited from Adam and the close communion that God still desired from humanity. This reveals that Cain's failure was not due to lack of access to divine wisdom but due to his orientation toward earthly solutions over heavenly guidance, not connecting the divine rain, God's wisdom, with the tilled, prepared earth in which he was toiling. The crucial difference between Cain's situation and his father Adam's lies in their location and orientation. Adam's original role as a tiller was rooted in communion with God within the garden of Eden, at the center where heaven and earth intersected harmoniously. Adam had initially received divine wisdom from above, successfully obeying God's commands in sacred space and properly ordering his environment. Adam was initially successful as a mediator, connecting heavenly wisdom with prepared earthly soil, cultivating his land and gathering a righteous yield.

## ABEL: THE RENEWER

Abel, as a keeper of sheep—a shepherd (Gen 4:2)—fulfilled the role of mediator in a fundamentally different way. The Bible frequently refers to God's followers as sheep, and shepherds represent those who gather and guide people toward divine wisdom. As a shepherd, Abel was gathering followers just as Adam had been called to do, creating a community of faithful people and offering sacrifices to God in the manner that divine wisdom expected from humanity. This explains why his sacrifice was favorable compared to Cain's.

Abel's role as shepherd represents movement toward center through proper mediation between heaven and earth. Unlike his brother, who inherited the burden of cursed ground and became trapped in earthly concerns, Abel's vocation freed him to focus on spiritual realities and proper orientation. His sacrifice of "the firstborn of his flock and of their fat" (Gen 4:4) represented the best of what he had been given, offered with proper reverence and faith.

The pattern reveals a profound principle: those who inherit earthly responsibilities often become so focused on managing inherited problems that they lose sight of their calling to mediation and faith in God over the works of one's hands. The elder brother's inheritance includes not just material possessions but spiritual burdens—the accumulated consequences of the fall, the expectation to maintain order in a disordered world, the responsibility to solve problems through earthly means. This situation creates what we might call "inheritance paralysis"—the elder becomes so focused on managing what has been inherited that he fails to seek divine wisdom for renewal and transformation.

## THE NEW TESTAMENT ON CAIN

The New Testament provides crucial insight into the dynamics of Cain's failure: "In this, the children of God and the children of the devil are manifest: whoever does not practice righteousness is not of God, nor is he who does not love his brother. For this is the message that you heard from the beginning: that we should love one another, not as Cain, who was of the wicked one and murdered his brother. And why did he murder him? Because his works were evil and his brother's were righteous" (1 John 3:10–12). This passage illuminates the principles at stake by connecting Cain's story to Christ's parable of the wheat and tares in Matt 13. Cain did not practice righteousness because he failed to integrate heavenly wisdom into his heart, express it properly in the world, and acquire a righteous "body" of followers from the Lord—spiritual offspring.

First John reinforces this interpretation by aligning it with Christ's teaching. The "children of the devil" referenced in 1 John 3 are equivalent to the "sons of the wicked one" mentioned in Matt 13:38. As a priest and mediator before God, Cain performed his role poorly by prioritizing earthly solutions over heavenly wisdom. Rather than prioritizing faith and proper orientation, Cain took matters into his own hands, believing he could solve his inherited problems by following the earthly work patterns he had learned from his father's pre-fall success in the garden. Jesus says, "Blessed are the meek, for they will inherit the earth" (Matt 5:5). Paul also provides the principle Cain needed to understand: "For with the heart one believes and is justified, and with the mouth one confesses and is saved" (Rom 10:10). Merely tilling the land and performing the inherited duties without faith and proper expression of divine wisdom would never be sufficient for successful mediation.

In many ways, Cain mirrors the Pharisees, whose focus on inherited religious traditions, legalistic views of their relationships with God, and uncharitable zeal toward those they rule, led them to miss God's renewal through Christ. The Pharisees became so concerned with managing and policing inherited religious systems that they lost sight of their calling to mediation—bringing God's love and grace to the world rather than merely maintaining traditional structures. Jesus rebukes them for also disregarding the proper sacrifice and orientation: "Woe to you, scribes and Pharisees, hypocrites! For you pay tithe of mint and anise and cumin, and have neglected the weightier matters of the law: justice and mercy and faith. These you ought to have done, without leaving the others undone" (Matt 23:23).

This wrongful orientation ultimately became a key factor in Cain's downfall much like the Pharisees. Christ's words would have offered Cain the wisdom and reorientation he needed to avoid his tragic path: "Therefore do not worry, saying, 'What shall we eat?' or 'What shall we drink?' or 'What shall we wear?' For after all these things the Gentiles seek. For your heavenly Father knows that you need all these things. But seek first the kingdom of God and His righteousness, and all these things shall be added to you" (Matt 6:31–33). This teaching reveals the fundamental principle: proper orientation toward divine wisdom (seeking first God's kingdom) ensures that earthly needs are met as secondary consequences, rather than making earthly concerns the primary focus.

Paul reinforces this orientation: "Set your mind on things above, not on things on the earth" (Col 3:2). This doesn't mean neglecting earthly responsibilities but approaching them from the perspective of the center rather than periphery. "By faith Abel offered to God a more excellent sacrifice than Cain, through which he obtained witness that he was righteous, God testifying of his gifts; and through it he being dead still speaks" (Heb 11:4). True communion with God must always take precedence over any works achieved through human effort alone.

This principle appears throughout Scripture: "If my people who are called by my name will humble themselves, and pray and seek my face, and turn from their wicked ways, then I will hear from heaven, and will forgive their sin and heal their land" (2 Chr 7:14). This analysis highlights how Cain's priorities were inverted, leading him down a path of resentment and exile to further separation rather than renewal and movement toward divine presence.

## ESAU AND JACOB: THE PATTERN CONTINUES

The brotherly pattern continues with Esau and Jacob, whose complex relationship further illuminates the themes of inheritance versus renewal, earthly power versus heavenly authority. Jacob, through his cunning and his mother's guidance, ultimately receives the firstborn blessing that belonged to Esau by natural inheritance. This story reveals additional layers of the principle at work. "Esau represents earthly power, and Jacob represents heavenly authority. Like Cain and Abel, Esau and Jacob are twin re-presentations of Adam's mediation. Therefore, their relationship mirrors the conflict between Cain and Abel after the fall."[3] As the natural heir, Esau holds significant earthly power due to his inheritance of the family's land and his father's favor.

However, his lack of wisdom becomes evident when he allows physical hunger to influence a decision as critical as giving up his birthright—the spiritual authority that comes with being the covenant bearer. Malachi 1:3: "But Esau I have hated, And laid waste his mountains and his heritage For the jackals of the wilderness." Jacob, like other younger brothers in this pattern, doesn't inherit the immediate earthly problems and responsibilities

3. Pageau, *Language of Creation*, 110.

that burden the elder, allowing him greater freedom to prioritize communion with God and reorientation over earthly concerns. The mysterious statement from 2 Esdras illuminates this principle: "Now Esau is the end of this age, and Jacob is the beginning of the age that follows" (2 Esd 6:9, NRSVUE). This suggests that Esau represents the culmination of earthly, material focus, while Jacob represents the beginning of renewed orientation toward divine purpose.

The famous scene of the birthright transaction reveals the dynamics at work: "Now Jacob cooked a stew; and Esau came in from the field, and he was weary. And Esau said to Jacob, 'Please feed me with that same red stew, for I am weary.' Therefore his name was called Edom. But Jacob said, 'Sell me your birthright as of this day.' And Esau said, 'Look, I am about to die; so what is this birthright to me?'" (Gen 25:29–32). The deeper meaning of this text reveals that Esau, having mismanaged his earthly inheritance and ruled poorly, ultimately found himself desperate and powerless. Near death, with his body weakened and his earthly resources apparently exhausted, he traded his calling—his right to serve as covenant mediator—for mere physical survival. This represents the ultimate triumph of earthly concerns over calling, of immediate material needs over spiritual inheritance. Jacob's position in this scene, as well as his later receiving of Isaac's blessing through Rebekah's devising in Gen 27, demonstrates the principle that the divine often works through unexpected means to accomplish renewal. As Matthieu Pageau observes, "Through his mother's cunning, Jacob inherited certain 'earthly attributes' from Esau. This dual inheritance granted Jacob not only heavenly authority but also earthly power."[4]

## JOSEPH AND HIS BROTHERS: THE PATTERN IN FULL DISPLAY

Perhaps nowhere is the inheritor/renewer pattern more dramatically illustrated than in the story of Joseph and his eleven brothers. The ten older brothers inherit the land of Canaan with all its tribal conflicts, family tensions, and earthly responsibilities. Joseph, as the eleventh son (younger than ten), receives instead the prophetic dreams that mark him as God's chosen renewer, destined to save both his family and the known world through elevation that transcends natural inheritance.

4. Pageau, *Language of Creation*, 110.

Joseph's dreams reveal the nature of his calling—sheaves bowing down, sun and moon, and eleven stars paying homage—imagery that transcends mere family dynamics and points to authority that will affect nations. The elder brothers, secure in their earthly inheritance, cannot comprehend that it bypasses natural succession. Joseph's interpretation of Pharaoh's dreams and his subsequent elevation to the second ruler of Egypt represent the fulfillment of the inheritor/renewer pattern. When the brothers come to Egypt seeking food, the irony becomes complete. Those who inherited the land cannot sustain life from it during famine, while the one they exiled has become the source of life for all nations. Joseph's response demonstrates the principle of the renewer: instead of revenge, he extends forgiveness and provision. "But as for you, you meant evil against me; but God meant it for good, in order to bring it about as it is this day, to save many people alive" (Gen 50:20).

## EPHRAIM AND MANASSEH: THE PATTERN TRANSMITTED

The story reaches its culmination when the aged Jacob, now called Israel, deliberately inverts the natural order by blessing Ephraim the younger over Manasseh the elder. This scene demonstrates Jacob's mature understanding of principles learned through his own experience of divine over natural inheritance. "When Joseph saw his father placing his right hand on Ephraim's head, he was displeased. Taking hold of his father's hand, he tried to move it from Ephraim's head to Manasseh's. 'Not so, my father,' Joseph protested, 'for this one is the firstborn; place your right hand on his head.' But his father refused, saying, 'I know, my son, I know. He too will become a people, and he too will be great. However, his younger brother will be greater than he, and his descendants will form a multitude of nations'" (Gen 48:17–19).

Jacob's response—"I know, my son, I know"—reveals deep understanding. Having personally experienced God's blessing of the younger over the elder, he now participates in transmitting this pattern to the next generation. In this act, Jacob moves from recipient to mediator, consciously transmitting the same principle that once overturned his own natural standing. The historical fulfillment confirms the significance of this blessing. Ephraim becomes the dominant tribe in the northern kingdom, often representing all Israel in prophetic literature, while Manasseh, though great, remains secondary. The pattern continues: divine accomplishes what natural inheritance could not.

## MOSES AND AARON

The relationship between Moses and Aaron presents a more complex example of the inheritor/renewer pattern, since both brothers serve crucial roles in God's purposes, yet Moses consistently receives greater authority despite being the younger brother. Aaron, as the elder, possesses natural qualifications for religious leadership—he speaks eloquently where Moses stammers, he understands priestly functions through family tradition, and he initially serves as Moses' spokesman before Pharaoh. The golden calf incident provides the clearest illustration of how inherited religious authority can fail under pressure. When Moses ascends Mount Sinai to receive the Law, Aaron inherits temporary leadership of the people. Faced with their demands for visible gods, Aaron chooses earthly expedience over faithfulness: "And Aaron said to them, 'Break off the golden earrings which are in the ears of your wives, your sons, and your daughters, and bring them to me'" (Exod 32:2). What they are doing is instead of putting faith in God, they are relying on their own self-determination, self-mediating how to preserve themselves. Stephen in Acts provides this insight: "And in their hearts, they turned back to Egypt, saying to Aaron, 'Make us gods to go before us; as for this Moses who brought us out of the land of Egypt, we do not know what has become of him.' And they made a calf in those days, offered sacrifices to the idol, and rejoiced in the works of their own hands" (Acts 7:39–41).

## DAVID AND HIS SEVEN BROTHERS: DIVINE CHOICE OVER HUMAN QUALIFICATION

When Samuel arrives at Jesse's house to anoint Israel's next king, he encounters the classic setup for the inheritor/renewer pattern. Seven older brothers possess all the natural qualifications for kingship—impressive physical stature, military bearing, and the dignity expected of rulers. David remains forgotten in the fields, fulfilling the humble occupation of shepherd at the periphery, tending his father's sheep far from the centers of political power. Samuel's initial response reveals how deeply human wisdom is influenced by earthly appearances: "So it was, when they came, that he looked at Eliab and said, 'Surely the Lord's anointed is before Him!'" (1 Sam 16:6). Eliab, as the eldest, possessed every earthly qualification for inheriting royal authority. Yet God's response establishes how he sees differently than man—"but the Lord looks at the heart" (1 Sam 16:7).

The significance of David's shepherding becomes clear when we recognize that it represents the ultimate form of mediation—gathering scattered sheep (people) toward divine protection and provision. Unlike his brothers, who would naturally focus on inheriting and managing earthly kingdoms, David's vocation trained him to prioritize the welfare of those under his care over his own advancement.

David's path to kingship follows the classic pattern of testing through apparent defeat and exile. While Saul represents the inheritor of earthly kingship through natural succession, David must flee to caves and wilderness, living as an outlaw at the periphery. Yet this exile becomes his preparation for authentic leadership. The psalms written during this period reveal David's orientation. Rather than focusing on earthly injustice or political strategy, David consistently appeals to divine righteousness and justice: "The Lord is my shepherd; I shall not want" (Ps 23:1). Having been a shepherd himself, David understands mediation from both perspectives—the care required to guide others and the trust required to be guided by divine wisdom.

## SOLOMON AND ADONIJAH: WISDOM VERSUS POLITICAL INHERITANCE

The pattern continues into the next generation with the succession struggle between Adonijah and Solomon. Adonijah, as David's fourth son but the eldest surviving after Amnon, Chileab, and Absalom, possessed a natural claim to inherit the throne through earthly succession. More importantly, he had the support of key political figures—Joab the military commander and Abiathar the priest—representing earthly power and religious authority. Adonijah's approach to securing the throne reveals the classic inheritor mentality: "Then Adonijah the son of Haggith exalted himself, saying, 'I will be king'; and he prepared for himself chariots and horsemen, and fifty men to run before him" (1 Kgs 1:5). His strategy depends entirely on earthly display and political maneuvering, attempting to secure divine calling through human effort and impressive appearances. Solomon, by contrast, receives the throne through divine wisdom channeled through Nathan the prophet and Bathsheba, his mother, representing the principle that spiritual authority transcends natural inheritance. The pattern teaches that authentic authority comes from heaven down to earth, not from earth striving upward toward heaven.

# 11

# Inheritor Versus Renewer in the New Testament

## JOHN THE BAPTIST AND JESUS

THIS PATTERN FINDS ITS fulfillment in the relationship between John the Baptist (the elder) and Jesus (the younger). John and Jesus are part of this larger pattern that traces back to Gen 4, especially since John declared, "There comes One after me who is mightier than I" (Mark 1:7), and humbly acknowledged, "He must increase, but I must decrease" (John 3:30). Most importantly, this resembles Jacob's blessing speech in Gen 48, suggesting that John recognized this same divine pattern at work in his time. There is clearly something John is seeing, considering he is using this same language. It seems that John understood his role as Israel's inheritor and why Christ was destined to renew and surpass him.

To begin with, the New Testament deliberately emphasizes the close relationship between John and Jesus. Their parents were relatives, and John "leapt in the womb" at the presence of Christ. John the Baptist was six months older than Jesus, signifying John as the older "brother." We are also told that John comes from a priestly lineage of Aaron (Luke 1:5). The principle of the firstborn inheriting the land versus the younger renewing it has been examined, leading one to ask: What impact does this have on Israel and their ministry? While John the Baptist is mentioned sparingly in the New Testament, his impact is profound. He willingly relinquished his ministry to make way for Jesus to flourish.

St. Ephrem emphasizes this significance, noting that Christ received his priestly line from John: "It was at His baptism that Jesus received the priesthood from John."[1] John is regarded as the greatest of men because, more than any inheritor, he demonstrated unparalleled humility and sacrifice, surrendering his authority and power for the good of Christ's ministry. From John's actions, it is evident that John the Baptist may have understood the inheritor/renewer pattern and recognized his role as the elder inheritor of Israel. As the son of the priest Zechariah, John was known throughout Israel from the time of his birth based on his miraculous birth and the pronouncement that went out throughout Judea.

John the Baptist, the last and greatest prophet of the old covenant, came from a priestly lineage yet rejected Jerusalem's religious establishment, ministering in the wilderness wearing camel's hair and eating locusts. Everything proclaimed: divine renewal comes from the periphery, not the center. His message confronted "inheritor" thinking directly: "Do not think to say to yourselves, 'We have Abraham as our father.' For I say to you that God is able to raise up children to Abraham from these stones" (Matt 3:9). Natural inheritance means nothing; spiritual life requires renewal from above. Jesus, the ultimate Renewer, came from Nazareth—"Can anything good come out of Nazareth?" (John 1:46). His entire ministry challenged the inheritor orientation. Pharisees trusted meticulous law observance, Abrahamic descent, theological knowledge, and religious position. Jesus consistently proclaimed this orientation disqualifies rather than qualifies: "Those who are well have no need of a physician, but those who are sick" (Mark 2:17). The church's composition makes the pattern unmistakable. Jesus calls fishermen, tax collectors, prostitutes, Samaritans, gentiles—those lacking religious inheritance. Meanwhile, those with every religious advantage largely reject him.

One significant example of John relinquishing his power and influence for Jesus is seen when he sent two of his disciples to follow Jesus (John 1:1–8). One of these disciples was Andrew, whose brother Peter became Jesus' leader of the church. Even in Acts, we find evidence that some of John's disciples later followed Jesus, demonstrating the success of John's ministry in pointing others to Christ, even after his death. John was the

1. Murray, *Symbols of Church*, 179.

witness through whom all might believe (John 1:1–8), fulfilling his divinely appointed role in preparing the way for Christ.

But also, John the Baptist, was the last prophet of the old covenant, calling Israel to turn back to God, for a new orientation. He prepared the way for the true King, whose grace would bypass the corrupted priesthood of the Pharisees and create a new people. This highlights John's greatness as the inheritor of Israel as a priest and the last prophet as a renewer. Many firstborns in the inheritor/renewer principle are thrown into the wilderness as part of their story, i.e., Cain, Esau (field). But John acted to overcome this pattern of exile and humbly passed this priestly line to Christ, giving him earthly power by bringing followers (body) to Christ. No inheritor was as selfless as John the Baptist, who so freely relinquished his power to allow the renewer to fulfill his divine purpose. John's greatness lies in the absence of rivalry with Christ. Even Christ himself declared John the greatest born of women, acknowledging that no man had so willingly surrendered his authority.

John's role was to point the way to the Messiah, and he found peace in performing that role honorably when he said, "He who has the bride is the bridegroom; but the friend of the bridegroom, who stands and hears him, rejoices greatly because of the bridegroom's voice. Therefore this joy of mine is fulfilled" (John 3:29). John's purpose was to prepare a body (the church) on earth for Jesus, a body that was cultivated and ready for him. Upon Jesus' baptism by John, Jesus inherited the priestly lineage from John, as seen in how, immediately after he came up out of the water, the Spirit led Jesus into the wilderness, the periphery, the sign of the firstborn, seen in many such as Cain (Gen 4:16) and Esau (Gen 25:24).

Once John was imprisoned, Jesus continued to gather a "body" (followers) and earthly power, taking on both roles as many protagonists in the Bible do, such as Jacob when he bargained for the firstborn birthright (Gen 25) and Joseph getting a double blessing (Gen 49). Jesus as Renewer of humanity, being the Second Adam, redeeming humanity. "But of Him you are in Christ Jesus, who became for us wisdom from God—and righteousness and sanctification and redemption" (1 Cor 1:30). The inheritor/renewer pattern doesn't denigrate inheritance itself—after all, Christ came through the inherited line of David (Matt 1:1). The pattern emphasizes how one must not prioritize inherited problems over performing heavenly duties, nor worry about discerning whether we are engaged in tasks that are "too low" or unworthy, which would show that we are trusting in inherited status apart from God's grace.

## CHRIST'S TEACHING: THE PRODIGAL SON

Jesus' parable of the prodigal son provides the most explicit teaching about the inheritor/renewer principle in the New Testament. Through this story, Christ reveals that he fully understood this pattern and intended his disciples to recognize its ongoing significance for understanding God's kingdom principles. The elder son represents the classic inheritor—faithful to inherited responsibilities and ensuring the earthly prosperity of his father's estate. His complaint reveals typical inheritor mentality: "Lo, these many years I have been serving you; I never transgressed your commandment; and yet you never gave me a young goat, that I might make merry with my friends" (Luke 15:29). His service is real and valuable, yet it remains focused on earthly reward and recognition rather than relationship.

The prodigal son, by contrast, begins with the classic renewer pattern of apparent failure and exile to periphery. His demand for inheritance—"Father, give me the portion of goods that falleth to me" (Luke 15:12)—represents rejection of inherited family structure in favor of autonomous self-determination. His subsequent wasteful living and reduction to feeding swine (the ultimate periphery for a Jewish audience) complete his exile from family and covenant community. Yet the prodigal's return demonstrates the authentic renewer pattern. His repentance—"Father, I have sinned against heaven, and before thee, and am no more worthy to be called thy son" (Luke 15:18–19)—represents recognition of failure and appeal to divine mercy rather than earthly entitlement. Unlike the elder brother, who appeals to his record of earthly faithfulness, the prodigal appeals solely to the father's character and grace.

The father's response reveals the principle that governs divine restoration: "But when he was yet a great way off, his father saw him, and had compassion, and ran, and fell on his neck, and kissed him" (Luke 15:20). The father's eagerness to restore relationship transcends questions of earthly fairness or earned reward, representing pure grace that renews relationship despite failure. "The older brother was thinking according to the laws of human justice, but the benevolent Father was acting according to His merciful, fatherly heart."[2] The celebration that follows—"bring forth the best robe, and put it on him; and put a ring on his hand, and shoes on his feet: And bring hither the fatted calf, and kill it; and let us eat, and be merry" (Luke 15:22–23)—represents complete restoration. The prodigal receives

2. Grēgorios, *Parable of the Prodigal*, 77.

not partial forgiveness but full restoration to sonship, symbolized by the robe (authority), ring (family identity), and shoes (honored status rather than servant position).

### The Elder Brother's Challenge

The elder brother's angry response to this celebration reveals the challenge that faces all inheritors: "But he was angry and would not go in. Therefore his father came out and pleaded with him" (Luke 15:28). His refusal to participate in the celebration represents the spiritual danger of inherited religious privilege—the tendency to view grace as unfair competition with earned righteousness. The father's final appeal—"Son, thou art ever with me, and all that I have is thine. It was meet that we should make merry, and be glad: for this your brother was dead, and is alive again; and was lost, and is found" (Luke 15:31–32)—reveals the invitation extended to inheritors. The elder brother can continue to enjoy his inheritance, but he's invited to transcend mere earthly possession by participating in the celebration of restoration and renewal.

## THE CHURCH: PHARISEES VS. OUTCASTS

The conflict between Jesus and the religious establishment provides another illustration of the inheritor/renewer pattern in the New Testament. The Pharisees represent the ultimate inheritors—possessing detailed knowledge of religious law, maintaining centuries-old traditions, and serving as respected guardians of covenant community identity. Tax collectors, prostitutes, and other social outcasts represent the ultimate periphery—excluded from religious community and considered spiritually hopeless by earthly standards.

Yet Jesus consistently demonstrates divine preference for the outcasts over the religious inheritors, revealing the principle that spiritual pride creates greater barriers to divine relationship than moral failure. Jesus' parable of the Pharisee and tax collector illustrates this inversion: "The Pharisee stood and prayed thus with himself, 'God, I thank You that I am not like other men—extortioners, unjust, adulterers, or even as this tax collector. I fast twice a week; I give tithes of all that I possess.' And the tax collector, standing afar off, would not so much as raise his eyes to heaven, but beat his breast, saying, 'God, be merciful to me a sinner!'" (Luke 18:11–13). The contrast is complete: the Pharisee appeals to his inherited religious advantages and earned righteousness, while the tax collector appeals solely to divine mercy from a position of acknowledged failure. Jesus' conclusion reveals the fundamental principle: "I tell you, this man went down to his house justified rather than the other; for everyone who exalts himself will be humbled, and he who humbles himself will be exalted" (Luke 18:14).

The Pharisee (Inheritor Orientation)

- Approached God with list of achievements
- Trusted religious pedigree and performance
- Compared himself favorably to "sinners"
- Expected acceptance based on status
- Left unjustified despite impressive credentials

The Tax Collector (Renewer Orientation)

- Approached God from distance, beating breast
- Had nothing to present but a need for mercy
- Made no comparisons, only confession
- Expected nothing but begged for grace
- Left justified despite occupation

Throughout the Gospels, Jesus consistently challenges the assumption that inherited religious knowledge and position automatically translate to spiritual blessing. The Pharisees' question about eating with tax collectors and sinners reveals their misunderstanding about leading Israel (Matt 9:11). Their accusation against Jesus, "This Man receives sinners and eats with them" (Luke 15:2), reveals their fundamental misunderstanding of mediation. Jesus' response exposes the principle at work: "When Jesus heard that, He said to them, 'Those who are well have no need of a physician, but those who are sick. But go and learn what this means: "I desire mercy and not sacrifice." For I did not come to call the righteous, but sinners, to repentance'" (Matt 9:12–13). The tragedy reaches its climax when the religious inheritors reject the ultimate Renewer. They cannot comprehend that divine love seeks to restore the lost rather than merely reward those of status. The pattern continues into the early church, where gentiles (outcasts with no religious inheritance) often respond to the gospel more readily than Jews (inheritors of covenant promises and religious tradition). Paul addresses this reversal extensively, explaining that "the gifts and calling of

God are without repentance" (Rom 11:29)—the inheritors retain their inheritance, but spiritual pride can temporarily blind them to renewal.

Peter's vision of the sheet with unclean animals represents the principle that grace transcends inherited religious categories: "What God has cleansed, you must not call common" (Acts 10:15). The expansion of the gospel to include gentiles demonstrates that it operates according to faith rather than inherited religious privilege. This "older brother" aspect of Israel is also noted by St. Jerome, who said, "The Jews are the first son; we are the last sons."[3] Paul describes the church as "the children of the promise," who are "counted as the seed," while "they are not all Israel who are of Israel" (Rom 9:6–9).

## CONCLUSION

The New Testament demonstrates that the inheritor-versus-renewer pattern established in Genesis continues with greater clarity and urgency. The contrast between John the Baptist and Jesus, between Pharisees and outcasts, between Israel and the church, reveals the orientation principle at redemptive-historical climax. This pattern runs from Abel over Cain, Jacob over Esau, David over his brothers, the tax collector over the Pharisee. This conflict between earned merit and unmerited grace drives story after story.

3. Manley, *Grace for Grace*, 30.

# 12

# The Three Curses as Foundational Conflicts

## FROM THREE PRINCIPLES TO THREE FRACTURES OF COMMUNION

We have reviewed the three principles drawn from Gen 1–4 and seen how they recur across Scripture:

- The Adam and Eve principle (authority)
- The tilling/rain/yield principle (cooperation)
- The inheritor-versus-renewer principle (orientation)

Together, these three principles make up the Genesis Conflict Framework, an interpretive method to read the Bible. Why did I choose these over other patterns? As seen below, the principles align with creation before the fall.

## BEFORE THE FALL

- Authority (God speaks → Adam obeys → Eve receives → creation ordered and prosperous)
- Cooperation functioning (man tills, God sends rain, ground yields)
- Orientation pure (everything received as a gift, no claiming merit)

To see why these three principles matter, we must first observe how they appear in their unbroken form before Gen 3. God created man as mediator to be fruitful and multiply and have dominion (Gen 1), having man cooperate in ordering the cosmos (Gen 2), being given everything freely. Scripture presents these principles first in their uncorrupted and ideal form. Because these principles appear already embedded in the created order of Gen 1 and 2, Gen 3 must show precisely how each one becomes fractured when communion with God is broken.

The three principles correspond to the three curses in Gen 3. When Adam and Eve sin, God's rebuke and the curses he pronounces upon them and the serpent each address a different mode of communion with him. Each curse reveals a mode of broken communion with God that began when Adam and Eve ate the fruit of the tree of knowledge of good and evil.

Humanity—and the biblical narrative as a whole—are structured around conflict in communion with God, particularly in relation to authority, cooperation, and orientation and how each story sees these modes of communion tested, broken or restored. This is why I call it the Genesis Conflict Framework. If Gen 1–2 presents these principles in harmony, Gen 3 reveals their disruption in parallel, with each curse touching the same structures of human existence, now rendered in distortion.

### After the Fall

- Authority broken: "Because you have heeded the voice of your wife" (Gen 3:17); "Your desire shall be for your husband, and he shall rule over you" (Gen 3:16).
- Cooperation burdened: "Cursed is the ground because of you" (Gen 3:17–18).
- Orientation distorted: "I will put enmity between you and the woman, and between your seed and her seed" (Gen 3:15).

## EXPLAINING EACH CURSE

Before examining each curse, we must recognize that each curse God pronounces contains all three modes corrupted, just with different emphases. St. Cyril of Alexandria states, "We had become accursed through Adam's transgression and had fallen into the trap of death, abandoned by God."[1] The serpent's curse primarily addresses orientation (lowered to belly, eating dust, earthly-minded) but also inverts authority (reduced to the lowest creature) and establishes generational conflict (seed warfare as an ongoing process). Eve's curse centers on authority ("he shall rule over you") but corrupts cooperation (painful childbirth) and extends temporally (sorrow "multiplied" across generations, highlighting orientation conflict). The ground curse of Adam emphasizes cooperation (toil, sweat, resistant earth) but begins by identifying authority failure ("heeded the voice of your wife") and concludes with orientation ("dust to dust"). Authority requires cooperation and orientation to function healthily. Cooperation needs authority and grace to avoid chaos. Orientation is expressed through submission and participation or remains mere sentiment.

Biblical narratives feel rich and layered because they reflect this complexity in reality. When Saul falls, authority breakdown dominates (obeying the people's voice), but cooperation failure is present (people demanding conformity to nations), and orientation corruption underlies it (trusting human patterns over divine election). This explains why seeing one mode of failure usually also means failures of the other two.

## The Serpent's Curse

We begin with the serpent, whose curse most directly addresses the distortion of orientation and the long war of "seed" that shapes the rest of Scripture. In his conversation with Eve, the serpent offers wisdom and to be like God apart from one's creator: "You will be like God" (Gen 3:5). Adam and Eve's orientation went from being given freely all but one tree, to taking pridefully, disobeying God's command. Grace is rejected in favor of entitlement and self-determination.

Next, God says to the serpent:

> Because you have done this, you are cursed more than all cattle,
> and more than every beast of the field;
> on your belly you shall go,
> and you shall eat dust all the days of your life.
> And I will put enmity between you and the woman,
> and between your seed and her Seed;
> He shall bruise your head,
> and you shall bruise His heel. (Gen 3:14–15)

1. Cyril of Alexandria, *On the Unity*, 105.

The serpent's curse does several things at once. It marks the serpent as uniquely cursed among the animals. It lowers him to the ground, an example of an orientation problem. Now he will be associated with "dust"—the very substance of materiality, another earthly reminder of the serpent's association. And it introduces enmity between seeds: a war of offspring that will stretch across history. This is the first fracture of communion. The serpent, who intruded into sacred space and inverted the order of obedience, becomes a permanent sign of conflict within that space. The creature that once spoke deceit is defined by its hostile relationship to humanity. This corresponds to the distortion of authority: a voice that should never have been heeded now becomes an ongoing adversary.

Since Adam received the garden freely, not as payment for labor, the tree of life stood available—eternal life offered, not achieved. Work itself was participation, not burden, but "to tend and keep it" (Gen 2:15). Tending the garden was participation in God's creativity, not toilsome obligation. Everything flowed from God's generosity. Therefore, every subsequent story must be about attempting to restore or further corrupt these three broken realities. Because these are the things that broke, they're necessarily the things God cares about restoring. Every story must necessarily engage these realities because these are the fundamental problems every human faces. Every conflict in the rest of Scripture finds its origin here, in Gen 3.

By speaking in terms of "seed," God frames the conflict not as a one-time event but as an unfolding struggle across generations, always grasping at status. Time itself becomes the medium of this enmity. This curse specifically targets what the inheritor/renewer principle requires: freedom to receive grace in each generation rather than being determined by inherited position. The serpent represents the "inheritor" because he tempts them with status ("You will be like God") and the curse establishes a "seed" war. This curse reveals spiritual reality: the serpent's seed will be earthly-minded, fixated on what's below, trusting accumulated advantage. Each generation inherits either blessing or curse, facing the choice between earthly orientation (serpent's seed) or heavenly dependence (woman's seed). The enmity unfolds across generations, with the past determining the present unless renewed by grace. John confirms this: "He who is of the earth is earthly and speaks of the earth. He who comes from heaven is above all" (John 3:31).

Adam and Eve are driven from the garden into exile. Time itself becomes corrupted—no longer the medium of continuous communion with God but the medium of distance and mortality. Past generations' sins now constrain future generations. Earthly inheritance (what passes from past to present) becomes corrupting, orienting the inheritor toward the earth.

## The Woman: Strained Union and Pain in Fruitfulness

When the serpent confronts Eve, he challenges God's word: "Has God indeed said?" (Gen 3:1). This is a direct assault on the structure of authority—who is heard and obeyed. Eve disobeys Adam; both should have mediated God's voice instead of listening to another. Headship is inverted; the creature leads, the man follows, and God is set aside.

To the woman God says:

> I will greatly multiply your sorrow and your conception;
> in pain you shall bring forth children;
> your desire shall be for your husband,
> and he shall rule over you. (Gen 3:16)

The curse reflects this breakdown with God rebuking Eve and the pain in childbirth and her desire being turned to her husband as intercessor who will rule over her. From this point on, authority becomes contested. Human relationships strain under the weight of competing voices. Authority is inverted: Eve listens to the serpent, Adam listens to Eve, neither listens to God. This loss of divine order is seen as the disruption of communion—the right relationship between Creator and creation.

When Adam ceases to mediate divine life to the world, the created order falls into disarray. And God specifically rebukes Adam, "Because you have heeded the voice of your wife, and have eaten from the tree of which I commanded you, saying, 'You shall not eat of it'" (Gen 3:17). The eventual restoration of authority, therefore, is not domination but restoration: humanity returning to its proper headship under God, where obedience becomes participation in divine wisdom.

Here fruitfulness that Adam and Eve were commanded in Gen 1—the very blessing of "be fruitful and multiply"—remains, but is now shot through with pain. Childbearing, which should have been pure joy, becomes costly. The fundamental relationship between man and woman is no longer seamless unity; it is marked by disordered desire and contested rule. This is the second fracture. What should have been a harmonious, complementary communion between Adam and Eve, working together to cultivate creation, now becomes strained. The Eve figure, who should receive wisdom and help preserve sacred order, now experiences a pull toward the Adam figure that is tangled with conflict, manipulation, and the temptation to invert roles.

### The Man: Futility in Work to Adam, God says

> Because you have heeded the voice of your wife,
> and have eaten from the tree of which I commanded you, saying,
> "You shall not eat of it":
> Cursed is the ground for your sake;
> in toil you shall eat of it
> all the days of your life.
> Both thorns and thistles it shall bring forth for you,
> and you shall eat the herb of the field.
> In the sweat of your face you shall eat bread
> till you return to the ground,
> for out of it you were taken;
> for dust you are, and to dust you shall return. (Gen 3:17–19)

God curses the ground itself. The space in which humanity dwells becomes resistant to fruitfulness. This is not merely a moral punishment but a structural corruption of physical space. Cooperation between human effort and divine provision—which once flowed naturally—now requires struggle, sweat, and uncertainty.

The key line is God's explanation: "Because you have heeded the voice of your wife." The curse on the ground is explicitly tied to an authority breakdown. Adam reverses the order—he listens to an earthly voice over the divine command—and the field itself begins to resist him.

Work becomes toil, sweat, frustration, and futility. Thorns and thistles stand as visible signs that creation itself now resists human efforts. And the shadow over everything is death: "dust you are, and to dust you shall return."

## THE CURSES AS A NARRATIVE FRAMEWORK

Once we see the three curses in this way, much of Scripture comes into focus. Nearly every story involves one or more of these fractures:

- A king who fails in authority, heeding the people's voice over God's command

- A people who fail in cooperation, grumbling about manna, resisting God's provision, or abusing the land
- A family or nation that fails in orientation, choosing the wrong heir, clinging to a corrupted inheritance, or rejecting the true renewer

The principles recur because they describe human existence in relationship to God. The rest of Scripture will show how God addresses these fractures through covenants, priests, kings, and prophets, until they are finally dealt with in Christ.

## THE STRUCTURAL CONSEQUENCES OF THE FALL

Genesis 3 does not simply record penalties; it reveals a fallen world. Each curse reshapes how humanity lives in relation to God, to one another, and to creation. Authority, cooperation, and orientation are three modes of reality. To see how the fall reshapes reality, we can set each curse alongside its corresponding principle and watch how the original order becomes inverted.

A helpful way to think about this is in terms of space, time, and relation:

- Space: Space no longer nourishes. The garden, a place of communion, becomes contested ground. The serpent crawls within it before humanity is expelled from it. The ground itself is cursed (Gen 3:17). Physical reality, which should yield to faithful cultivation, now resists. Every subsequent biblical story involves where God's presence dwells and whether that space is honored or defiled.
- Time: The human story is now bounded by death. "All the days of your life" (Gen 3:14, 17) marks existence as temporary. Succession is corrupted—each generation inherits either the serpent's curse or the woman's blessing. Will the past determine the future (inheritor), or will God's grace break in fresh (renewer)? Pain, labor, and decay mark "all the days" of life. Succession is corrupted; each generation receives or resists grace based on being either the seed of the serpent or the seed of woman.
- Relational: The fundamental relationships—God-human, man-woman, human-creation—are now marked by mistrust, conflict, and misalignment. Marriage and all hierarchical structures of human organization are continually corrupted by tyranny or inversion of authority.

Scripture reinforces these same three fractures through the symbolic language of the human body, using head, hands, and feet to depict authority, cooperation, and orientation.

## HEAD, HANDS, AND FEET

One of Scripture's most profound patterns is the way it uses different parts of the body to reveal the inner structure of a person's vocation. When the Bible describes a person's head, hands, or feet, it is not merely recording anatomy. It is telling us about authority, action, and direction, the three conflicts of humanity's relationship with God that were fractured by the fall.

The head represents authority, discernment, and direction: God "set [Christ] as head over all things to the church" (Eph 1:22), and a husband is called "head" as Christ is head of the church (Eph 5:23), so when a head fails, the whole body is misled. The hands represent agency and works—what a person actually does with the power entrusted to them. The psalmist prays, "Establish the work of our hands" (Ps 90:17), and Ecclesiastes exhorts, "Whatever your hand finds to do, do it with your might" (Eccl 9:10); James even uses "cleanse your hands" as a picture of moral repentance (Jas 4:8). The feet represent a person's path, walk, and direction in life. Scripture repeatedly speaks of "walking" in God's ways, and God's word is "a lamp to my feet and a light to my path" (Ps 119:105). When a biblical character's head is deceived, their hands become instruments of disorder, and their feet walk down a crooked path, we are watching their mediating role disintegrate; when their head receives God's wisdom, their hands serve his purposes, and their feet walk in his ways, we are seeing the three dimensions of their vocation aligned.

Head (Authority Principle): Authority, Discernment, Leadership, Source

- Ephesians 1:22–23—Christ is "head over all things to the church."
- Colossians 1:18—"He is the head of the body, the church."

Hands (Cooperation Principle): Actions, Works, Cooperation, Stewardship

- Psalm 90:17—"Establish the work of our hands."
- Ecclesiastes 9:10—"Whatever your hand finds to do, do it with your might."

- James 4:8—"Cleanse your hands, you sinners" (repent from sinful deeds).

Feet (Orientation): Direction, Path, Purpose

- Proverbs 4:26–27—"Ponder the path of your feet. . . . Do not turn to the right or the left."
- Psalm 119:105—"A lamp to my feet and a light to my path."

When all three parts of a person's body fail, it means a complete collapse, highlighting that all three modes of communion are broken: "From the sole of the foot even to the head, there is no soundness in it" (Isa 1:5–6). This is also seen in the consecration of the priesthood on the ear, thumb, and toe (Exod 29:20) and in the Seraphim vision of Isaiah (Isa 6:1-2).

## ASCENDING THE MOUNTAIN

Some readers may wonder: Isn't reducing biblical narratives to three principles overly simplistic and reductionist? Does it risk flattening the richness of Scripture into a few abstract categories?

To answer this, I would reply with what Jesus himself does. When asked which commandment is greatest, He distilled the entire Law and the Prophets into two commands:

> "You shall love the Lord your God with all your heart, with all your soul, and with all your mind." This is the first and great commandment. And the second is like it: "You shall love your neighbor as yourself." On these two commandments hang all the Law and the Prophets. (Matt 22:40)

Jesus did not erase the 613 commandments or the vast wisdom and insight of the Old Testament. He revealed its underlying architecture. Jesus distilled the entire Law and the Prophets into two Old Testament commands, love of God (Deut 6:5) and love of neighbor (Lev 19:18), revealing the underlying structure that all the Law and Prophets derive from. In the same way, I am drawing three principles out of God's cursing and pronouncement on Adam, Eve, and the serpent (Gen 3:14–19); not adding to Scripture but using them to highlight the deep patterns that organize the Bible's narrative conflicts. This book attempts something similar, but at the level of narrative rather than ethics. The Genesis Conflict Framework attempts to follow Jesus' precedent. If Gen 1–4 establishes Scripture's constitutional patterns, the foundational architecture on which later narratives are built, then we should expect to find generative principles in these opening chapters. The apparent simplicity is not reductionism; it is revelation of deep structure. Jesus distilled the law's moral commands (what to do). Here we are distilling Genesis's narrative curses (what broke and recurs). This is parsimony—when a small number of principles accounts for a large range of phenomena, allowing one to see the Bible's unity and coherence. Jesus showed the law's moral framework; likewise, this work attempts to map Scripture's narrative structure, allowing one to see the unity of Scripture by showing the conflicts that make up each story. The Adam/Eve principle (authority and mediation), the tilling/rain/yield principle (divine-human cooperation), and the inheritor/renewer principle (grace-based versus merit-based orientation) function in narrative precisely as Jesus' distillation functioned in ethics: they show how surface complexity "hangs" on deeper structure. Far from replacing other ways of reading, this framework offers a way to "step back" and see the larger pattern and deeper reality that connects the Bible.

### Jesus and the Apostles

Jesus himself consistently practiced this pattern recognition. On the Emmaus road, "beginning at Moses and all the Prophets, He expounded to them in all the Scriptures the things concerning Himself" (Luke 24:27), demonstrating a unified pattern running through diverse texts. The apostles continued this method. Peter saw typological correspondence between Noah's ark and baptism—"There is also an antitype which now saves us—baptism" (1 Pet 3:21)—perceiving how physical and spiritual realities mirror the same underlying pattern. The writer of Hebrews described the law as "having a shadow of the good things to come, and not the very image of the things" (Heb 10:1), explicitly teaching that earlier narratives operate as patterns revealing later realities. These weren't interpretive innovations but recognitions of patterns in Scripture that are intentionally embedded.

## GOD'S FIRST COMMAND: THE BIBLICAL FOUNDATION

God himself established humanity's calling in Gen 1: "Then God blessed them, and God said to them, 'Be fruitful and multiply; fill the earth and subdue it; have dominion over the fish of the sea, over the birds of the air, and over every living thing that moves on the earth'" (Gen 1:28). This directive isn't merely about biological reproduction—it's the mapping for all human flourishing. With this command, the rest of the Bible flows downstream of this command, allowing us to examine whether humanity is following God's word or not. We can see in this command embedded the three inseparable modes of communion with God:

### Authority: "Have dominion"

This establishes a clear hierarchy—God speaks, humanity receives and obeys. The command assigns humanity the mediatorial role between heaven and earth, ordering creation according to divine wisdom. Before any breakdown occurred, this is what authority looked like: God → humanity → creation. This is the Adam and Eve principle in its unfallen form.

### Cooperation: "Be fruitful and multiply"

The dual nature reveals divine-human synergy. "Be fruitful" requires human action—the tilling, the faithful work, the preparation. "Multiply" describes divine response—the rain, the supernatural increase beyond human capacity. One couple becomes a family, a family becomes a nation, a nation fills the earth. This is the tilling/rain/yield principle in its fundamental expression: human faithfulness + divine blessing = abundant fruit.

### Orientation: "God blessed them"

God blessed humanity even before commanding it to be fruitful, even before man had worked the ground, giving all of creation as a gift. Humanity received dominion not from merit, but by grace. We receive it as a blessing when faithfully fulfilling our role. The command itself assumes God's enabling power, not human self-sufficiency. This is the "renewer" posture from the beginning: receiving and stewarding what God provides rather than claiming what we've achieved.

Having traced how the three curses structure all biblical conflict—breaking authority, corrupting cooperation, and distorting orientation toward merit—we can now understand why Christ's work required such a comprehensive scope. Each curse demands a specific remedy, which is why Christ restores this in his incarnation and his threefold office as king, priest, and prophet.

13

# King, Priest, and Prophet

## HOW CHRIST OVERCOMES THE CURSES

God's answer to the threefold rupture is a threefold restoration. Since authority broke, Christ rules as king. Since cooperation failed, Christ comes as a priest from the line of Melchizedek. Since the orientation of man was fractured, Christ comes as a prophet to turn us back to God. Christ inhabits all three offices, which allows communion with God to be restored. These mediating offices are structural responses to the original rupture in Eden. Christ restores what was corrupted in Adam by assuming our fallen condition and healing it from within, transfiguring its consequences through his death and resurrection. Believers then participate in this restoration. Where prophecy describes what might come, structure demands what must come. This moves beyond prophetic fulfillment and becomes structural fulfillment. Structural fulfillment occurs when Christ does not merely correspond to earlier events or satisfy individual prophetic predictions but resolves the deeper structure those events reveal. The three-fold fracture of human communion with God—broken authority, corrupted cooperation, distorted orientation—cannot be healed by anyone but the God-man who embodies all three offices.

## THE GENESIS FOUNDATION OF THE KING, PRIEST, AND PROPHET

Each curse from Gen 3 corresponds to a divine office that will one day restore what was lost.

Why these three offices specifically? Because the fall created three specific problems:

- Authority crisis → Requires a king to restore proper mediation of God's rule
- Cooperation crisis → Requires a priest to bridge the divine-human gap through perfect sacrifice
- Orientation crisis → Requires a prophet to call humanity back from merit to grace

Scripture explicitly identifies Jesus in all three offices: king, priest, and prophet. Moses declares him prophet: "The Lord your God will raise up for you a Prophet like me from your brethren. Him you shall hear" (Deut 18:15). Hebrews identifies him as priest: "Seeing then that we have a great High Priest who has passed through the heavens, Jesus the Son of God" (Heb 4:14). Revelation crowns him king: "And He has on His robe and on His thigh a name written: KING OF KINGS AND LORD OF LORDS" (Rev 19:16). Every biblical narrative contains one or more of these foundational conflicts:

- King (authority)—the crisis of rightful rule
- Priest (cooperation)—the crisis of divine-human partnership
- Prophet (grace)—the crisis of heart orientation and grace

The king reorders authority, the priest restores cooperation, and the prophet renews grace. The gospel, therefore, is not a patchwork remedy but a comprehensive restoration of order. At the cross, the three offices are perfected. As king, Jesus submits to the Father's authority: "Not My will, but Yours, be done" (Luke 22:42). As priest, he obeys and toils to his death. As prophet, he calls the lost back to God: "For the Son of Man has come to seek and to save that which was lost" (Luke 19:10). The result is a comprehensive restoration. "For there is one God and one Mediator between God and men, the Man Christ Jesus, who gave Himself a ransom for all" (1 Tim 2:5–6). One Mediator—authority restored. Gave himself—perfect sacrifice, cooperation accomplished. Ransom for all—grace offered. All three are necessary because the fall broke all three modes. Self-mediation replaced God-headship, requiring a king. Self-sufficiency replaced divine-human cooperation, requiring a priest. Merit-claiming replaced grace-receiving, requiring a prophet. Only when all three unite in one Person is communion fully restored.

- King without priest = Tyranny prevails, authority without cooperation
- Priest without prophet = Empty ritual, cooperation without proper orientation
- Prophet without king = Powerless proclamation (orientation without authority to enforce

## Why a King: Restoring Authority

God's answer is kingship: "You shall surely set a king over you whom the Lord your God chooses" (Deut 17:15). The king mediates God's authority: God → king → people. But every king fails: Saul feared the people over God, others abandoned God's word for idols or heeded other voices.

Jesus fulfills this, as he states, "The Son can do nothing of Himself, but what He sees the Father do" (John 5:19), and as Paul states, "Now I praise you, brethren, that you remember me in all things and keep the traditions just as I delivered them to you. But I want you to know that the head of every man is Christ, the head of woman is man, and the head of Christ is God" (1 Cor 11:3). Since "all authority has been given to [Christ] in heaven and on earth" (Matt 28:18), Christ restores the structure of authority. God's rule now flows rightly through the King.

## Christ Restores Authority

Where Adam failed to uphold God's wisdom against Eve's counsel, Christ maintains divine wisdom against all temptation, whether from Satan, Peter, or the crowds. He succeeds where the first Adam failed. The curse introduced harsh rule, but Christ reverses this by demonstrating that true greatness is service. "Yet it shall not be so among you; but whoever desires to become great among you, let him be your servant" (Matt 20:26). He washes his disciples' feet and gives his life for the church, showing that authority is meant for self-sacrifice, not domination. The relationship between Christ and the church reveals the restored pattern. The church willingly submits to Christ's loving leadership, orienting herself toward his mission. This isn't forced subjugation but a joyful partnership, fulfilling Eve's original role as helpmate and sustainer.

## Serpent Temptation: Authority Affirmed (vs. Inverted Headship)

The serpent's second attack was on authority—"Has God indeed said . . . ?" (Gen 3:1)—an attempt to insert doubt and invert the divine hierarchy. Satan's second temptation is a perverse echo of this, quoting Scripture to manipulate the structure of authority: "If You are the Son of God, throw Yourself down" (Matt 4:6). It is a challenge asking Jesus to perform a miracle rather than rely on God's timing; it's the serpent testing the Head rather than submitting to him. Jesus' response restores the proper order: "You shall not tempt the Lord your God" (Matt 4:7). He refuses to invert the divine structure, affirming perfect submission to the Father's authority.

## Why a Priest: Accomplishing Cooperation

Expelled from Eden, humanity cannot produce fruit on its own. "All our righteousness are like filthy rags" (Isa 64:6). Divine rain without faithful tilling yields nothing at best and wickedness at worst. The priestly system is introduced: "He shall put his hand on the head of the burnt offering, and it will be accepted on his behalf to make atonement" (Lev 1:4). The offering must be right, and God must accept it. But Jesus serves as high priest: "He humbled Himself and became obedient to the point of death, even the death of the cross" (Phil 2:8) and "offered Himself without spot to God" (Heb 9:14). Cooperation is restored in the Priest.

## Christ Restores Cooperation

The crown of thorns shows Christ literally wearing the symbol of Adam's cursed ground. In Gethsemane, his sweat of agony becomes like drops of blood, transforming Adam's sweat of toilsome labor into the sacrifice that becomes the Bread of Life. In the parable of the sower, Christ is the Sower who works the field of the world. He acknowledges the curse's realities—thorns and resistant ground—but unlike Adam, he produces an abundant yield. Christ's work was also toilsome, culminating in his cry, "It is finished" (John 19:30). But unlike Adam's labor, which ended in death, Christ's labor was completed and produces eternal fruit—the church. Through participation in Christ, believers' work can again become fruitful, not by eliminating struggle, but by infusing it with grace and purpose. Lastly, Adam's curse ended in death, but Christ defeated it through his resurrection. As Paul states, "For as in Adam all die, even so in Christ all shall be made alive" (1 Cor 15:22). His resurrection is the "firstfruits," guaranteeing a future harvest for all who are in him. Each temptation Satan brings against Christ maps precisely onto the sequence and manner of the serpent's assault in Gen 3.

## Serpent Temptation: Cooperation Defended (vs. Self-Sufficiency)

The serpent's first lie was an attack on cooperation: "You will not surely die" (Gen 3:4), a promise of life apart from dependence on God. Satan's first temptation of Jesus mirrors this: "If You are the Son of God, command that these stones become bread" (Matt 4:3). It is a temptation to use divine power for self-provision, to act in self-sufficiency rather than in cooperation with the Father's timing. Jesus' response restores the principle: "Man shall not live by bread alone, but by every word that proceeds from the mouth of God" (Matt 4:4). He affirms that true life comes not from self-effort ("tilling" alone), but from complete dependence on God's provision ("rain").

## Why a Prophet: Correcting Orientation

Adam and Eve cover themselves (Gen 3:7). Cain expects acceptance based on firstborn status and the yield of his own toil. Israel boasts, "The temple of the Lord" (Jer 7:4). The Pharisees say, "We have Abraham as our father" (Matt 3:9). The prophets confront this inheritance mindset: "Do not remember the former things. . . . Behold, I will do a new thing" (Isa 43:18–19) and "I will make a new covenant . . . not according to the covenant that I made with their fathers" (Jer 31:31–32). Jesus rebukes the inheritor mindset: "Unless one is born again, he cannot see the kingdom of God" (John 3:3). Grace replaces entitlement—Jesus says in Revelation 21:5, "Behold, I am making all things new."

The prophetic office did not begin with Abraham or Moses but with Abel, whose grace-oriented offering—and whose murder by his inheritance-claiming brother—established the pattern Jesus identifies as the central, recurring tragedy of human history. Jesus has a confusing statement where he connects the persecution of the prophets who call Israel to repentance and return to God, to Abel, highlighting that Abel in Gen 4, from the foundation of the world, was acting in this office: "Therefore the wisdom of God also said, 'I will send them prophets and apostles, and some of them they will kill and persecute,' that the blood of all the prophets which was shed from the foundation of the world may be required of this generation, from the blood of Abel to the blood of Zechariah who perished between the altar and the temple" (Luke 11:50–51). He is telling the Pharisees in this context that their rejection of him is not a new event. He identifies the inheritor-versus-renewer dynamic as the central, recurring tragedy of human history, starting with Cain murdering his brother Abel. They are participating in the same pattern of the entitled "inheritor" rejecting God's "renewer" that began with the first murder. Abel acted as a renewer from the beginning and like the prophets was killed in this role.

## Serpent Temptation: Orientation Maintained (vs. Grasping at Status)

The serpent's final offer was an attack on orientation: "You will be like God" (Gen 3:5), a promise of achieved status for the inheritor who grasps at power. Satan's final temptation is the ultimate version of this offer: "All these things I will give You if You will fall down and worship me" (Matt 4:9). It is a shortcut to kingship, an invitation to seize a kingdom rather than receive it by grace. Jesus' response is the perfect anthem of the renewer: "You shall worship the Lord your God, and Him only you shall serve" (Matt 4:10). He affirms that his authority and identity come from the Father alone and will be received in the Father's way, not grasped through a deal with a rival power. Christ's victory in the wilderness is the definitive answer to the serpent's original assault. From the very beginning of his ministry, he demonstrates that he is the one who will restore the architecture of humanity's relationship with God. Where Adam and Eve failed across all three modes, Christ succeeds across all three. The architecture of redemption mirrors the architecture of the fall.

Spatial: the church as body in space (communities gathering, sacraments in material space)

Temporal: the church across time (tradition, liturgical calendar, eschatological hope)

Relational: the church ordered by authority (hierarchies, priesthood, prophetic witness)

The church doesn't just spiritualize these modes; it practices their restoration.

| Principle | Function | Curse | Christ's Office |
|---|---|---|---|
| Adam/Eve | Structure (authority) | Eve's relational | King (maintains authority) |
| Tilling/Rain/Yield | Process (cooperation) | Adam's ground | Priest (restores cooperation) |
| Inheritor/Renewer | Preservation (orientation) | Serpent's lowliness and seed warfare | Prophet (corrects orientation) |

## 1 JOHN PARALLEL

A parallel can be seen between when the serpent was speaking to Eve—"So when the woman saw that the tree was good for food, that it was pleasant to the eyes, and a tree desirable to make one wise, she took of its fruit and ate" (Gen 3:6)—and the apostle John's warning about the three conflicts one must overcome since they are from the foundation of the world: "Do not love the world or the things in the world. If anyone loves the world, the love of the Father is not in him. For all that is in the world—the lust of the flesh, the lust of the eyes, and the pride of life—is not of the Father but is of the world" (1 John 2:15–16). John isn't inventing categories—he's recognizing that Gen 3:6's three desires still constitute the conflict of what was disordered in Genesis.

- "Good for food" = "Lust of the flesh" (physical/fleshly desire)
- "Pleasant to the eyes" = "Lust of the eyes" (coveting against what God forbids)
- "Desirable to make one wise" = "Pride of life" (claiming self-determination)

The curses of Gen 3 aren't arbitrary punishments—they are the direct consequences of violating the three modes of communion with God that structured Eden. Authority is inverted. Cooperation is fractured. Grace is replaced with self-determination and pride. From this point on, every biblical story will echo one or more of these same tensions, and every promise of redemption will answer them. What the serpent unraveled in a garden, Christ will restore at the cross.

## JESUS CROWNED AND PIERCED

What is astonishing is that when Jesus is crucified, he is wounded in the head, hands, and feet, revealing that his crucifixion is not random suffering but deliberate alignment of the three fundamental fractures of human mediation discussed. He is crowned with thorns upon his head, pierced through his hands, and nailed through his feet. On the cross, Jesus is pierced for humanity's transgressions of proper authority, cooperation, and orientation at the points where Adam's race was shattered.

- Head: Christ's head is crowned with the very sign of Adam's failed rule.
- Hands: At the cross, his pierced hands become the place where human labor is redeemed.
- Feet: Christ's feet are nailed to the cross, bearing the full weight of humanity's disordered orientation.

The hands of Christ never grasped selfishly; he came "not to be served but to serve" (Mark 10:45). His hands touched the leper, lifted the sinking disciple, blessed the children, broke the bread, and washed the feet of his followers. These hands—offered freely in obedience—are pierced and fastened to the wood of the cross. In that moment, the curse of frustrated labor is undone. The hands that cooperated perfectly with the Father's will now bear the nails that atone for every misuse of our own. The second principle—cooperation with divine life—is restored in the body of the true Worker, whose hands labor in perfect harmony with his Father.

The third wound completes the pattern. In Scripture, the feet represent the path a person walks, the orientation of a life, the direction of desire. The righteous are those who "walk in His ways," guided by the word that is "a light to [the] feet" (Ps 119:105). The wicked are described as having "feet swift to shed blood" (Rom 3:15), wandering ever farther from God's presence. Adam, once placed in the garden to walk with God, soon walks into exile. Cain goes out "from the presence of the Lord" (Gen 4:16). Israel repeatedly "walks after other gods" (Deut 8:19). The story of humanity is the story of misdirected steps and disordered loves.

Jesus' feet are pierced so that every exile may come home. The one whose feet carried him along the dusty roads of Galilee, who walked the path of obedience his entire life, now has those feet fixed to the beams of the cross. The nails that hold him there are the nails that reorient humanity's path. He becomes the way by which every prodigal son and daughter can return. He is crowned on his head to restore fallen authority. He is pierced through his hands to redeem human cooperation. He is nailed through his feet to heal disordered orientation. The three great fractures of Gen 3 are redeemed in the three great wounds of the crucifixion, showing how Christ's incarnation reveals the divine economy of salvation.

## Heart: The Darkened Nous Restored Through the Pierced Side

Yet these three wounds—head, hands, feet—point to a deeper reality that integrates them all. After Jesus dies, "one of the soldiers pierced His side with a spear, and immediately blood and water came out" (John 19:34). This fourth wound strikes at the fundamental fracture underlying all three principles: the darkened nous, the corrupted spiritual perception that was humanity's deepest loss in Eden.

The heart in Scripture represents not merely emotion but the nous—the faculty of spiritual perception through which Adam was meant to discern God's will and maintain communion. When God "breathed into his nostrils the breath of life" (Gen 2:7), the divine breath animated not just Adam's body but his nous, creating the capacity for spiritual sight. This faculty enabled Adam to perceive divine wisdom, to discern truth from deception, to see creation rightly and order it accordingly.

The fall darkened this faculty completely. As we established earlier in this book, "the Fathers teach that with the Fall, the human nous became darkened. Adam's nous became darkened. The Fathers are not concerned with Adam per se, but with Adam's nous and the sickness that followed from the darkening of his nous."[1] This darkening didn't merely affect one

1. Romanides, *Patristic Theology*, 32.

aspect of human life—it corrupted the integrating center through which all three modes of communion function.

Authority operates rightly only when the nous perceives God's voice clearly and can distinguish divine wisdom from earthly counsel. Adam's darkened nous made him vulnerable to the serpent's deception and unable to maintain proper ordering. Cooperation flows only when the nous discerns how to participate with divine grace rather than relying on autonomous effort. The darkened nous cannot perceive where God's rain falls or how to position oneself to receive it. Orientation aligns only when the nous sees truly—distinguishing eternal from temporal, grace from merit, God's ways from serpent wisdom. The darkened nous inevitably orients toward dust, toward what appears good to earthly perception.

This explains why the heart piercing is not merely a fourth wound parallel to the other three, but the wound that reveals their integrating center. The head governs rightly only when the heart perceives truly. The hands cooperate faithfully only when the heart directs wisely. The feet walk the right path only when the heart orients correctly. Christ's pierced heart restores what Adam's darkened nous lost. Where Adam's heart became closed to spiritual perception through disobedience, Christ's heart remains open even in death. The spear that pierces it reveals not darkness but abundant life—blood and water flowing freely to restore what was lost.

Both sacraments of Baptism and Communion flow from the pierced heart because both address the darkened nous—the root problem underlying all three principles. Without restored spiritual perception, authority remains corrupted, cooperation remains broken, and orientation remains earthward. But with the nous healed through what flows from Christ's heart, all three begin functioning properly. This explains why Jesus declares, "Out of his heart will flow rivers of living water" (John 7:38), and John clarifies, "But this He spoke concerning the Spirit, whom those believing in Him would receive" (John 7:39). The pierced heart becomes the source from which the Spirit flows to the church, continuously restoring what the darkened nous lost.

The true Adam stands where the first Adam fell, embodying perfect headship, perfect obedience, perfect work, perfect trust, and perfect direction. In him, the human vocation is not discarded—it is rebuilt. This is why the crucifixion is not merely the forgiveness of sins but the reconstitution of humanity. His head, aligned with the Father, becomes the source of our renewed discernment. His hands, offered in obedience, become the source of our restored work. His feet, steadfast in the path of God, become the source of our reoriented desires. Everything broken in Eden is healed on Golgotha. Christ's wounds are more than historical details. St. Irenaeus writes, "This is why He [Jesus] passed through all the ages of human life, restoring to all men communion with God."[2] The resurrected Christ bears the marks of authority healed, cooperation redeemed, and orientation restored. In his body, humanity is made whole again.

## CONCLUSION: CHRIST AND HIS BRIDE

The relationship between Christ and his bride completes the biblical narrative's trajectory from Genesis to Revelation. What began with Adam and Eve in Eden—the pattern of head and body in sacred communion—finds its ultimate fulfillment in Christ and the church. "Let us be glad and rejoice and give Him glory, for the marriage of the Lamb has come, and His wife has made herself ready" (Rev 19:7). For "the peace that Christ brought by becoming human is acquired through repentance."[3] History culminates with a wedding feast—perfect communion between Christ and his bride, the goal toward which all patterns have pointed. "Then I, John, saw the holy city, New Jerusalem, coming down out of heaven from God, prepared as a bride adorned for her husband" (Rev 21:2). From the beginning, earthly marriage served as a type pointing toward the ultimate reality: Christ as Head united with his bride in perfect communion.

The church as Bride represents all three principles restored and functioning properly. Authority is perfected: Christ serves as faithful Head, never heeding voices below but maintaining perfect submission to the Father while providing perfect guidance to his body. The church responds as faithful bride, neither pressuring Christ toward compromise nor rebelling against his headship, but submitting gladly to his loving leadership. The authority inversions that plagued every previous Adam figure—Aaron yielding to the people, Saul fearing popular opinion, Solomon swayed by foreign wives—find no place in Christ's headship.

Cooperation is accomplished: The church doesn't produce fruit autonomously but only as branches abiding in Christ the Vine. Believers till through faithful obedience, Christ provides divine rain through his Spirit, and fruit results—"love, joy, peace, longsuffering, kindness, goodness,

2. Irenaeus, *Scandal of the Incarnation*, 59.

3. Grēgorios, *Divine Liturgy*, 111.

faithfulness, gentleness, self-control" (Gal 5:22–23). The cooperation that broke when the ground was cursed is restored through union with Christ. Our work matters but produces genuine yield only through his enabling grace. Orientation is corrected: the church approaches Christ not claiming merit but receiving grace. "We love Him because He first loved us" (1 John 4:19). There's no inheritor mindset claiming to deserve Christ's love through spiritual achievement. Every blessing flows from his sacrifice, every spiritual gift comes from his grace, and every fruit results from his life flowing through us. The church embodies renewer orientation—all is received, nothing is earned.

The church must cleave wholly to Christ, her Head, like God first stated in Genesis for man to cleave to his wife. This cleaving is not passive; it's the cooperation of divine grace (Jesus) and human freedom (church). Individually, we cleave through faith and ascetic practice; corporately, the church cleaves through fidelity to the apostolic tradition and the sacraments, since in the Orthodox Church, salvation is not an individual pursuit. "An individualistic Christianity is a contradiction in terms to the Orthodox. Although the Christian God is a personal God and desires to have a personal relationship with each believer, Orthodox Christians believe they are being saved together in the Church, not in isolation."[4] The church, as a corporate body with many members, worships and partakes in communion with God, awaiting Christ's promise to be with us to the end of the age (Matt 28:20). The Eucharist is the supreme act of cleaving. In the Divine Liturgy, the bride unites herself to the bridegroom in the most intimate way: "He who eats my flesh and drinks my blood abides in me, and I in him" (John 6:56). Here the church's cleaving is not only spiritual but sacramental, as the faithful are made "one Body" by partaking of the one Bread (1 Cor 10:17).

4. Tibbs, *A Basic Guide to Eastern Orthodox Theology*, 29.

# 14

# The Serpent—Character Versus Circumstance

The serpent's curse in Gen 3:14—"Upon thy belly shalt thou go, and dust shalt thou eat" and "I will put enmity between you and the woman, and between your offspring and her offspring; he shall bruise your head, and you shall bruise his heel" (Gen 3:15)—establishes two opposing lineages. The serpent's offspring represents the ultimate inheritor—the line of rebellion, pride, and self-reliance that seeks to claim authority on its own terms. Understanding the serpent's strategy is crucial for recognizing how temptation operates throughout Scripture. The serpent never forces Eve to eat; he simply provides an alternative interpretation of God's command. This is the pattern of temptation: not overpowering human will but offering a competing voice that sounds reasonable.

Throughout biblical narratives, the "serpent" appears not as a literal snake but as any voice—internal or external—that offers earthly wisdom in place of divine instruction. Sometimes it's a wife (Delilah to Samson), sometimes it's the people (Israel to Moses), sometimes it's our own disciple (Peter to Jesus), sometimes it's our bodily desires (Esau's hunger). The common element is not the specific form but the dynamic: a voice that bypasses proper authority and offers what seems good from an earthly perspective. Learning to recognize this pattern helps you identify temptation in your own life: whenever you face a voice suggesting that God's command doesn't really mean what you thought, or that circumstances justify an exception, or that your immediate needs outweigh your long-term obedience—that's the serpent's strategy recurring.

The woman's offspring points to the ultimate Renewer (Christ), who crushes the serpent's head through humility and sacrifice, renewing creation. But the serpent's offspring can be seen in two distinct forms of serpent-like existence throughout Scripture: those who choose deception (character-based) and those who inherit fallen conditions (circumstance-based). The original serpent chose deceptive mediation, corrupting authority above it, which had dominion over it. Its punishment—reduction from upright movement to crawling on its belly—"upon your belly shalt thou go"—establishes the foundational pattern: corrupted mediation results in loss of proper upright existence. The dust that the serpent shall eat are beings that don't have the breath of life in them.

When God created Adam, he gathered dust and breathed into his nostrils the breath of life, making him human. Throughout Scripture, dust marks the state of life apart from divine breath (Gen 2:7; Ps 104:29; Eccl 3:20). To eat dust, then, is to consume what has lost the Spirit's animation—a condition of spiritless existence. The curse isn't about diet but dominion: the serpent feeds on lifelessness. The curse also created conditions where others inherit serpent-like circumstances—inability to walk upright, reduction to ground-level existence, exclusion from sacred space—without possessing the serpent-like character of eating the dust. Their condition results from living in a world where original mediation failed, inheriting the consequences of others' corrupted choices. This distinction proves crucial for understanding biblical healing narratives and the broader pattern of divine restoration operating throughout Scripture.

## CHARACTER-BASED SERPENTS: CHOSEN DECEPTION AT CENTER

Character-based serpents actively choose deceptive mediation, following the original serpent's pattern. These figures possess serpent-like traits—cunning, manipulation, resistance to divine truth—yet often occupy positions of authority at the center rather than the periphery. The center represents proximity to sacred space (Eden, the tabernacle, the temple, Jerusalem). Pharisees in the Gospels are a clear example: guardians of the law who, while standing at the center, "shut up the kingdom of heaven against men" and become "blind guides" (Matt 23:13, 16).

They are not victims of serpent-like circumstances; they embody serpent-like character. They twist truth while claiming to defend it, leading people away from God while insisting they represent him. This is the original serpent's sin in human form.

## CIRCUMSTANCE-BASED SERPENTS: INHERITED CONSEQUENCES

Circumstance-based serpents experience serpent-like conditions without choosing deceptive character. Their "crawling" or exclusion is inherited, not self-inflicted. They live in a fallen world where mediation has already failed, and they suffer the consequences. They are pushed to the periphery: exile (Cain wandering, Israel in Babylon), social marginalization (lepers outside the camp, tax collectors excluded from synagogue), or physical limitations (the lame, the blind) that restrict access to sacred space. These figures are not enemies to be destroyed but sufferers to be restored. Recognizing this distinction reshapes how we read many healing narratives: God is not merely fixing bodies; he is reversing serpent-like conditions for those who never chose serpent-like rebellion.

## MEPHIBOSHETH: PERIPHERY TO ROYAL COURT

Among those who embody this peripheral, serpent-like condition without personal guilt stands Mephibosheth. Mephibosheth's lameness resulted not from personal sin but from inherited catastrophe. When his nurse fled upon hearing of Saul and Jonathan's deaths, five-year-old Mephibosheth fell, becoming permanently lame (2 Sam 4:4). He bore the consequences of his grandfather Saul's corrupted kingship—a circumstance-based serpent condition. The fall that crippled him was itself a bringing low—from royal heir to disabled outcast in a single moment, echoing the serpent's curse in the garden.

His exile to Lo-debar (2 Sam 9:5) reveals the depth of peripheral existence. The name means "no pasture"—a place far from the center, dusty and desolate. Physical separation from the royal court (power center) and social and status exclusion all combined to create a periphery existence. His lameness trapped him there, unable to journey toward the center due to being of the wrong lineage, the line of the fallen King Saul. He had been brought low in every sense: physically (the fall), socially (exile), politically (from royal house to obscurity), and spiritually (dwelling where God's word doesn't reach).

When David sought to show kindness "for Jonathan's sake" (2 Sam 9:1), messengers brought Mephibosheth from Lo-debar to Jerusalem. The text emphasizes his humility by lowering himself upon arrival: "Now when Mephibosheth the son of Jonathan, the son of Saul, had come to David, he fell on his face and prostrated himself" (2 Sam 9:6). Already confined to ground-level existence by lameness, Mephibosheth humbled himself further, later stating, "What is your servant, that you should look upon such a dead dog as I?" (2 Sam 9:8). Years of exclusion, inherited shame, and physical limitation had humbled Mephibosheth. This humility—this recognition of complete dependence on royal mercy—positioned him to receive what he could never earn or demand.

David's response demonstrates mercy extended not for Mephibosheth's merit but "for Jonathan's sake"—a pattern prefiguring divine grace: "Do not fear, for I will surely show you kindness for Jonathan your father's sake, and will restore to you all the land of Saul your grandfather; and you shall eat bread at my table continually" (2 Sam 9:7). The king's mercy flows from prior relationship and covenant love, not from the recipient's worthiness. As believers receive mercy "for Christ's sake" (Eph 4:32), Mephibosheth received restoration "for Jonathan's sake." David's mercy was transforming: geographical location changed to Jerusalem instead of Lo-debar, social status elevated (king's table instead of exile), economic security restored (family lands returned), and relational identity redefined (adopted son rather than enemy's descendant). The phrase "he shall eat at my table, as one of the king's sons" (2 Sam 9:11) represents complete movement from periphery to center. The one brought low—through childhood fall, years of exile, and humble prostration—was raised to the king's table.

## DAVID'S COVENANT MERCY: BREAKING THE SERPENT'S TEMPORAL CHAINS

The serpent's curse in Gen 3:15 establishes precisely this pattern of generational warfare where past enmity perpetuates into present conflict. "I will put enmity between your seed and her seed" creates a temporal structure where each generation inherits either blessing or curse based on lineage rather than personal choice. The curse orients humanity earthward and backward, trapped by accumulated consequences of ancestral decisions. The past becomes prison, and inheritance becomes inescapable destiny.

David's action shatters this temporal determinism through covenant mercy that transcends generational consequences. When he sends messengers to bring Mephibosheth from Lo-debar to Jerusalem, David acts not based on what the past requires but on what covenant love enables. Saul attempted to murder David repeatedly. Saul's house lost the kingdom through disobedience. Saul's descendants represent potential rivals to David's dynasty. Every earthly calculation, every inherited enmity, every lesson from the past suggests David should eliminate or ignore Saul's surviving line. The serpent's temporal logic demands that past hostility determine present action.

Yet David asks, "Is there still anyone who is left of the house of Saul, that I may show him kindness for Jonathan's sake?" The question itself reverses the curse's orientation. David looks not at what the past dictates but at what covenant enables. His relationship with Jonathan creates an obligation that supersedes the enmity between their houses. The covenant between David and Jonathan was explicitly generational: "You shall not cut off your kindness from my house forever" (1 Sam 20:15). David's faithfulness means that Jonathan's seed receives blessing despite belonging to Saul's fallen house.

The phrase "for Jonathan's sake" establishes that grace can flow through covenant relationships to benefit those who possess no personal merit or claim. Mephibosheth receives blessing not because of anything he has done but entirely through what his father meant to David—and despite what his grandfather did. This breaks the serpent's temporal logic where accumulated disadvantage perpetuates generationally. Covenant mercy intervenes in the generational transmission of curse, redirecting inheritance from judgment to blessing based on relationship rather than lineage.

This principle that David enacts toward Mephibosheth becomes the very pattern by which God treats Solomon generations later. When Solomon's heart turns after foreign gods and he builds high places for Chemosh and Molech, he commits precisely the kind of corporate failure that cost Saul his kingdom. Solomon inverts proper authority by allowing foreign wives to redirect his worship, yields to corrupted voices rather than maintaining divine wisdom, and leads Israel into idolatry through his example. The structural violation mirrors Saul's authority breakdown when he heeded the people's voice rather than God's command.

Yet God's response to Solomon differs dramatically from his judgment of Saul. God declares, "Because you have done this, and have not kept My covenant and My statutes, which I have commanded you, I will surely tear the kingdom away from you and give it to your servant. Nevertheless I will not do it in your days, for the sake of your father David; I will tear it out of the hand of your son" (1 Kgs 11:11–12). The preservation operates entirely through David's covenant rather than Solomon's merit. The text reinforces this principle: "However I will not tear away the whole kingdom; I will give one tribe to your son for the sake of My servant David" (1 Kgs 11:13).

## DAVID, THE BLIND AND THE LAME, AND THE GREATER SON

When David comes to take Jerusalem, the Jebusites mock him: "You will not come in here, but the blind and the lame will ward you off" (2 Sam 5:6). They boast that even their weakest can keep God's anointed king out. Their taunt becomes a proverb: "The blind and the lame shall not come into the house" (v. 8). This is not a divine hatred of the disabled but a symbolic judgment on proud, serpent-like character in the stronghold. They use "blind" and "lame" as a badge of mockery; David uses it as a marker of what must be cleansed from the holy hill—false confidence, false mediation, self-secure blindness.

Later, when David welcomes Mephibosheth—the "lame" grandson of Saul—to "eat at my table continually" (2 Sam 9:7), he enacts the other side of the pattern. The proud mockers are driven from the walls; the humbled lame man is seated at the table. The stronghold is cleansed of character-based serpents and filled with restored circumstance-based sufferers. David's city becomes a picture: "the blind and the lame" of pride are excluded; the blind and lame of inheritance are welcomed by grace.

Centuries later, the greater Son of David repeats and fulfills this pattern. Entering the temple, Jesus drives out those who commercialize worship and corrupt mediation. Then, immediately, "the blind and the lame came to Him in the temple, and He healed them" (Matt 21:14). Cleansing and restoration now occur together: false mediators removed, wounded sufferers restored. Zion becomes not only the city of a king but the dwelling place of mercy.

## THE LAME BEGGAR AT THE TEMPLE: SACRED ACCESS RESTORED

Another example of a circumstance-based serpent was the lame man at the temple gate in Acts 3, who experienced healing that specifically enabled worship—movement from exclusion to participation in sacred space itself. His condition matched the paralytic's severity: "And a certain man lame from his mother's womb was carried, whom they laid daily at the gate of the temple which is called Beautiful, to ask alms from those who entered the temple" (Acts 3:2). Congenital lameness from birth, complete dependence on others for movement, daily positioning at a fixed location—all characterized peripheral existence.

The geographical detail is significant; he couldn't enter the temple courts where worship occurred at the center of sacred space. The "gate called Beautiful" marked the boundary between the accessible outer court and sacred inner spaces reserved for covenant people. For forty years—"the man was above forty years old" (Acts 4:22)—he had occupied this liminal space: close enough to observe worship, far enough to be excluded from participation. Each day brought the same routine—"whom they laid daily"—parallel to the laying, horizontal existence the serpent was cursed with. He possessed no independent access to the sacred center, no ability to respond to divine summons through his own mobility.

When Peter and John approach, the lame man responds normally: "Seeing Peter and John about to go into the temple, [he] asked for alms" (Acts 3:3). But "then Peter said, 'Silver and gold I do not have, but what I do have I give you: In the name of Jesus Christ of Nazareth, rise up and walk.' And he took him by the right hand and lifted him up, and immediately his feet and ankle bones received strength. So he, leaping up, stood and walked and entered the temple with them—walking, leaping, and praising God" (Acts 3:6–8).

The healing accomplished what even David's mercy for Mephibosheth could not: physical transformation enabling independent movement. The progression reveals systematic reversal of serpent-like reduction: from ground-level existence to upright human dignity through leaping up, standing, and walking. But the geographical transformation matters equally: the man "entered the temple with them." For forty years, the Beautiful Gate marked his exclusion. Now he passed through it, not carried but walking, not as a beggar but as a worshiper. His response—"walking, leaping, and praising God"—demonstrates complete restoration. The leaping literally fulfills Isaiah's prophecy: "Then shall the lame man leap as an hart" (Isa 35:6). His praise reveals that the healing is not merely physical but recognized as divine action, drawing him into restored communion with God and participation in his glory.

## THE MAN BORN BLIND: WHEN CIRCUMSTANCE TEACHES CHARACTER

The blind beggar in John 9 is another example of healing by Jesus, representing restoration. But equally significant is that a circumstance-based serpent (blind beggar) instructs character-based serpents (Pharisees) about Jesus, exposing who truly sees and who remains blind. This scene demonstrates that circumstance-based serpents can possess greater spiritual sight than character-based serpents who occupy positions of religious authority—a complete inversion of expected order. His condition matched the others' severity: "Now as Jesus passed by, He saw a man who was blind from birth" (John 9:1). Blindness meant he had never navigated independently, living in darkness, never seeing the path toward the temple or any center of communal life. His peripheral position appears immediately when disciples ask, "Rabbi, who sinned, this man or his parents, that he was born blind?" (John 9:2). Jesus' response establishes the critical distinction: "Neither this man nor his parents sinned, but that the works of God should be revealed in him" (John 9:3).

The man's blindness resulted from living in a fallen world where the serpent's curse affects all creation, not from chosen deception. Next, Jesus applies mud to his eyes and sends him to wash in Siloam's pool: "He went his way therefore, and washed, and came seeing" (John 9:7). When neighbors question whether this is the same beggar, he confirms: "I am he" (John 9:9). They ask how his eyes opened, and he describes the healing but identifies Jesus simply as "a man called Jesus" (John 9:11)—initial recognition at the human level. His sight is brand new; his understanding is forming step by step.

The Pharisees summoned him for interrogation and pressed for judgment on Jesus' identity. His understanding deepens: "He is a prophet" (John 9:17). The man who had been blind from birth now sees more clearly than Israel's religious leaders. His recognition progresses naturally—from "a man" to "a prophet"—as he considers what only divine authority could accomplish. The contrast between the healed man and the Pharisees becomes devastating. Those who should mediate divine wisdom to Israel demonstrate willful blindness: "Some of the Pharisees said, 'This Man is not from God, because He does not keep the Sabbath'" (John 9:16). They possess religious knowledge, occupy the religious center, and hold authority to interpret Torah.

Yet they cannot see what the formerly blind beggar perceives immediately—that power to heal congenital blindness reveals divine presence. The Pharisees' blindness is character-based, not circumstantial. They choose not to see because seeing would require relinquishing their position and authority. When some Pharisees express doubt about their conclusion, others dismiss the healing entirely: they call the man's parents to verify he had actually been blind, hoping to discredit the miracle itself (John 9:18–23).

The parents confirm their son's condition but refuse to explain the healing: "He is of age; ask him. He will speak for himself" (John 9:21). John notes explicitly: "His parents said these things because they feared the Jews, for the Jews had agreed already that if anyone confessed that He was Christ, he would be put out of the synagogue" (John 9:22). The Pharisees' character-based corruption extends to terrorizing the community, using their central authority to maintain control through fear.

The Pharisees summon the healed man a second time: "Give God the glory! We know that this Man is a sinner" (John 9:24). The command reveals their blindness—they've already reached their conclusion and demand he confirm it. But the circumstance-based serpent, newly freed from blindness, speaks truth: "Whether He is a sinner or not I do not know. One thing I know: that though I was blind, now I see" (John 9:25). His response cuts through to praising the mercy and restoration he received. The Pharisees are the inheritors of the traditions; they claim a comprehensive understanding. He experienced undeniable grace.

When they demand again how the healing occurred—"What did He do to you? How did He open your eyes?" (John 9:26)—highlighting who is actually blind, the beggar's patience breaks: "I told you already, and you did not listen. Why do you want to hear it again? Do you also want to become His disciples?" (John 9:27). The question is profound: the man who lived in darkness—who has been blind his entire life, who begged at roadsides, who occupied the lowest social position—asks the Pharisees if they want to become disciples of Jesus. He recognizes what they refuse to see: that following Jesus is the logical response to witnessing divine power. His mockery exposes their hardened hearts.

The Pharisees' response reveals they are the character-based serpent: "Then they reviled him and said, 'You are His disciple, but we are Moses' disciples. We know that God spoke to Moses; as for this fellow, we do not know where He is from'" (John 9:28–29). They claim certainty about the past while refusing to see the present. This scene is absolutely full of irony: we have the physically blind "serpent" helping the spiritually blind "serpent" about who Jesus truly is. What follows is extraordinary—the formerly blind beggar instructs the religious authorities in theology: "Why, this is a marvelous thing, that you do not know where He is from; yet He has opened my eyes! Now we know that God does not hear sinners; but if anyone is a worshiper of God and does His will, He hears him. Since the world began it has been unheard of that anyone opened the eyes of one who was born blind. If this Man were not from God, He could do nothing" (John 9:30–33). The man uses their own theology against them: God doesn't empower sinners to perform miracles.

The circumstance-based serpent, freed from blindness hours earlier, sees Christ and his ministry more clearly than those who've studied Torah their entire lives. The Pharisees' response exposes character-based corruption completely: "'You were completely born in sins, and are you teaching us?' And they cast him out" (John 9:34). Unable to refute his logic, they attack his person—claiming his congenital blindness proves he was "born in sins," therefore unqualified to teach them anything. They revert to the disciples' original false assumption—that circumstance-based conditions prove character-based sin—because acknowledging the truth would cost them their position. By casting him out, they attempt to restore him to the periphery. The man who spoke truth must be exiled from the center, silenced, excluded. Character-based serpents at the center cannot tolerate circumstance-based serpents speaking truth—it exposes the inversion, revealing that the periphery sees more clearly than the center.

## The Final Recognition: From Circumstance to Worship

But this attempted re-exile creates the condition for ultimate restoration: "Jesus heard that they had cast him out; and when He had found him, He said to him, 'Do you believe in the Son of God?' He answered and said, 'Who is He, Lord, that I may believe in Him?' And Jesus said to him, 'You have both seen Him and it is He who is talking with you.' Then he said, 'Lord, I believe!' And he worshiped Him" (John 9:35–38). Physical healing enabled seeing Jesus' face. Spiritual healing enabled recognizing Jesus' identity.

Jesus' concluding statement carries weight: "For judgment I have come into this world, that those who do not see may see, and that those who see may be made blind" (John 9:39). The Pharisees, overhearing, ask with apparent confusion, "Are we blind also?" (John 9:40). The question reveals they still don't understand the distinction between circumstance and character, between inherited conditions and chosen corruption. Jesus' response cuts to the heart: "If you were blind, you would have no sin; but now you say, 'We see.' Therefore your sin remains" (John 9:41). If they suffered circumstance-based blindness—if they genuinely couldn't see—they would be innocent like the beggar was innocent of his condition. But their blindness is character-based. They say "we see"—being proud, claiming comprehensive understanding, religious authority, spiritual insight—while rejecting the divine presence standing before them. Their claimed sight is their condemnation because it's willful blindness masquerading as knowledge.

The complete inversion is now visible: the circumstance-based serpent who inherited blindness gains both physical and spiritual sight, recognizes divine presence, teaches theological truth, and worships God incarnate. The character-based serpents who possess religious authority, occupy the center, and claim comprehensive sight remain spiritually blind, reject divine presence, revile theological truth, and cast out those who see clearly. This is the ultimate demonstration of restoration's power: healing bodies or repositioning people, but reversing the fundamental disorder where the periphery sees truth while the center clings to deception, where inherited suffering produces spiritual sight while chosen authority produces spiritual blindness, where circumstance-based serpents worship while character-based serpents curse.

## THE LORD'S PRAYER AND COVENANT FORGIVENESS

This pattern finds its fullest expression in Jesus' teaching on forgiveness within the Lord's Prayer. When Christ instructs us to pray "forgive us our debts, as we forgive our debtors" (Matt 6:12), he establishes the same covenant principle that David enacted toward Mephibosheth and that God applied to Solomon. The petition operates on covenant logic rather than transactional justice.

The Lord's Prayer petition thus reverses the serpent's temporal curse at the relational level. The curse establishes enmity between seeds that perpetuates generationally, creating inherited hostility where past offenses determine present relationships. Covenant forgiveness interrupts this temporal chain. When we forgive those who trespass against us, we refuse to let their past actions determine our present response or their future possibilities. We break the deterministic pattern where accumulated grievance becomes inherited enmity, choosing instead the covenant mercy pattern where relationships create possibilities that transcend strict justice.

This explains why Jesus emphasizes the principle immediately after teaching the prayer: "For if you forgive men their trespasses, your heavenly Father will also forgive you. But if you do not forgive men their trespasses, neither will your Father forgive your trespasses" (Matthew 6:14–15). This is not arbitrary divine condition but structural reality. Those who refuse to extend covenant mercy to others demonstrate they have not understood or embraced the covenant mercy pattern by which they themselves receive forgiveness. They remain trapped in the serpent's temporal logic where past determines present and strict accounting governs all relationships.

Christ represents the ultimate reversal of the principle that past determines present. He enters human history bearing the full weight of accumulated generational curse—all the enmity, all the consequences, all the inherited disadvantages that the serpent's seed has perpetuated since Eden. Yet he breaks the temporal chain completely. "Therefore, if anyone is in Christ, he is a new creation; old things have passed away; behold, all things have become new" (2 Cor 5:17). The past no longer defines those united to him because he has absorbed its consequences and broken its determinative power.

The resurrection particularly manifests this temporal reversal. Death represents the ultimate expression of the serpent's curse—the final consequence that has passed to all humanity through generational transmission. Christ's resurrection breaks this temporal progression. He enters death bearing all inherited curse but emerges alive, demonstrating that the past's determinative power has been shattered. Those who belong to him participate in this resurrection life, liberated from the principle that ancestral failure must determine descendant destiny.

## CONCLUSION: THE PATTERN REVEALED

The lame man begging at the temple gates observes worship but cannot enter. Like Mephibosheth, who dwelling in Lo-debar ("no word/pasture") experienced both physical and spiritual barrenness but received kindness for Jonathan's sake, we now receive mercy for Christ's sake (Eph 4:32). Restoration consistently moves people from the periphery toward the center, reversing the curse's effects. This movement represents more than physical healing—it signifies restored access to divine presence, renewed community participation, and recovery of humanity's original calling to mediate between heaven and earth at the sacred center where God meets his people, ultimately experiencing communion with God. The serpent's curse brought humanity low, excluded us from sacred space, and blinded us to divine presence. These healings demonstrate systematic reversal: from crawling to leaping, from periphery to center, from blindness to sight, from exile to communion. Character-based serpents who choose deception face judgment unless they repent. Circumstance-based serpents who inherit consequences receive divine mercy and restoration. Both point toward ultimate restoration when the crawling imposed by Gen 3:14 will be permanently replaced by upright praise.

15

# Seed, Offering, and the Orientation of the Heart

## CAIN AND ABEL AND THEIR OFFERINGS

When Adam and Eve were cast out of the garden, a fundamental shift occurred. In Eden, they had freely available fruit from the trees—fruit that nourished both body and spirit. But their disobedience led to God cursing the ground: "Cursed is the ground because of you; through painful toil you will eat food from it all the days of your life. It will produce thorns and thistles for you" (Gen 3:17–18). The earth would no longer yield provision easily. Having rejected God's direct provision, humanity would now learn through grinding struggle that true sustenance must come from God, not from earthly effort alone.

The next generation, Cain and Abel, are now having to survive in a world that is no longer abundant. They now present offerings to God—our first glimpse of what God deems acceptable worship. Offering reveals the direction of one's being (orientation principle). Worship is never neutral; it reflects whether one's life participates in restoring order or perpetuating disorder. Their sacrifices reveal whether worship will express faith in God as the source of life and blessing or whether humanity will act in self-determination, securing provision autonomously. The distinction centers on a single biblical principle: seed represents life-transmission—the capacity to generate future from present. This principle, established in Cain and Abel's story, becomes the pattern for understanding acceptable offerings throughout Scripture. To see how Scripture frames this life-bearing principle, we must return to the seed categories established in Gen 1.

Genesis 1:11–12 introduces three botanical categories defined by seed-bearing capacity: grass (seed absent and temporary), herb-bearing seed (middle category), and the fruit tree with "seed in itself" (the highest category). Scripture consistently treats seed as the life-principle within plants—the capacity to generate future from present. Seed is your future in concentrated form. This makes Gen 4's wording all the more striking. "And in the process of time it came to pass that Cain brought an offering of the fruit of the ground to the Lord" (Gen 4:5). Cain offers "fruit of the ground"—a phrase that departs from Gen 1's seed-based designations. Where Gen 1 defines plants by seed-bearing capacity, Gen 4 defines Cain's offering by origin (cursed ground) and function (consumable), with no mention of seed. The linguistic shift matters: from life-generating to life-consuming, from God's creative abundance to human labor's terminal product. When you harvest grain, you can either keep it in seed form or process it into meal or flour. By distinguishing "fruit of the ground" from "seed," the narrative implies a product stripped of its reproductive power. In the language of Leviticus, this shifts the category from "firstfruits" to "grain offering" (flour), which requires oil to be acceptable. Cain provides the material, but without the mechanism of life (seed) or the witness (oil).

Because herbs bearing seed do not contain their seed "within themselves" the way fruit trees do (Gen 1:11–12), the seed is normally separated during harvest through threshing or winnowing (Ruth 3:2; Isa 28:27–28). When Cain brings his offering "in the process of time" (Gen 4:3)—a phrase indicating the harvest cycle had ended—it is likely that the life-bearing seed has already been removed or stored. This fits the narrative context of Cain's offering. What remained was produce without seed, a terminal product lacking the life-principle. It is important to note that "fruit of the ground" can indeed be acceptable to God, as shown in Israel's commanded grain offerings (Lev 2:1–14), but only when the seed remains intact or when oil—the sign of the Spirit's consecrating witness—is added. Cain's offering, on this reading, lacked both.

Leviticus makes this distinction explicit:

- Flour with oil: "When anyone offers a grain offering to the Lord, his offering shall be of fine flour. And he shall pour oil on it" (Lev 2:1).

- Full heads: "If you offer a grain offering of your firstfruits to the Lord, you shall offer . . . grain beaten from full heads" (Lev 2:14).

Seed represents the human act of trusting God for future provision—surrendering what could secure one's own tomorrow. Oil represents the Holy Spirit's witness that the offering is consecrated and accepted. Together, they complete the cooperation of sacrifice: human faith meets divine confirmation. If Cain offered without seed and without oil, his offering, at least in terms of the Levitical code, was not acceptable.

The law reveals an underlying principle: acceptable offerings require life in biological form (seed/blood) or the Spirit's witness (oil/fat), never terminal products stripped of both. This is why Scripture never pits grain offerings against animal offerings (Deut 22:11). The central question is not the material offered but whether life is present within it. Deuteronomy 26:1–2 commands bringing "the first of all the produce of the ground" (v. 2), not leftovers from a completed harvest. Scripture establishes that life resides in specific places and requires specific offerings. In animals, "the life of the flesh is in the blood" (Lev 17:11)—a bloodless animal is a corpse, not a sacrifice. In plants, life to multiply resides in the seed: "Unless a kernel of wheat falls to the ground and dies, it remains only a single seed. But if it dies, it produces many seeds" (John 12:24).

This distinction is seen in Abel's offering: he brings "the firstborn of his flock and their fat" (Gen 4:4). Abel's offering reflects both elements; Cain's reflects neither. The offering embodies the offeror. Where Cain withheld both seed (life) and oil (Spirit-witness), Abel gave both blood (life itself) and fat (the oil analogue, representing Spirit-blessed consecration).

When grain is processed into flour, its biological life is destroyed; the seed can no longer germinate. Biological life is absent, so the Spirit's witness—symbolized by oil or fat—must be present. "The Spirit bears witness with our spirit that we are children of God" (Rom 8:16). This same pattern appears in Israel's worship: God commands the Zadokite priests to "offer to Me the fat and the blood" (Ezek 44:15), confirming that acceptable offerings must present biological life (blood), biological life in plants (seed), and the Holy Spirit's witness (oil or fat).

Each brother's offering revealed his heart's orientation. Hebrews 11:4 confirms: "By faith Abel offered to God a more excellent sacrifice." The issue was faith in God versus self-reliance, life surrendered versus life withheld. The New Testament reinforces this reading. John writes that Cain "was of the wicked one and murdered his brother. And why did he murder him?

Because his own works were evil and his brother's righteous" (1 John 3:12). Notice the sequence: John interprets the murder in light of the works—the offering precedes and explains the violence. The phrase "was of the wicked one" indicates Cain proceeded from a source devoid of life.

Though Abel was martyred, he "still speaks" (Heb 11:4)—as Tertullian states, "The blood of the martyrs is the seed of the Christians," since seed and blood contain life.[1] The principle that acceptable worship requires offering the life-source—whether in biological or spiritual form—finds its most dramatic expression in Abraham's supreme test. Isaac represents not merely Abraham's son but his entire future—God's promise made flesh—making this the ultimate seed-offering that reveals heart orientation.

## THE ULTIMATE TEST: ABRAHAM AND ISAAC (GEN 22)

The most profound test of this principle is the binding of Isaac. Isaac was a son; he was the child of the promise, the "only son . . ., whom you love" (Gen 22:2). More importantly, he was the "seed" through whom God had promised "all nations of the earth shall be blessed" (Gen 22:18). Isaac embodied the entire future of the covenant; he was the life-principle of God's redemptive plan. This is precisely why God asks for Isaac, because he is the seed—which Jesus reveals must die and fall into the ground to produce (John 12:24). This is the ultimate test of the Cain/Abel dynamic. Abraham is asked to sacrifice, in radical faith, his life-bearing seed, placing his entire future in God's hands. He demonstrates his complete trust that God, not his heir, is the ultimate source of life, even "concluding that God was able to raise him up, even from the dead" (Heb 11:19), since seed, which Isaac was repeatedly identified as, must die to have life.

When God provides a substitute, he is not rejecting the offering but affirming the heart behind it. He confirms the principle: "Because you have done this and have not withheld your son . . . in your seed all the nations of the earth shall be blessed" (Gen 22:16–18). The principle holds: the willingness to offer the seed—the life-source itself—is the ultimate expression of faith, which God meets with covenantal blessing. Jephthah is a distortion of this principle. He doesn't vow to offer seed but, "whatever comes out" (Judg 11:31). The result is not life through surrender, but death through hedging and irresponsibility—Abraham offers in faith; Jephthah in ignorance.

1. Tertullian, *Apology*, 117.

Ontologically, the tests reveal that the promise is not secured by withholding the seed but by participation in God, from whom all life proceeds.

## THE WIDOW OF ZAREPHATH (1 KGS 17:8–24)

The seed principle reaches its sharpest test not in abundance but in famine. During a drought, Elijah encounters a widow preparing a final meal for herself and her son: "I have only a handful of flour in a bin, and a little oil in a jar; and now I am gathering a couple of sticks that I may go in and prepare it for myself and my son, that we may eat it, and die" (1 Kgs 17:12). Her handful of flour is the end of all sowing—grain ground down, incapable of germination. It is life reduced to residue. But notice that she has also oil (the very substance that makes flour acceptable as offering); she still possesses the oil that carries life in spiritual form. She has flour (processed grain, seed destroyed) and oil (the Spirit-substance required for an acceptable offering). What Cain withheld in abundance, she offers in poverty.

Elijah's request is staggering: "Make me a small cake from it first, and bring it to me; and afterward make some for yourself and your son" (v. 13). He asks her to offer what cannot be reproduced, to surrender the last barrier between her household and death. Here, faith is tested at its most elemental: whether she will cling to what remains or release it God. And "the bin of flour was not used up, nor did the jar of oil run dry" (v. 16).

Then the test deepens. Her son—the last seed of her lineage—falls ill and dies. The seed now lies lifeless. Elijah carries the child to the upper room and cries, "O Lord my God, let this child's soul come back to him" (v. 21). The Lord hears; the child revives, and Elijah returns him to the woman. This echoes Abraham's test—but now the resurrection happens literally, not metaphorically. This is the first resurrection in Scripture, demonstrating God can bring even dead seed back to life. Life is preserved only by relinquishing control of it. To die in faith is to release control, to yield what we can no longer sustain into the hands of God. The seed loses autonomy when it falls into the ground; only then can God give it new form. So too the widow: she relinquishes her last measure of control, and that surrender becomes the doorway through which divine provision flows. "Whoever seeks to save his life will lose it, and whoever loses his life for My sake will find it" (Luke 9:24).

The two miracles, the jar that never empties and the son restored, reveal one pattern: what is offered in faith is sustained, and what dies in faith is raised. The contrast with Cain is profound. He guarded the seed and reaped curse; she gave the flour and received resurrection. Her faith prefigures Christ—the true Seed who, in the poverty of flesh, offers himself to the Father and becomes the living Bread of the world. This connects the arguments of faith and offering, both being important to God, since the substance reflects the faith (offering the seed = faith; withholding/processing it = lack of faith).

## THE WIDOW'S MITE (LUKE 21:1–4)

Jesus makes this principle explicit at the temple. He contrasts two types of offerings. The rich contribute large sums from their "abundance"—their surplus. They are offering a "terminal product" after their own seed is secured. Their offering requires no faith. A poor widow, however, gives "two mites." Jesus' verdict reveals God's economy: "Truly I say to you that this poor widow has put in more than all; for all these out of their abundance have put in offerings for God, but she out of her poverty put in all the livelihood that she had" (Luke 21:3–4). She offered her life-principle. She held nothing back. Giving from the surplus is a transaction; giving the "seed" is an act of total trust. "In return, God offers us His entire life, 'so that we may receive life in return for life, the eternal in return for the temporal.'"[2] Jesus communicates this principle, stating, "For everyone to whom much is given, from him much will be required; and to whom much has been committed, of him they will ask the more" (Luke 12:48). Showing why the seed is the future-securing portion that cannot be held back, he says, "Assuredly, I say to you that it is hard for a rich man to enter the kingdom of heaven" (Matt 19:23). Since the rich man has more, he is required to give more. All these examples demonstrate positive seed-offering, but the pattern also illuminates failure. Ananias and Sapphira's tragedy reveals what happens when the opposite orientation dominates—when the appearance of generosity masks actual withholding, when the seed is kept while ostensibly being offered.

2. Grēgorios, *Divine Liturgy*, 69.

## THE NEGATIVE EXAMPLE: ANANIAS AND SAPPHIRA (ACTS 5:1–11)

This story is the New Testament's chilling parallel to Cain's failure. In a community moved by the Spirit to share all things (Acts 4:32), Ananias and Sapphira sell property. Their sin is not in keeping a portion—Peter makes it clear the land was theirs to control: "While it remained unsold, did it not remain your own? And after it was sold, was it not at your disposal?" (Acts 5:4). Their sin, like Cain's, is in the deception. They "kept back part of the proceeds" but "brought a certain part and laid it at the apostles' feet," presenting it as if it were the whole (Acts 5:2). This is the exact pattern: a pretense of total generosity while secretly withholding the life-resource for their own security. They wanted the reputation of Abel with the self-securing heart of Cain.

Peter's verdict is devastating: "Ananias, why has Satan filled your heart to lie to the Holy Spirit . . . You have not lied to man but to God" (Acts 5:3–4). This phrase—"lying to the Holy Spirit"—is critical in light of the oil principle. Throughout Scripture, oil represents the Holy Spirit, the life-giving presence that consecrates all acceptable offerings (Gen 2:7; John 6:63). To lie about your offering is to lie to the Spirit—the very reality that the oil represents. As discussed, oil represents the Holy Spirit, and the Spirit's role is to bear witness to truth. To lie about your offering is to lie to the Spirit himself—to falsify the very witness that makes offerings acceptable. They pretended to pour out everything (claiming the Spirit witnessed their total devotion) while secretly keeping back (the Spirit's witness was absent, making their claim false).

This explains why Peter specifically invokes the Holy Spirit rather than simply calling it a lie to the apostles. The sin is not merely interpersonal deception—it's an offense against the very principle of acceptable worship. The Spirit who gives life brings death when offerings are made in his name but without his presence, when sacrifice is claimed but the oil is withheld or falsified. They pretended to pour out everything while secretly withholding, claiming Abel's complete surrender while practicing Cain's self-securing hedging. They wanted the blessing oil brings (community honor, spiritual reputation) without offering the life oil requires (genuine surrender, total trust).

Peter's verdict reveals the sobering truth: you cannot fake the oil. The Holy Spirit knows what is truly offered. To lie to him about your offering—to claim you've poured out the oil when you've actually withheld it—is to commit Cain's sin in its most explicit form. The result is immediate judgment: death (Acts 5:5, 10). It is the same spiritual consequence Cain's offering produced, demonstrating that a feigned sacrifice—a terminal product offered in place of life-bearing seed, a false claim made to the Oil himself—is a fatal lie. Where Cain's rejection came through silent divine disfavor, Ananias and Sapphira's comes through immediate judgment, but the principle is identical: offerings that falsify the Spirit's presence receive death, not life.

This pattern illuminates why Jesus describes blasphemy against the Holy Spirit as uniquely unforgivable (Matt 12:31–32). The Pharisees attributed the Spirit's work to Satan—the ultimate falsification of the Oil—calling the very principle of life-giving consecration demonic. Like Cain offering grain without oil, or Ananias lying to the Oil himself, they rejected the Spirit's testimony while maintaining religious form. The unforgivable nature stems not from divine unwillingness but from human impossibility: if you reject the very principle that consecrates offerings (the Spirit/Oil), no offering can be acceptable. If you call the Oil demonic, you cannot be consecrated by it. The sin is unforgivable because the sinner has rejected the only means of forgiveness—the Spirit's testimony to Christ and his consecrating work in believers.

## THE PATTERN MADE EXPLICIT: JESUS, BONES, AND THE GRAIN OF WHEAT (JOHN 12:24–25)

Jesus makes this principle explicit: "Unless a grain of wheat falls into the ground and dies, it remains alone; but if it dies, it produces much grain" (John 12:24). We must realize, a grain of wheat is a seed. The seed secured above ground "remains alone"—produces nothing. The seed surrendered to death multiplies. The seed principle appears at Golgotha. When soldiers came to hasten death by breaking legs, "they did not break His legs . . . that the Scripture should be fulfilled, 'Not one of His bones shall be broken'" (John 19:33, 36). "Christ was born and dedicated to God as the firstborn and the first-fruits of the new creation."[3]

Christ's sacrifice succeeds because the Seed remains intact even through death. His bones—the structural, life-bearing core—preserved their integrity, ensuring resurrection and multiplication. Just as a seed must remain whole to germinate, the Messiah's unbroken bones signify the

3. Grēgorios, *Divine Liturgy*, 68.

integrity of the Seed who will rise to multiply. Christ is the Seed of the woman (Gen 3:15). God promised the Seed of the woman would crush the serpent's head. The irony is that the serpent attempts to crush the Seed with death, but the Seed remains intact while crushing the serpent.

The Passover context deepens this meaning. God's original command regarding the Passover lamb specified "nor shall you break one of its bones" (Exodus 12:46). The lamb whose blood saved Israel from death had to remain structurally whole. Why? Because the lamb pointed forward to Christ, the true Lamb of God. The blood provides covering (life poured out for others); the unbroken bones provide integrity (life preserved through death for resurrection). Both elements matter. A broken lamb would signify a corrupted sacrifice, a compromised offering, seed destroyed rather than surrendered.

## CONCLUSION

We face Cain's temptation, constantly offering God our resources after we've secured our futures, our devotion after we've secured our comforts. We wait until "the end of days"—until the process is complete, the decisions are made, the seed is stored—before approaching God with what remains. But even when we do offer, we often offer like Cain: processed products of our labor without the oil of Spirit dependence, achievements of our effort without the fat of surrender.

But God desires Abel's offering, not Cain's. He desires the life-source offered immediately, before we know if more will come. He desires first-fruits, not leftovers; living seed or oil-consecrated flour, not processed meal offered bare. He desires the seed that could produce our future crop, not the meal we've already ground for our own consumption. This is why Jesus calls us to "seek first the kingdom of God" (Matt 6:33)—not seek our own kingdom first and then offer God the surplus. This is the sin of the Holy Spirit that Peter called out in Acts. The sin is the false claim of complete offering, pretending to pour out everything (Abel's faith) while actually withholding (Cain's self-security). This is why Paul calls us to present our bodies as "living sacrifices" (Rom 12:1)—not dead products of our completed efforts. What is offered in faith, God multiplies; what falls into the ground in trust, he raises to life that outlasts us. From Cain to Abraham to Christ, Scripture reveals that God receives offerings only when life is surrendered in faith rather than secured in self-reliance.

# 16

# Trees and the Cross

## TREES, HERBS, AND GRASS

Genesis 1 establishes three botanical categories distinguished by their relationship to seed—the life-principle within plants: "Then God said, 'Let the earth bring forth grass, the herb that yields seed, and the fruit tree that yields fruit according to its kind, whose seed is in itself, on the earth'" (Gen 1:11). This threefold distinction is not incidental. Trees bear fruit "whose seed is in itself"—the life-principle contained within, elevated above the ground. Herbs yield seed but spread horizontally across the earth's surface. Grass (with no seed emphasized) sprouts, is consumed, and vanishes.

Scripture maintains these categories from Genesis to Revelation. The righteous are "like a tree planted by streams of water, which yields its fruit in season" (Ps 1:3), while the wicked are "like chaff which the wind drives away" (Ps 1:4). Isaiah declares that "all flesh is grass. . . . The grass withers, the flower fades, but the word of our God stands forever" (Is 40:6–8). Jesus teaches that the kingdom begins smaller than herbs but "when it is grown it is greater than the herbs and becomes a tree" (Matt 13:32). Revelation restores access to "the tree of life, which bore twelve fruits" for "the healing of the nations" (Rev 22:2).

This botanical hierarchy reflects a hierarchy of spiritual nourishment. Trees bridge heaven and earth—roots drawing from deep sources below, branches reaching toward heaven above. Their fruit hangs elevated, requiring effort to reach, and carries seed with capacity to generate new life. This vertical structure makes trees natural symbols of *mediation*: the very function Adam was created to perform and failed, and which Christ perfects.

What trees provide might be called "head food," nourishment that transforms identity rather than merely sustaining the body. Unlike herbs that address immediate physical needs, tree fruit carries life-bearing potential that reshapes the consumer from within. The seed requires digestion and integration; it changes not just what a person has but who a person is. The distinction matters because the Bible's central conflict is never over what people eat physically but over what they allow to form them spiritually. Head food engages the nous, the faculty of spiritual perception that is for cultivating wisdom, discernment, and orientation toward or away from God.

Herbs, by contrast, spread horizontally across the earth's surface. They are fruitful and necessary—useful for healing, practical sustenance, earthly knowledge—but they operate at ground level and produce their yield seasonally. At the lowest level, grass satisfies momentarily but leaves no lasting nourishment: "The life of mortals is like grass; they flourish like a flower of the field; the wind blows over it and it is gone, and its place remembers it no more" (Ps 103:15–16).

This framework illuminates the two trees at Eden's center. God "made all kinds of trees grow out of the ground—trees that were pleasing to the eye and good for food. In the middle of the garden were the tree of life and the tree of the knowledge of good and evil" (Gen 2:9). Both were trees—both offered head food capable of fundamental transformation. The question was never whether eating would change Adam and Eve, but *how* it would change them and through what channel the transformation would come.

## The Tree of Knowledge

The tree of knowledge of good and evil was not biologically poisonous. No toxin killed Adam and Eve; they lived centuries after eating. The tree killed through transformation, not chemistry; this was head food reshaping identity from within. The serpent understood this: "Your eyes will be opened, and you will be like God, knowing good and evil" (Gen 3:5). He promised not nutrition but fundamental reorientation through consumption. And the promise proved accurate—though not as Eve anticipated.

The immediate aftermath demonstrates the tree's head-food nature: "The eyes of both of them were opened, and they knew that they were naked; and they sewed fig leaves together and made themselves coverings" (Gen 3:7). The transformation was instant and real. They genuinely gained knowledge they hadn't previously possessed. But this new knowledge brought shame rather than wisdom, hiding rather than communion, death rather than life. Consider what actually changed. They had always been naked—their bodies were identical before and after eating. The tree didn't alter their flesh; it altered how their heads perceived their flesh. Shame occurs only in the head; it marks a disconnect between head and body, a fracture in integrated perception.

Before eating, their nous perceived their bodies rightly—as good, natural, part of God's creation. After eating, the head became alienated from the body it was meant to govern.

This head/body fracture is the signature of corrupted head food. It doesn't poison the flesh but darkens the nous, destroying the integrated perception that characterized Eden. The tragedy is that the tree offered genuine transformation through the wrong channel. God designed humanity to receive transformative wisdom through communion with him—knowledge through relationship, wisdom through obedience. The forbidden tree promised the same transformation through autonomous grasping. Both paths reshaped identity. Only one maintained proper ordering.

Adam and Eve's exile curses humanity to earthly knowledge we obtain through sweat since they lost access to elevated food (trees) and are reduced to ground-level sustenance: "You shall eat the herb of the field" (Gen 3:18). The fall moves humanity from transformative communion to mere survival—from head food that reshapes identity to body food that merely sustains existence.

In stark contrast, those who eat of the tree of life receive transformation that orients toward God rather than away from him. Jesus identifies himself with this tree: "Unless you eat the flesh of the Son of Man and drink His blood, you have no life in you" (John 6:53). This is head food that heals the nous rather than darkening it, restoring the integrated perception Adam lost and reuniting head and body, heaven and earth, in proper ordering.

## DANIEL IN BABYLON

Daniel, taken as a youth from Judah to Babylon, enters a world where headship is now represented by a foreign king. The way of life in exile is corrupting, and food and wine at the king's table ismeant to impress and assimilate. Every dish carries not just nourishment but a worldview and integration, a subtle invitation to internalize the empire's values. "But Daniel resolved that he would not defile himself with the king's food, or with the wine that he drank" (Dan 1:8). In terms of our tree/herb/grass framework, the king's delicacies function as Babylonian "head food"—they are not just calories but covenantal participation in the king's table and values. Daniel therefore chooses herb-level, non-assimilating food: nourishment that sustains the body without letting Babylon's "seed" enter his inner life.

Daniel's refusal is deliberately choosing herbs over trees—choosing temporary sustenance over transformative intake that would reshape his identity under a foreign head. He requests vegetables and water—simple, humble, "body" foods. This choice is radical. It reflects discernment, an understanding that what enters the body can shape the soul. Daniel then receives from God literature, wisdom and understanding in visions and dreams. Yet he refuses what would contaminate his spiritual integrity, the spirit of Babylon, being the wine and the food of the king, being internal and deep "Babylonic" wisdom containing the "seed" from its head, the king. After ten days, Daniel and his companions appear healthier and more vigorous than those who consumed the king's delicacies: "At the end of ten days they looked healthier and better nourished than any of the young men who ate the royal food" (Dan 1:15).

This demonstrates the principle of head food vs. body food: different types of food are different types of knowledge and nourishment that can transform the person. The simple vegetables Daniel chose, like herbs, could be impressive but lacked the internalizing, spirit-transforming quality of wine and meat. Daniel ensured God provided the wisdom of Babylon, not Babylon formation. Scripture not only distinguishes between trees and herbs; it also distinguishes between different kinds of trees. Some trees symbolize immediate crisis leadership, others long-term covenant rooting. The different trees represent different kinds of mediators. Understanding these patterns allows one to understand why certain leaders rise and merely perform their duty, while others are transformative and their enduring actions impact across generations.

## PALM TREES AND OAKS AS PATTERNS OF MEDIATION

Scripture does not use trees as random decoration. When someone appears under a specific tree, it often reflects something deeper about their role in God's story. The natural differences between palm trees and oaks mirror two different kinds of leaders and two different ways God restores order to his people. Palms highlight a single elevated mediator raised up in a moment of crisis. Oaks symbolize deep, generational roots that shape a whole people over time. A palm tree grows from one spot at its very top—its "crown." Everything depends on that one point for life to continue to flourish. Palms do not grow rings, do not thicken through the trunk, and do not renew strength from below. If the top is harmed, the tree cannot continue growing. A palm's entire life flows through one singular elevated point.

This biological reality makes the palm a natural symbol of a single leader raised up in crisis, someone God lifts above the disorder to bring clarity when everything else collapses. This is why Deborah judges Israel under a palm tree (Judg 4:5). Israel is spiritually scattered, leaderless, and confused. In that moment, Deborah becomes the lone point of clarity and righteousness. The people "come up to her," just as the life of a palm rises to its single crown. She is not building a dynasty or establishing a long-term institution; she is stabilizing Israel in a chaotic moment.

Palm imagery consistently points to this pattern:

- "The righteous flourish like the palm tree" (Ps 92:12): upright and visible
- Palm branches at Jesus' triumphal entry: the whole city turning toward one King
- Palms carved in the temple: one central house where all Israel gathers
- Jericho, "the city of palms": the head-fortress; cut off the head, and the land opens

In Scripture, palms represent singular headship, a single mediator God raises to restore order when the broader body fails. Judges is a book where the "Adam role" is repeatedly abandoned. Leaders are passive. Men refuse responsibility. Israel is directionless. When the Adam role collapses. God raises a renewer to restore clarity. Deborah steps into the Adam role precisely because the appointed leaders will not. She discerns God's will, speaks with authority and calls Barak forward, and directs the battle, which restores order. Deborah shows that when the structure fails, God appoints a figure—male or female—to serve as the necessary leader in a crisis. Her being placed under a palm reinforces this: she becomes the single elevated mediator God uses to realign Israel.

Another obvious palm tree figure is Samson, who lives in a time of turmoil where the Philistines and Israel are at constant war with one another. Samson is raised up as a solitary deliverer when Israel is oppressed and leaderless. Being a Nazirite, his uncut hair is his "crown" that gives him power. When his hair is cut, the whole structure collapses; once the crown is cut, his strength withers instantly. Samson does not build a lineage, establish institutions, or create generational stability. He rises in a moment of crisis, acts with singular force, and then falls. His story embodies the palm pattern perfectly: one elevated mediator whose impact comes in a single vertical surge rather than slow, generational rooting.

Oaks grow in the opposite way. Their trunks widen year after year, forming rings—layers of memory and history. Oaks renew strength from the bottom upward and through the whole tree. They endure for centuries. Oaks are symbols of rootedness, stability, covenant, and the formation of a people, not simply the acts of one person. This explains why Abraham meets God at oaks—Moreh, Mamre, Shechem. Abraham's role is not crisis oriented. It is generational. He becomes the root, the trunk, the father of a people through whom God will work for centuries. Abraham's life matches the character of the oak: deep, steady, slow, and enduring. Oaks represent corporate identity, enduring covenant, and long-term formation.

Other oak scenes reinforce this:

- Jacob buries his household's idols under an oak—an entire family changing direction (Gen 35:4).
- Joshua renews Israel's covenant under an oak—a national commitment meant to last (Josh 24:26).
- Isaiah calls God's restored people "oaks of righteousness"—a community shaped over time (Isa 61:3).

These two trees reveal two ways God works in Scripture:

Palm → renewer principle (singular figure entering crisis)

Oak → inheritor principle (deep roots, continuity, covenant stability)

Palm-type leaders (like Deborah):

- One elevated leader
- Crisis mediation
- Concentrated clarity
- A "crown-only" pattern of life
- A leader raised up when all else collapses

Oak-type leaders (like Abraham):

- Generational formation
- Corporate identity
- Stability spread among a people
- Strength built over time
- A leader who roots God's people in the land

Throughout Scripture, no single mediator holds both patterns simultaneously. Deborah delivers Israel from crisis but establishes no lasting house; her work ends when the threat passes. Abraham roots a people across generations but does not rise to judge Israel's immediate chaos. The pattern reveals a profound limitation: human mediators, constrained by mortality and finitude, can be raised up for crisis or planted for generations, but not both fully. This very limitation points forward, creating a space only the God-man can fill.

## Absalom Caught in the Oak: A Man Fighting the Structure Itself

The narrative emphasizes the precise manner of Absalom's downfall: "His head caught in the thick branches of a great oak, and he was left hanging between heaven and earth" (2 Sam 18:9). This is not presented as a random accident. At the very moment he attempts to seize the kingdom from his father, King David, Absalom collides with the very structure he is rebelling against. The oak—symbol of long-standing covenant order—becomes the means through which his illegitimate attempt at headship is exposed. He is not struck down by a soldier or cut down in combat; he is stopped by the branches of the tree itself, as if the order God planted will not allow him to climb past it.

Throughout the narrative, Absalom's hair functions as a symbol of his self-exaltation. Scripture underscores its weight, beauty, and public admiration; it is the emblem of his charisma and the false "crown" by which he seduced Israel. Absalom's uprising represents a corrupted form of the renewer figure—someone who attempts to seize the Adam role through manipulation rather than divine appointment. His "glory" becomes the instrument of his downfall. In biblical terms, the head that attempted to usurp the kingdom is caught and immobilized by a tree that represents enduring, covenant-rooted authority.

Absalom's entanglement shows that he is fighting against something larger than David—he is fighting against the structure of rightful authority. Scripture uses trees to reveal the stability and rootedness of God's design, and Absalom attempts to rise outside that structure. His hair, the symbol of his self-created glory, becomes the mechanism by which he is ensnared. The one who tried to elevate himself and overshadow the rightful king is caught by a branch because he attempted to climb where he did not belong. He is a shoot pushing against the trunk, trying to grow apart from the rooted order that God established. The oak resists him. It does not hold him up or support his ascent; it halts him because he is trying to rise through illegitimate means. In this sense, Absalom's death is not caused by nature but revealed by structure. He finds himself suspended precisely because the structure he opposed will not bear his weight.

## CHRIST—THE TREE OF LIFE

The curses upon fallen humanity and its restoration ultimately converge at the tree of the cross. Christ, the Second Adam and ultimate renewer, has become a curse for us (Gal 3:13). He is now the tree of life. He wears the "crown of thorns" (Matt 27:29)—the very yield of the cursed ground—upon his head, a crown that is similar to the top of a palm tree, which we have established highlights singular headship. In doing so, he elevates the lowest sign of the curse into the highest symbol of holiness. Through his perfect obedience on this new "tree," Christ restores our communion with God and grants access to the true and eternal, like an oak tree bringing blessings across generations.

Next, in his resurrection and the sending of the Spirit, he becomes the oak-like root of a new people, the vine from which all branches draw life across every generation. No previous mediator could hold both patterns: Deborah was raised for crisis but established no dynasty; Abraham rooted a people but did not adjudicate Israel's chaos. Christ alone is both the palm and the oak, because he alone is the God-man who can be simultaneously the singular mediator in crisis and the eternal root of a corporate people. Christ is not raised for one crisis, only to then pass away; he is the eternal vine into which every generation is grafted. The palm-crisis opens into oak-rootedness. The singular mediator becomes the corporate source. This is the mystery that human limitation could not achieve: one person holding both patterns fully. The church, the new Eve, is now called to be a branch of the true Vine, as Christ said: "I am the vine; you are the branches" (John 15:5).

Authority principle:

- John 15:1: "I am the true vine, and My Father is the vinedresser."
- John 15:5: "I am the vine, you are the branches" shows proper authority structure: Father (vinedresser) → Son (vine) → us (branches).

Cooperation principle:

- John 15:4: "Abide in Me, and I in you"—human action abiding/participating with Christ (abiding/tilling).
- John 15:5: "Without Me you can do nothing"—divine provision essential (rain).
- John 15:5: "He who abides in Me . . . bears much fruit"—yield from cooperation.

Orientation principle:

- John 15:16: "You did not choose Me, but I chose you"—grace (renewer), not merit (inheritor).

We don't achieve fruitfulness; we receive it through abiding. This is Jesus' explicit teaching on all three principles simultaneously—the tree of life offered to disciples. This fulfills another parallel: just as the first Eve was taken from the side of the sleeping Adam, the church fathers taught that the new Eve—the church—was born from the water and blood that flowed from the pierced side of the Second Adam in the sleep of his death on the cross (John 19:34). The fulfillment of Scripture's heavenly nourishment arrives in Christ, who declares in John 6:51: "I am the living bread that came down from heaven. Whoever eats this bread will live forever. This bread is my flesh, which I will give for the life of the world." Here, the text makes clear that life is in his flesh. Just as manna sustained the Israelites, Christ offers a sustenance that is eternal and transformative, but unlike manna, it is not provisional; it is the very life of God, which is everlasting.

## THE DISCIPLES AS BRANCHES: THOSE WHO ALIGN WITH THE STRUCTURE

If Absalom is the man who opposes the structure and is stopped by it, the disciples are the men who align with the structure and therefore live from it. Jesus' teaching, "I am the vine; you are the branches" (John 15:5), makes this contrast unmistakable. A branch does not fight the tree. A branch does not compete with the trunk or attempt to take the headship for itself. A branch receives its life, direction, and fruitfulness from the structure it abides in. This is exactly what the disciples do. They do not grasp for authority or attempt to elevate themselves over Christ; they remain connected to him, drawing life from the order he has established.

This is why the vine-and-branches imagery works with such clarity: a branch flourishes only when it abides, when it remains oriented toward the source rather than attempting to become the source. Christ explicitly links bread and wine to his life and blood: "Then He took bread, gave thanks and broke it, and gave it to them, saying, 'This is my body given for you; do this in remembrance of me.' Likewise, the cup after supper, saying, 'This cup that is poured out for you is the new covenant in my blood'" (Luke 22:19–20). In the Orthodox tradition, the bread and wine are the real presence of Christ. Jesus reinforced this by stating, "Most assuredly, I say to you, unless you eat the flesh of the Son of Man and drink His blood, you have no life in you" (John 6:53). Since "the life of the flesh is in the blood" (Lev 17:11), to drink Christ's blood is to partake of his very life. St. Ignatius of Antioch emphasizes this, warning against those who deny it: "They abstain from the Eucharist and from prayer because they refuse to acknowledge that the Eucharist is the flesh of our Savior Jesus Christ."[1] Here, the pattern of integration is clear: the faithful partake of Christ himself. The Eucharist is the head food, transforming and nourishing both body and soul.

1. Holmes, *Apostolic Fathers in English*, 123.

## THE EUCHARIST: WHERE ALL THREE PRINCIPLES MEET

- Authority is exercised in consuming the Eucharist, as Christ as Head feeds his body. "This is my body"—his authoritative word creates reality. Hierarchical structure is maintained (priest consecrates, people receive). Proper ordering: heaven → earth, God → man, spirit → matter.
- Cooperation is enacted. Human preparation (fasting, confession, liturgical participation) = tilling. Divine response (presence, Holy Spirit) = rain. Union with Christ (Communion) = yield.
- Our orientation is corrected because we receive life as pure gift. No merit earns this, only grace provides. We acknowledge, "Lord, I am not worthy": since we know, "For not as common bread nor common drink do we receive these; but since Jesus Christ our Savior was made incarnate by the Word of God, and had both flesh and blood for our salvation."[2]

The Emmaus road shows what the Eucharist accomplishes. Two disciples leave Jerusalem in grief. A stranger joins them and opens the Scriptures, yet they do not recognize him. At the table, he takes, gives thanks, and breaks the bread and everything changes: "their eyes were opened and they recognized him" (Luke 24:31). The phrase is not accidental. In Eden, Adam and Eve eat which opens their eyes to shame—the nous darkened, perception fractured, the body estranged from the head meant to govern it. At Emmaus, eating opens the eyes to recognition—the nous restored, perception healed, communion overcoming separation.

The church today acknowledges the oak and palm mediation patterns of Jesus. We honor Christ's singular, unrepeatable sacrifice that accomplished salvation "once for all" (Heb 10:10). Yet we abide in the Vine (John 15:4), receiving nourishment that transforms. We are called to be "oaks of righteousness, the planting of the Lord" (Isa 61:3)—rooted in him, spreading his healing to the nations, bearing fruit that endures. Where eventually "a great multitude which no one could number, of all nations, tribes, peoples and tongues, standing before the throne and before the Lamb, clothed in white robes, with palm branches in their hands" (Rev 7:9) is praising Jesus as Lord.

2. Justin Martyr, "First Apology," 55.

17

# Complaint Versus Lament

HAVING SEEN HOW GRUMBLING corrupts authority at personal, marital, and corporate scales (chapter 2), this chapter demonstrates lament as the proper alternative—vertical speech to God that maintains communion even in distress. We'll trace lament across the same scales where grumbling failed, showing how proper orientation of speech preserves rather than destroys divine order.

As Adam named the animals in Gen 2, this brought order to the world, acting similarly to how God spoke creation and order into the cosmos in Gen 1. Naming is a form of discernment and separating between those who can build up the kingdom and those who wouldn't. We now have a creature (serpent) using speech in a counterproductive way. The first complaint does not appear in the wilderness but in Eden. The serpent's dialogue with Eve (Gen 3:1–5) establishes the template of destructive complaint: the questioning undermines the ordering God and Adam performed, creating a conflict over God's authority structure of God to Adam and Eve to animals. The question the serpent asked could be interpreted as an inquiry into God's "fasting requirements," as only one tree was forbidden. The serpent then explicitly lies to Eve: "You shall not surely die. For God knows that in the day you eat of it, your eyes will be opened, and you will be like God, knowing good and evil" (Gen 3:4–5). This lie is a corruption since to believe this goes against the order God created.

Next, Eve perceived the tree as "good for food, that it was pleasant to the eyes, and a tree desirable to make one wise" (Gen 3:6). Her reliance on her own faculties of vision, often linked to understanding, reveals a lack of spiritual discernment and suggests that what appears good to us may still be fatal, underscoring our inability to fully grasp God's perspective on true good and evil. For Eve, obedience should have trumped her own reasoning and the complaints the serpent brought before her. Instead, she allowed the fruit's allure to distract her from God's clear instruction. We see the serpent performs a counterproductive speech, something that doesn't build up God's kingdom. This Edenic complaint is not random—it becomes the archetype of grumbling throughout Scripture.

## COMPLAINT SUMMONS SERPENTS: FROM EDEN TO THE DESERT

The serpent in Eden spoke the first complaint. This complaint speech pattern—questioning divine truthfulness and authority, denying divine consequences, undermining and lying about God's motives, and grumbling about one's place as subordinate rather than ruler—establishes a template we can see in other stories. In Num 21, exhausted in the wilderness, Israel adopted this same pattern, and they complained: "Why have you brought us up out of Egypt to die? There is no food and no water, and our soul loathes this worthless bread" (Num 21:5). Notice the serpent-speech structure: questioning God's guidance ("Why have you brought us?"), denying God's provision (when he literally provided manna daily), and despising God's gift (calling heaven's bread "worthless").

God's response exposes the spiritual reality behind their words: "So the Lord sent fiery serpents among the people, and they bit the people; and many of the people of Israel died" (Num 21:6). The biting the serpents did here could be seen as injecting poison into the people bitten, which led them to die in the wilderness, probably believing they should turn back to go to Egypt. This is parallel to Eve integrating (eating) the lies (poison) of the serpent about eating the fruit, which led to her dying (eventually) in exile (wilderness).

The physical serpents made visible what had already occurred spiritually: serpent speech produces serpent character. When you speak like the serpent, you align yourself with the serpent's character, and God reveals this alignment through serpent consequences that bring death. The remedy

God provides carries profound typological significance. Next, "Therefore the people came to Moses, and said, 'We have sinned, for we have spoken against the Lord and against you; pray to the Lord that He take away the serpents from us.' So Moses prayed for the people" (Num 21: 7). The people, instead of complaining, decided to ask humbly within their hierarchy for healing. They oriented themselves and their pain upwards, where healing can occur. They lamented. God then instructs Moses, "Make a fiery serpent, and set it on a pole; and it shall be that everyone who is bitten, when he looks at it, shall live" (Num 21:8). The bronze serpent wasn't merely a cure but a confrontation: those who complained like serpents had to look directly at a serpent lifted high.

Healing required acknowledging what their speech had made them become; they needed to reorient themselves, asking Moses for intercession and allowing healing to occur outside of their understanding. This is precisely the pattern and ultimate irony Christ fulfills. When Jesus declares, "As Moses lifted up the serpent in the wilderness, even so must the Son of Man be lifted up, that whoever believes in Him should not perish but have eternal life" (John 3:14–15), he identifies himself with that bronze serpent. But the connection runs deeper than mere typological parallel.

Paul explains the shocking reality: Christ "became sin for us, who knew no sin" (2 Cor 5:21). After all the grumbling done against God—in Eden, in the desert—that God did respond to the grumbling of humanity by sending his only Son. Jesus, the one who never complained, never questioned God's goodness, never spoke accusatory words, takes upon himself the full weight of humanity's serpent character formed through a whole history of complaints. But Jesus, who knew no sin, doesn't just bear our sins—he becomes the serpent itself. The healing comes through looking to him lifted up—not at our own righteousness or religious performance, but at the one who became serpent-cursed for us. Just as Israel had to look at the bronze serpent (the very image of what was killing them) to live, we must look at Christ crucified (bearing the full weight of our complaint-formed serpent character) to find life.

## APPLICATION—LAMENT IS SPEAKING TO GOD

Have you complained to God and thought he wasn't listening? By contrast with complaint/grumbling, which we have identified in the Bible as complaint about God, lament represents complaint and distress reoriented toward God. It is vertical, relational, and covenantal. Lament names suffering honestly but addresses it to God, preserving the dialogue rather than breaking it. Psalms are the primary biblical corpus demonstrating this:

Psalm 13:1: "How long, O Lord? Will you forget me forever?" Here, the psalmist expresses frustration and sorrow while still invoking God's presence and trust.

Psalm 142:1–2: "I cry out to the Lord with my voice; With my voice to the Lord I make my supplication. I pour out my complaint before Him; I declare before Him my trouble."

Jeremiah 12:1: "Righteous are you, O Lord, when I complain to you." The prophet openly challenges God, yet in a framework of recognition of divine justice.

Even Jesus models lament. In Gethsemane (Matt 26:39), he expresses desire for relief but submits fully to the Father: "Not as I will, but as you will." On the cross, he quotes Ps 22:1: "My God, my God, why have you forsaken me?" (Matt 27:46)—a cry of anguish that simultaneously preserves covenantal trust and anticipates redemption.

## Key Structural Difference

Both complaint and lament express pain, fear, or dissatisfaction, but the direction and form of the speech determine its effect. Importantly, lament transforms grief into trust and deepens communion with God.

### *Grumbling/Complaint = Rebellion Against Divine Order*

- Direction: attacks God's character, timing, or authority
- Purpose: seeks to change God's mind or reject his plan entirely
- Form: chaotic, destructive speech that tears down cosmic harmony
- Audience: often expressed to others about God rather than to God directly
- Timing: seasonally inappropriate—demanding spring harvest in winter preparation periods
- Character: questions divine goodness and wisdom rather than seeking understanding

*Lament = Appeal Within Divine Order*

- Direction: cries to God while acknowledging his ultimate authority
- Purpose: seeks divine comfort and understanding within existing covenant relationship
- Form: structured prayer that maintains cosmic harmony even in distress
- Audience: addressed directly to God in proper sacred context
- Timing: seasonally appropriate—accepts divine timing while expressing need
- Character: maintains trust in God's goodness while honestly expressing confusion or pain

| Complaint | Lament |
|---|---|
| Blames God | Cries to God |
| Alienates | Draws near |
| Distorts truth | Speaks truth (however painful) |
| Echoes serpent's voice | Echoes faith's trust |

## The Canaanite Woman: Transforming Apparent Rejection

The encounter in Matt 15:21–28 provides Scripture's most striking example of proper response to seemingly harsh divine treatment. When Jesus appears to call the woman a "dog," she faces a moment that could easily provoke grumbling. The Canaanite woman could have responded with a complaint. She could have taken offense at the name given by the authority above. She could have questioned the character of God and his mediator, broadcast her grievance to others, or demanded justification for the treatment she received.

But instead, her response was a proper lament:

- "Yes, Lord"—Accepts the designation without offense, maintains proper relationship and authority. Maintains worship posture throughout interaction.
- "Yet even the dogs eat the crumbs"—Works creatively within the limitation. Demonstrates faith rather than demanding action.

Jesus' validation: "O woman, great is your faith! Be it done for you as you desire." Her daughter receives immediate healing. The same apparent rejection produces opposite outcomes based purely on response orientation.

## LAMENTING ACROSS SCALES OF REALITY

### Person Scale of Reality

Job: After losing everything—children, wealth, health—Job's response demonstrates proper individual lament: "Then Job arose, tore his robe, and shaved his head; and he fell to the ground and worshiped. And he said: 'Naked I came from my mother's womb, and naked shall I return there. The Lord gave, and the Lord has taken away; blessed be the name of the Lord'" (Job 1:20–21; 3:1–3).

Later, Job expresses deep anguish: "May the day perish on which I was born, and the night in which it was said, 'A male child is conceived.' May that day be darkness; may God above not seek it, nor the light shine upon it." Job's lament is raw, honest, even shocking in its intensity—yet it remains directed toward God. He doesn't blame his wife (though she suggests cursing God), doesn't curse his circumstances to others, and doesn't seek human solutions. His complaint flows upward in prayer, not outward in rebellion. This maintains the vertical channel of communion even in extreme suffering. The book's lengthy dialogues show Job wrestling with God, not abandoning him. Lament brings us into the presence of God; grumbling drives us from it.

### Marital/Couple Scale of Reality

Hannah: Her barrenness creates similar anguish, but her response demonstrates proper marital-scale lament: "And she was in bitterness of soul, and prayed to the Lord and wept in anguish. Then she made a vow and said, 'O Lord of hosts, if You will indeed look on the affliction of Your maidservant and remember me, and not forget Your maidservant, but will give Your maidservant a male child, then I will give him to the Lord all the days of his life'" (1 Sam 1:10–11).

When accused of drunkenness by Eli, she explains: "No, my lord, I am a woman of sorrowful spirit. I have drunk neither wine nor intoxicating drink, but have poured out my soul before the Lord. Do not consider your maidservant a wicked woman, for out of the abundance of my complaint and grief I have spoken until now" (1 Sam 1:15–16). The contrast with Rachel is profound. Both women experience the same suffering—barrenness in a culture where it meant social shame and threatened their place in redemptive history. But Rachel demands from Jacob ("Give me children, or else I die!"), treating her husband as if he held God's power. Hannah "poured out her soul before the Lord," directing her complaint vertically. Notice the language: "abundance of my complaint and grief." Lament isn't emotionless acceptance—it's bringing the full weight of suffering *to God* rather than demanding human solutions. Hannah's story also shows that proper lament produces proper fruit: Samuel becomes one of Israel's greatest prophets, given back to God in thanksgiving. Rachel's grumbling produces Bilhah's sons through human scheming, creating family strife that echoes through generations.

## National Scale of Reality

Israel in Egypt: Before the grumbling in the wilderness, Israel demonstrated proper corporate lament in Egyptian slavery: "Now it happened in the process of time that the king of Egypt died. Then the children of Israel groaned because of the bondage, and they cried out; and their cry came up to God because of the bondage. So God heard their groaning, and God remembered His covenant with Abraham, with Isaac, and with Jacob. And God looked upon the children of Israel, and God acknowledged them" (Exod 2:23–25). The text emphasizes the vertical direction of Israel's cry: "Their cry came up to God." They didn't plot rebellion against Pharaoh, didn't organize political resistance, didn't complain to each other that God had abandoned them. They cried to God about their suffering. The result? "God heard . . . God remembered . . . God looked . . . God acknowledged." Four verbs of divine response, triggered by proper lament. This demonstrates the principle: lament opens the channel for divine intervention; grumbling closes it.

The contrast with their later wilderness grumbling is sharp. In Egypt, they cry to God about genuine oppression—and he delivers them. In the wilderness, they complain about God to each other regarding perceived threats—and judgment follows. Same people, same God, different direction of speech, opposite outcomes. This establishes that God's character doesn't change; our orientation toward him determines whether we experience mercy or judgment.

## LAMENT, NOT DESTRUCTIVE COMPLAINT

The Parable of the Persistent Widow is another example of lament, not destructive complaint. The crucial distinction lies in the speech's direction and form: while grumbling severs a relationship by questioning authority indirectly, as Israel did in the wilderness (Num 21:5), lament confronts authority directly to demand justice, as the psalmist does: "How long, O Lord?" (Ps 13:1).

The widow's method is a perfect example of faithful lament. She goes repeatedly *to* the "unjust judge" (Luke 18:2), demanding, "Grant me justice against my adversary" (Luke 18:3). Her cry is vertical and direct; she acknowledges the judge's authority by appealing to his office, even while challenging his personal inaction. This tenacious engagement stands in stark contrast to serpent-like complaint, which undermines authority and breaks communion. Jesus uses her success to frame his central point: if persistent lament can move a corrupt judge, how much more will the righteous Father respond to the cries of his elect (Luke 18:7)? The widow, therefore, models not annoyance but tenacious faith expressed through proper lament. Her story teaches that bringing our needs directly and persistently before God is a powerful, divinely encouraged form of prayer that moves the heavens.

## CONCLUSION

Throughout the Bible, the theme of temptation highlights the struggle between obedience to God and the allure of earthly desires or self-reliance. God's chosen people, including his mediators (priests), are called to maintain unwavering faith. Yet, many are tempted to stray—some by the promise of worldly pleasures, others by the misguided belief that their own efforts can replace divine intervention during difficult times. Temptation often serves as a test, a hurdle to overcome in order to preserve one's communion with God. This Genesis template of complaint versus lament provides the lens through which we must evaluate subsequent biblical narratives, particularly when apparent followers question divine authority.

# 18

# Applying the Framework

## THE LORD'S PRAYER

HAVING SEEN HOW GEN 3 fractured the three modes of communion we can now recognize something remarkable. Prayer is a form of communion with God. St. John Chrysostom says, "There is nothing more worthwhile than to pray to God and converse with Him, for prayer unites us with God as His companions."[1] Specifically, Jesus structured the Lord's Prayer as the precise restoration of the three Genesis curses. They are mirror images—the fall's curse and Christ's cure in perfect structural opposition.

### Restoring Authority (Gen 3:16–17)

The curses reveal authority inverted: "Your desire shall be for your husband, and he shall rule over you" (Gen 3:16). Eve's desire creates tension in the authority structure, introducing conflict where partnership should exist. God explicitly rebukes Adam: "Because you have heeded the voice of your wife, and have eaten from the tree of which I commanded you" (Gen 3:17). The mediator listened to the wrong voice. The head followed the body rather than maintaining order and obedience to God. Authority

1. Constas, *Light of the World*, ix.

was inverted; this is why the first line of the Lord's Prayer does not ask for provision or forgiveness. It reasserts the proper order of being.

Jesus teaches us to reverse this precisely:

> Our Father in heaven,
> Hallowed be Your name.
> Your kingdom come.
> Your will be done
> On earth as it is in heaven. (Matt 6:9–10)

The prayer begins exactly where restoration must begin—with proper authority reestablished. We acknowledge God as Father (headship restored), we hallow his name (reverence for divine authority), and we submit to his kingdom and will (hierarchy corrected).

The phrase "on earth as it is in heaven" directly addresses the authority inversion. Heaven is the realm where God's authority functions perfectly. Earth is where it was rejected. We ask that earth's broken authority structure be restored to match heaven's perfect ordering—divine wisdom flowing from above to below, from head to body, exactly as Adam was meant to mediate but failed. This isn't just acknowledging God exists. It's liturgically reversing the authority inversion of Gen 3. Every time we pray these opening words, we're verbally reestablishing what the fall broke: God as supreme authority, our willing submission, proper hierarchical ordering restored.

## Restoring Cooperation (Gen 3:17–19)

The ground curse shattered divine-human partnership: "Cursed is the ground for your sake; in toil you shall eat of it all the days of your life. Both thorns and thistles it shall bring forth for you. . . . In the sweat of your face you shall eat bread" (Gen 3:17–19). What once flowed naturally—human preparation meeting divine provision to produce abundant fruit—now requires agonizing struggle. The harmony between tilling and rain was destroyed. Work became burden. Provision became uncertain. Cooperation fractured into isolated human effort against resistant creation.

Jesus restores these modes with stunning simplicity: "Give us this day our daily bread" (Matt 6:11). This single petition redeems the cooperation curse. The wording assumes human participation. Bread still requires sowing, kneading, baking—human labor meeting divine provision. The petition restores the Gen 2 dynamic where God provides rain and humanity cultivates the earth in faithful response. "Give us" acknowledges that provision ultimately comes from God, not from our sweat alone. "This day" emphasizes present dependence rather than anxious accumulation. "Our daily bread" points to what we actually need, not what we can hoard. But notice the brilliance: the petition doesn't ask God to provide while we remain passive. It assumes cooperation. We are working, we are tilling, we are faithfully preparing. The prayer doesn't say "give us bread while we sleep"—it says "give us our daily bread" with the implicit understanding that we're doing our part. We're asking divine provision to meet our faithful effort. We're requesting rain to bless our tilling so yield can result. By asking for "daily" bread, Jesus also dissolves the anxiety born from the curse's uncertainty. What once required anxious toil is now received with steady trust. This is the restoration of partnership.

## Restoring Orientation (Gen 3:14–15, 19)

The curses corrupted orientation toward death, earthly fixation, and inherited accusation. The serpent was lowered: "On your belly you shall go, and dust you shall eat" (Gen 3:14)—earthbound, unable to lift head toward heaven. The seed enmity established generational warfare: "I will put enmity between your seed and her seed" (Gen 3:15)—each generation inheriting conflict, past determining present. Adam's identity was reduced to dust: "For dust you are, and to dust you shall return" (Gen 3:19)—orientation toward death and material decay rather than eternal communion.

These curses reoriented humanity earthward, toward dust and toil. Jesus reorients us heavenward through the prayer's final petitions:

> And forgive us our debts,
> As we forgive our debtors. (Matt 6:12)

This breaks the accusation cycle Gen 3 established. When Adam and Eve sinned, blame immediately cascaded—Adam blamed Eve, Eve blamed the serpent. The pattern of accusation became humanity's inheritance. Jesus teaches us the opposite: extending forgiveness, receiving grace. We don't claim merit (inheritor posture) but acknowledge need for mercy (renewer posture). And critically, we do this corporately—"forgive us" not "forgive me"—reversing the isolation Gen 3 created.

> And do not lead us into temptation,
> But deliver us from the evil one. (Matt 6:13)

These final words complete the orientation reversal. Rather than claiming self-sufficiency ("you will be like God, knowing good and evil"), we admit vulnerability and dependence. Rather than trusting accumulated advantage (inheritor mindset), we appeal for divine guidance and deliverance (renewer posture). Rather than facing the evil one (the serpent and his seed) in our own strength, we ask protection. This is the opposite of Gen 3's orientation—not dust returning to dust in futile self-reliance, but dependent creatures looking upward for daily guidance and deliverance from the ancient enemy whose enmity began at the fall.

## The Pattern of Restored Communion

What makes the Lord's Prayer so significant for understanding biblical patterns is this: Jesus doesn't teach us to pray randomly. He teaches us to pray in a way that restores what Gen 3 fractured. This is why liturgy matters; we're enacting restored communion verbally. The prayer isn't just making requests; it's rehearsing the pattern of restored communion, addressing each mode of communion. "Prayer is the light and life of the soul. It is an everlasting bond uniting us to God. Whoever does not pray or has no desire to enjoy communion with God, is already lifeless and dead."[2]

We begin with God, reestablishing proper authority, because that relationship must be right before anything else can be restored. We address our material needs through renewed cooperation between divine provision and human faithfulness. We extend to our relationships with others through grace rather than accusation. And we acknowledge our ongoing need for guidance and protection, maintaining proper dependence.

This structural alignment cannot be accidental. Jesus, as the Second Adam who succeeded where the first Adam failed, knows exactly what broke and exactly how to restore it. The prayer he teaches is the verbal pattern of that restoration. When we pray the Lord's Prayer, understanding its structure, we're not just reciting familiar words—we're participating in the reversal of the Gen 3 curses. We're rehearsing the pattern of restored communion, training ourselves to approach God rightly (authority), to receive provision through partnership (cooperation), and to depend on his grace and guidance (orientation).

Every time we pray it, we're rejecting the fall's pattern and embracing the restoration Christ offers. We're reversing the curse verbally, preparing

2. Constas, *Light of the World*, x.

our hearts for the kingdom where communion with God functions perfectly across all three modes—authority properly ordered, cooperation joyfully renewed, orientation fixed on heaven rather than dust. The most prayed prayer in Christian history is the most prayed because it is structurally complete—it addresses comprehensively what Gen 3 broke, point by point, mode by modes, curse by curse. Two thousand years of Christian liturgy have preserved what theology is only now articulating: Jesus gave us the verbal pattern of redemption itself.

## THE QUESTION

As stated in the introduction, an answer is only as significant as the question it addresses. How does communion with God—fractured at every level simultaneously in Gen 3—get restored? That is the question every biblical story is asking in its own way, at its own scale. The framework exists to show that every story's conflict is a local expression of that question, and Christ and ministry is its complete answer. While Christians know Christ is the answer, his true significance is often discounted. We can read a Bible story, see how Jesus resolves a specific conflict, and correctly identify him as the "answer" for that story, yet still not understand the underlying question being addressed. What is the deeper reality this scene is confronting? Stories rarely state their structural problem explicitly; without a diagnostic framework, readers often perceive the symptoms but miss the underlying fracture. Many times, we sense that something more is being communicated beneath the surface. We might even know Jesus resolves the conflict, but without understanding the conflict's nature, we don't grasp the full weight of what he's answering. The foundational principles from Genesis help illuminate these deeper realities.

Every story's central conflict can be traced to one of three Genesis principles: a conflict of *authority*, a conflict of *cooperation*, or a conflict of *orientation*. These principles function as a lens, allowing us to identify the specific, underlying source of the story's dramatic tension—whether proper authority, cooperation, or orientation are happening or being inverted. The three principles provide the very "rules of the game" for the biblical world, establishing its internal coherence and logic, generating its dramatic tension. The Bible is not a random collection of stories, but a unified narrative operating with a consistent logic of how characters in the story respond to a conflict in their communion with God along these three modes. This allows these stories to feel coherent, seeing how their outcomes logically follow from their premises.

The Genesis Conflict Framework provides consistent criteria showing the Bible's internal coherence. This framework provides:

- Recognition (What pattern is this?)
- Explanation (Why does this happen?)
- Anticipation (What consequence follows?)
- Application (What does this teach me?)

In the quest to understand the Bible as a single, coherent story, readers have long employed interpretive lenses to perceive its "greater unity." Typology reads the Old Testament as a book of shadows pointing forward to Christ. Complementing this, the Genesis Conflict Framework examines the internal coherence and dramatic tension of each story on its own terms. While typology provides the architectural blueprint of salvation history, the Genesis Conflict Framework offers a lens to interpret the narratives themselves. Used together, they provide a richer, more holistic understanding of Scripture.

This framework and hermeneutical method sees the Bible's foundational grammar in Gen 1–4 as a discerning lens, meaning there is a conflict that needs to be uncovered. These three principles work together to provide a comprehensive falsifiable reading of most stories while being exegetically faithful to the Bible, deriving this lens from Genesis. Since, God highlights the threefold rupture of authority, cooperation, and orientation that occurred in Gen 3.

The framework operates through textual markers—specific words and phrases biblical authors use to signal which principles are in play. These lenses highlight the internal coherence of the dynamics of authority, cooperation, and orientation that were ruptured in Gen 3. This combined method equips the reader to see the greater unity not just between stories, but within them, revealing how God's redemptive work is always a complete and comprehensive restoration of all that was lost. Primarily diagnostic, this lens asks not "How does this point to Christ?" but "What is the core conflict, and which foundational relationship is being tested or broken?"

## HOW TO REMEMBER THE FRAMEWORK

Three questions for any biblical story:

1. Authority: Whose voice is being followed? (Authority: head → body operating correctly?) Authority markers to be aware of: "saw" (trusting sight over command); "heeded the voice" / "listened to"; "let us make" / "make a name"; "feared the people"; "no king in Israel"; silence of the one who should speak.
2. Cooperation: Is human action partnering with divine power? (Cooperation: tilling + rain = yield?) Cooperation markers to be aware of: garden imagery; rain/water from above; tilling/labor/sweat; fruit/yield/harvest; "under the sun"; thorns and thistles; seed/oil/firstfruits.
3. Orientation: Is an inheritor claiming or renewer receiving? Is this about earning or receiving? Orientation markers to be aware of: "you will be like God"; "right in his own eyes"; elder/younger dynamics; dust/death language; "we have Abraham as father"; wilderness/periphery movement.

## TEST CASE: THE GOOD SAMARITAN

Applying the framework to another story that is not analyzed in the book: The parable of the good Samaritan (Luke 10:25–37). This parable serves as a test case because Jesus tells it to an "expert in the law"—an "inheritor"—who is testing him about authority and righteousness.

1. The Adam and Eve principle (authority/structure)

   This principle highlights the conflict of "Whose voice is being followed?" The priest and the Levite are the established "Adam figures" in this story—the official mediators of God's covenant and law. The priest and the Levite invert the divine hierarchy. They are the leaders responsible for "tending and keeping" the covenant community. However, when confronted with the broken man, they "pass by on the other side" (Luke 10:31, 32).

   The "voice": Instead of heeding God's higher command for mercy, they are likely heeding a "corrupted" voice of earthly wisdom—their own voice of self-preservation (fear of robbers) or the voice of ceremonial law (fear of defilement from a corpse). By failing in their mediatorial role, they demonstrate a breakdown of the authority structure they represent.

2. The tilling/rain/yield principle (cooperation/process)

   The priest and Levite refuse to "till." They perform no human action, so no "yield" of mercy is produced. The Samaritan's cooperation: The Samaritan embodies the principle perfectly. Tilling (human action): He sees the man, feels compassion, goes to him, bandages his wounds, and takes him to an inn.

   Rain: He provides the "rain" himself, pouring on oil and wine—the very elements of his own provision and healing.

   Yield (spiritual result): The "yield" is life. The man, who was "left for dead" is preserved and restored. The Samaritan's faithful cooperation with the spirit of the law produces life, while the priest's adherence to the letter produces nothing.

3. The inheritor-versus-renewer principle (orientation/grace)

   This highlights the conflict between the entitled "inheritor" (who relies on status and merit) and the humble "renewer" (who is chosen by grace and often an outcast). This is the core conflict of the parable. The inheritors: The priest and the Levite are the ultimate "inheritors." They possess the religious pedigree, the theological knowledge, and the "religious position." They are the "older brothers" who trust in their "inherited status." The renewer: The Samaritan is the ultimate "renewer" or "outcast." To Jesus' audience, Samaritans were heretics, half-breeds, possessing zero religious inheritance.

   The inversion: Jesus masterfully inverts the entire system. The "inheritors," who should be the model of righteousness, demonstrate their hearts are oriented toward merit and status. The "renewer" (the outcast) is the only one who acts with true, grace-based compassion. Jesus forces the lawyer (the inheritor) to admit that the outcast was the one who fulfilled the law.

## EXPANDING THE LENS

Based on all the material we have reviewed that is either explicitly or implicitly linked to Genesis, one can add those insights to understand more of the message communicated in any passage in the Bible. Since many stories contain details that readers gloss over due to not knowing their significance, one must try to understand any story or passage from a maximalist reading, taking into account all particularities, which allows one to comprehend more meaning from the story. We can now have a lens that adds even more detail. These are five questions to ask when reading a passage. These questions form a diagnostic lens that reveals structural meaning beneath narrative surface.

1. Which principle/conflict is operating?

   Authority conflict? (Adam/Eve)

   Cooperation conflict? (Tilling/rain/yield)

   Orientation conflict? (Inheritor/renewer)

2. What symbols appear?

   Trees/herb/grass? (What type of tree—oak, palm, etc.? What characteristics are being emphasized?)

   Seeds/oil? (Inheritance or grace? Faith or life-principle acknowledged?)

   Body parts? (Head/hands/feet imagery?)

3. What scale is this?

   Individual, marital, corporate, national, cosmic?

4. How does Christ address it?

   As king? (Authority)

   As priest? (Cooperation)

   As prophet? (Orientation)

5. What is being complained about vs. lamented?

   Complaint = demands God change circumstances (murmuring, grumbling)

   Lament = grieves within God's sovereignty (Psalms, prophetic grief)

   Complaint inverts authority (people → leader → God)

   Lament maintains authority (person → God directly)

## Test Case: Luke 15:11–32 (Prodigal Son)

Let's apply all five questions to this parable.

1. Which principles/conflicts are operating?

   The parable's primary conflict is orientation—inheritor versus renewer—though authority and cooperation are also present. The younger son begins as a false kind of "renewer," resisting the structure of inheritance by demanding what is not yet his: "Father, give me the portion of goods that falls to me" (Luke 15:12). He rejects the authority of his father, choosing autonomy over communion. His departure enacts Adam's leaving the garden—seeking life outside the Father's presence—and his attempt at self-determination collapses quickly. When "there arose a severe famine in that land" (Luke 15:14), his self-made renewal reveals itself as mere rebellion.

   The older son embodies the inheritor posture—trusting in merit, accumulated faithfulness, and status. His words expose this: "Lo, these many years I have been serving you . . . yet you never gave me a young goat" (Luke 15:29). His obedience has become a claim, something that puts the father in his debt.

   By contrast, the father embodies proper authority and the divine pattern of grace. He allows freedom without coercion, receives repentance without hesitation, and confronts entitlement without harshness. He is the still point around which the sons' distorted orientations become visible.

2. What symbols appear?

   The central symbol is inheritance, functioning like "seed" elsewhere in Scripture. When the younger son demands his portion prematurely (Luke 15:12), he grasps at the seed before its time—echoing Cain's offering of processed yield rather than seed and life (Gen 4:3–4). His journey into the "far country" (Luke 15:13) is a movement into wilderness, a return to territory east of Eden where no fruit trees grow and nothing yields its increase. His descent is marked by food imagery. Starving, he longs to eat the "pods that the swine ate" (Luke 15:16). Pig food is an image of dust food—the diet of the serpent (Gen 3:14). It symbolizes the lowest orientation imaginable: a human being reduced to eating what sustains beasts.

   The father's house, by contrast, is a place of abundance. When the younger son returns, the father calls for the "best robe," a ring, and sandals (Luke 15:22). These items signal restored authority, renewed cooperation, and reoriented identity. The killing of the "fatted calf" (Luke 15:23) is sacrificial feast language—an image of restored communion, echoing every moment in Scripture when God's presence results in shared table fellowship.

Even bodily movement is symbolic. When the son resolves, "I will arise and go to my father" (Luke 15:18), the word arise captures an upward orientation, a reversal of the downward trajectory toward dust. When the father "fell on his neck and kissed him" (Luke 15:20), the authority relationship that had been inverted is suddenly healed. The father again becomes head; the son again becomes son.

3. What scale is this?

   Individual: two sons' personal orientations toward father

   Corporate: parable addressed to Pharisees/scribes (Luke 15:1–2)

   - Pharisees = older son (inheritors grumbling about tax collectors/sinners)
   - Tax collectors/sinners = younger son (prodigals returning)

   Cosmic: father = God's grace toward both Jews (older son) and gentiles (younger son)

   Fractal connection: personal parable → corporate reality (Pharisees vs. sinners)

4. How does Christ address it?

   As prophet (primary):

   - Calls both sons to right orientation
   - Younger son: from merit, self-determination, and pride to grace (undeserving return)
   - Older son: from merit ("I've served you faithfully") to grace ("all I have is yours")

   As king (secondary):

   - Represents God's rightful authority
   - Father's authority not tyrannical (lets son go) but also not abdicated (sets terms of restoration)

5. What is being complained about vs. lamented?

   The younger son shows *no complaint* when he suffers. He does not blame famine, misfortune, or his employer. Instead he arrives at lament: "I have sinned against heaven and before you, and am no longer worthy to be called your son" (Luke 15:18–19). This lament is the turning point, because lament directs its grief upward toward the Father rather than outward toward circumstances. Lament maintains proper authority.

The older son's response is pure complaint. He refuses to enter the feast (Luke 15:28), lectures his father, and distances himself from his brother: "This son of yours" (Luke 15:30). Complaint inverts authority—it places the self above the father, merit above grace, and bitterness above reconciliation.

The father's answer—"Son, you are always with me, and all that I have is yours" (Luke 15:31)—exposes the tragedy: the older son has lived in the house of grace while perceiving it as a house of wages. Thus the story shows that complaint belongs to the inheritor; lament belongs to the renewer. Only lament can lead to restoration.

### Conclusion of the Prodigal Son

The parable of the prodigal son is not simply the story of a wayward youth returning home. It is the story of Eden replayed in miniature. One son grasps at inheritance, wanders into exile, and tastes the dust of serpent food before turning his steps back toward communion. The other clings proudly to merit and cannot bear the wideness of the father's grace. The father stands in the center, restoring authority, renewing cooperation, and reorienting both sons toward the feast of life.

Through the five-question lens, the parable becomes a concentrated revelation of Gen 3 healed: authority restored through the father's embrace, cooperation renewed through shared celebration, and orientation transformed from resentment to grace. Jesus tells this story so we can see ourselves—not only in the sons but in the father who longs to restore all things in love.

## APPLICATION BEYOND NARRATIVE: THE PRINCIPLES ACROSS THE BIBLE

While this book focuses primarily on biblical narratives from Genesis through the Gospels, the three principles established in Gen 1–4 apply across all biblical literature because they reflect fundamental theological realities rather than merely narrative conventions. These principles describe how God relates to humanity: through proper authority structures, divine-human cooperation, and grace-based orientation. Since these realities pervade all Scripture, they illuminate wisdom literature, psalms, prophetic oracles, and the epistles just as they do narrative passages. Every biblical genre engages these principles because every genre addresses the divine-human relationship.

Wisdom literature is especially compatible with the Genesis Conflict Framework because it describes life not as disconnected moral teachings but as the ongoing outworking of Eden's ruptured structure. Proverbs exemplifies all three principles operating simultaneously. The book's framework assumes proper authority: "My son, hear the instruction of your father, and do not forsake the law of your mother" (Prov 1:8). This establishes the Adam/Eve dynamic—divine wisdom flows through human mediators (parents, teachers) to those who receive it. The warnings against the "strange woman" who leads men astray directly parallel Eve's role in Gen 3, where earthly persuasion corrupts divine order. The entire book assumes that when authority structures collapse—when fools reject correction or when the seductive voice supplants wisdom—chaos and death follow.

The tilling/rain/yield principle appears throughout Proverbs' theology of work and blessing. "Honor the Lord with your possessions, and with the firstfruits of all your increase; so your barns will be filled with plenty, and your vats will overflow" (Prov 3:9–10) perfectly captures the pattern: human preparation (offering firstfruits) meets divine response (abundant yield). The book never suggests pure works-based righteousness nor passive fatalism, but rather synergy: "The hand of the diligent makes rich" (Prov 10:4) cooperates with "the blessing of the Lord makes one rich" (Prov 10:22).

The inheritor/renewer distinction structures Proverbs' contrast between the wise and the fool. "There is a way that seems right to a man, but its end is the way of death" (Prov 14:12) describes the inheritor orientation—trusting earthly wisdom and inherited assumptions. Meanwhile, "The fear of the Lord is the beginning of wisdom" (Prov 9:10) captures the renewer orientation—approaching God with humility rather than presumption, seeking divine wisdom rather than relying on accumulated human knowledge.

Ecclesiastes demonstrates what happens when humanity operates with inverted principles. Solomon, the ultimate inheritor—possessing inherited kingdom, wisdom, and wealth—discovers that inheritance without proper orientation toward God produces vanity. His repeated phrase "under the sun" describes life lived with man as authority rather than God, where human effort (tilling) operates without divine rain, producing only weariness. His conclusion—"Fear God and keep His commandments, for this is man's all" (Eccl 12:13)—returns to proper ordering (divine authority), cooperation (keeping commandments), and orientation (fear of God).

The psalms constantly engage these principles. Lament psalms cry out when authority breaks down (enemies triumph, wicked prosper), while praise psalms celebrate proper order restored. "They that sow in tears shall reap in joy" (Ps 126:5) explicitly uses agricultural language for the tilling/rain/yield principle applied to spiritual life. Throughout, the psalms contrast those who trust in earthly power (inheritors) with those who seek God's face (renewers).

Psalm 1 functions as the constitutional gateway to the entire Psalter, and all three principles structure its theology. The psalm begins with authority: "Blessed is the man who walks not in the counsel of the ungodly, nor stands in the path of sinners, nor sits in the seat of the scornful" (Ps 1:1). This progression—walks, stands, sits—depicts increasing settlement into corrupted authority. The "counsel of the ungodly" parallels the serpent's counsel to Eve; the man who heeds earthly wisdom over divine command experiences the same authority breakdown that destroyed Eden.

The Inheritor/Renewer contrast structures the entire psalm: "The ungodly are not so, but are like the chaff which the wind drives away" (Ps 1:4). It's what remains after the seed (life-principle) is removed. The wicked produce chaff because they operate by works without faith, by inheritance without renewal. Meanwhile, the righteous are fruitful trees because they maintain proper orientation toward God's law as a gift rather than a burden. The psalm concludes: "The Lord knows the way of the righteous, but the way of the ungodly shall perish"—the ultimate distinction between renewer (known by God) and inheritor (self-justified but perishing).

# Author's Note

THIS PROJECT BEGAN WHEN I became fascinated with the Eastern Orthodox Church and felt a desire to engage more deeply and meaningfully with my Christian faith. Prayer has always been a challenging practice for me, and I hoped that some of the Orthodox approaches to prayer might be helpful for me having a stronger prayer life. Many of their practices and beliefs were unfamiliar to me, as I had spent fifteen years in a Protestant tradition. In my upbringing, the use of images in prayer was discouraged; icons were often considered idolatrous, violating the commandment against graven images.

At the time, I attended a contemporary Protestant church that, in many ways, was far removed from the sacramental and mystical faith of Orthodox Christianity. The Orthodox tradition, with its rich use of icons, candles, and incense, presented a radically different approach. These elements create an immersive, multisensory prayer experience, making spiritual life tangible and present. I was drawn to the participatory nature of Orthodox worship, where believers share sacred space with the saints themselves, and I hoped that engaging with these practices might renew my faith, which had grown somewhat dull. Wanting to jump in, I purchased a few icons online—what I thought of as a starter set for my home space: Christ, Mary, John the Baptist, St. George, and the angel St. Michael. I approached this purchase naively, unaware of the deeper symbolism embedded in these images. My first encounter with John the Baptist's icon was shocking. The icon depicted John with angel wings, holding a platter with his own severed head, staring directly at me. To my twenty-first-century sensibilities, this was repulsive, unsettling, and deeply disrespectful to John the Baptist. The image clashed with my expectations of Christian art as solemn, serene, and comforting.

I later learned that Orthodox icons use reverse perspective, a technique in which figures appear to follow the viewer, in contrast to the linear perspective common in Western art. This method emphasizes symbolism over realism, representing a reality beyond our physical sight. In this light, John the Baptist seemed less like a static figure and more like a presence confronting me directly, adding to the otherworldly and charged nature of the encounter. Fr. Alexander Schmemann states, "Therefore, icons are more than images. According to the teaching of the Orthodox Church, they make truly present those whom they represent, they are a spiritual reality and not a mere symbol."[1] Applying this to a beheaded John initially felt wrong and disturbing. I had so many questions. Why was this image part of Orthodox tradition? What deeper meaning did John holding his own head convey? I discovered that this scene—John's beheading as described in Mark 6—has been a recurring subject in Christian art for centuries. Following Christ and Mary, John the Baptist is perhaps the most depicted biblical figure, particularly in images of martyrdom. Stories of his severed head appear in art, legend, and even accounts of hauntings. I realized that this unsettling imagery must carry profound spiritual significance, just as the brutality of the crucifixion points to life, salvation, and purpose.

Through research and reflection, I began to understand that icons are not meant to merely replicate historical events but to symbolize deeper truths. The Bible often speaks of "sight" as spiritual understanding, the ability to perceive beyond what is immediately visible. In this sense, my initial discomfort reflected a limited spiritual sight, unprepared to grasp the layers of meaning in the icon. The beheaded John, far from being a grotesque spectacle, became an invitation to explore spiritual reality, to see beyond appearances, and to confront truths that may at first seem disturbing or even terrifying.

I studied the Scriptures, focusing on stories with the head and body, the role of John the Baptist, and the ways in which separation and martyrdom convey spiritual lessons. I explored passages such as Matt 3:7, where John calls the Pharisees a "brood of vipers," and considered the implications of authority, witness, and prophetic courage. These studies illuminated the rich symbolic language of icons, revealing that what initially seems dreadful can point toward transformation, insight, and salvation. This book is the fruit of that experience. It grew from a single encounter with a shocking icon into a broader meditation on how God calls us to see beyond the

1. Schmemann, *Liturgy and Life*, 36.

surface, to discern spiritual truths in scenes that might at first appear repulsive or unsettling. The images and stories I encountered in the Orthodox tradition revealed that what may initially seem dreadful can carry profound spiritual significance, offering lessons about faith, courage, and the deeper realities of truth. It reminded me of the story of Eve in the garden of Eden, who saw the fruit as pleasing to the eye but deadly in consequence, and how this pattern pervades the Bible. These reflections were all things floating in my head during my study of the Bible, and this book is the fruit of that initial encounter and meditation. I know I needed to understand the stories of the Bible deeply.

Through this journey, I have come to appreciate the power of icons, the richness of Orthodox symbolism, and how Christian art can invite us to a fuller, more contemplative vision of faith. What began as curiosity—and even discomfort—has become a deeper engagement with the mysteries of prayer, the presence of the saints, and how God communicates through images, stories, and symbols to see beyond appearance.

# Bibliography


Adar, Zvi. *The Biblical Narrative*. Trans. Misha Louvish. Jerusalem: Department of Education and Culture, 1959.

Alter, Robert. *The Art of Biblical Narrative*. New York: Basic, 2011.

Anderson, Gary A. *The Genesis of Perfection: Adam and Eve in Jewish and Christian Imagination*. Louisville: Westminster John Knox, 2001.

Armatas, Evan. *Toolkit for Spiritual Growth II: A Practical Guide to Scripture, Confession, and Time*. Chesterton, IN: Ancient Faith, 2025.

Brand, Chad, et al., eds. *Holman Illustrated Bible Dictionary*. Nashville: B&H, 2015.

Brock, Sebastian. *The Luminous Eye: The Spiritual World Vision of Saint Ephrem the Syrian*. Kalamazoo: Cistercian, 1992.

Burke, Tony, and Brent Landau, eds. *New Testament Apocrypha: More Noncanonical Scriptures*. Grand Rapids: Eerdmans, 2024.

Constas, Maximos, trans. *The Light of the World: Prayers to Our Lord and Savior Jesus Christ*. Columbia, MO: Newrome, 2020.

Crowe, Brandon D. *The Last Adam: A Theology of the Obedient Life of Jesus in the Gospels*. Grand Rapids: Baker Academic, 2017.

Cyril of Alexandria. *On the Unity of Christ*. Crestwood, NY: St. Vladimir's Seminary Press, 1995.

Ellis, Edward E. *The Old Testament in Early Christianity: Canon and Interpretation in the Light of Modern Research*. Tübingen: Mohr, 1991.

Fokkelman, J. P. *Reading Biblical Narrative: An Introductory Guide*. Louisville: Westminster John Knox, 1999.

Foster, Thomas C. *How to Read Literature Like a Professor*. New York: Harper, 2003.

Grēgorios. *The Divine Liturgy: A Commentary in the Light of the Fathers*. Mount Athos: Cell of St. John the Theologian, 2009.

———. *Parable of the Prodigal Son: A Commentary in the Light of the Fathers*. Translated by Stelios Zarganes. Columbia, MO: Newrome, 2013.

Gregory of Nazianzus. *On God and Christ: The Five Theological Orations and Two Letters to Cledonius*. Translated by Frederick Williams and Lionel Wickham. Crestwood, NY: St. Vladimir's Seminary Press, 2002.

Gregory of Nyssa. *Saint Gregory of Nyssa Collection: 7 Books*. London: Aeterna, 2016.

Holmes, Michael W., ed. *The Apostolic Fathers in English*. Translated by Michael W. Holmes. 3rd ed. Grand Rapids: Baker Academic, 2006.

Holy Transfiguration Monastery. *A Prayer Book for Orthodox Christians*. Brookline, MA: Holy Transfiguration Monastery, 1987.

Irenaeus. *The Scandal of the Incarnation: Irenaeus Against the Heresies*. Edited by Hans Urs von Balthasar. Translated by John Saward. San Francisco: Ignatius, 1990.

Josephus, Flavius. *The Complete Works of Josephus*. Translated by William Whiston. Nashville: Thomas Nelson, 1998.

Justin Martyr. "First Apology." In *The Faith of the Early Fathers*, edited and translated by William A. Jurgens, 1:50–57. Collegeville, MN: Liturgical, 1970.

Kaiser, Walter C., Jr. *The Messiah in the Old Testament*. Grand Rapids: Zondervan, 1995.

Kapsanēs, Geōrgios. *Theosis: The True Purpose of Human Life*. Mt. Athos: Holy Monastery of St. Gregorios, 2023.

Keener, Craig S., and John H. Walton, eds. *NKJV Cultural Backgrounds Study Bible*. Grand Rapids: Zondervan, 2017.

Laird, Martin S. *Gregory of Nyssa and the Grasp of Faith: Union, Knowledge, and Divine Presence*. Oxford: Oxford University Press, 2004.

Lossky, Vladimir. *The Mystical Theology of the Eastern Church*. Crestwood, NY: St. Vladimir's Seminary Press, 1976.

Manley, Johanna, ed. *Grace for Grace: The Psalter and the Holy Fathers; Patristic Christian Commentary, Meditations, and Liturgical Extracts Relating to the Psalms and Odes*. Forestville, CA: Monastery, 1992.

Meyer, Marvin, ed. *The Nag Hammadi Scriptures: The Revised and Updated Translation of Sacred Gnostic Texts*. San Francisco: HarperOne, 2007.

Murray, Robert. *Symbols of Church and Kingdom: A Study in Early Syriac Tradition*. London: T&T Clark, 2004.

Orthodox Eastern Church. *The Festal Menaion*. Translated by Mother Mary and Kallistos Ware. South Canaan, PA: St. Tikhon's Seminary Press, 1990.

Pageau, Matthieu. *The Language of Creation: Cosmic Symbolism in Genesis*. Self-published, CreateSpace, 2018.

Pentiuc, Eugen J., et al, eds. *Studies in Orthodox Hermeneutics: A Festschrift in Honor of Theodore G. Stylianopoulos*. Brookline, MA: Holy Cross Orthodox, 2016.

Reardon, Patrick H. *Creation and the Patriarchal Histories: Orthodox Christian Reflections on the Book of Genesis*. Ben Lomond, CA: Conciliar, 2008.

Romanides, John S. *Patristic Theology: The University Lectures of Protopresbyter John S. Romanides*. Translated by Alexios Trader. Crestwood, NY: Uncut Mountain, 2008.

Sarna, Nahum M. *Understanding Genesis: The Heritage of Biblical Israel*. New York: Schocken, 1970.

Schmemann, Alexander. *The Eucharist: Sacrament of the Kingdom*. Translated by Paul Kachur. Crestwood, NY: St. Vladimir's Seminary Press, 2003.

———. *For the Life of the World: Sacraments and Orthodoxy*. Crestwood, NY: St. Vladimir's Seminary Press, 1973.

———. *Liturgy and Life: Christian Development Through Liturgical Experience*. Syosset, NY: Department of Religious Education, Orthodox Church in America, 1993.

"The Secret Book of James." In *The Nag Hammadi Library in English*, edited by James M. Robinson, 29–37. 3rd ed. San Francisco: HarperSanFrancisco, 1990.

Stylianopoulos, Theodore G. *The New Testament: An Orthodox Perspective*. Brookline, MA: Holy Cross Orthodox, 1997.

Symeon the New Theologian. *The First-Created Man: Seven Homilies*. Translated by Seraphim Rose. Platina, CA: Saint Herman of Alaska Brotherhood, 1994.

Tertullian. *Apology*. In *The Faith of the Early Fathers*, edited and translated by William A. Jurgens, 1:111–61. Collegeville, MN: Liturgical, 1970.

Tibbs, Eve. *A Basic Guide to Eastern Orthodox Theology: Introducing Beliefs and Practices*. Grand Rapids: Baker Academic, 2021.

Velimirović, Nikolai. *Prayers by the Lake*. Alhambra, CA: Sebastian, 2018.

———. *The Universe as Symbols and Signs: An Essay on Mysticism in the Eastern Church*. South Canaan, PA: St. Tikhon's Seminary Press, 2010.

Vlachos, Hierotheos, and Bartholomew. *"I Know a Man in Christ": Elder Sophrony, the Hesychast and Theologian*. Edited by Effie Mavromichali. Translated by Pelagia Selfe. Levadia, GRC: Birth of the Theotokos Monastery, 2015.

Walton, John H. *The Lost World of Adam and Eve: Genesis 2–3 and the Human Origins Debate*. Downers Grove, IL: IVP Academic, 2015.

Walton, John H., and Victor H. Matthews. *The IVP Bible Background Commentary: Genesis–Deuteronomy*. Downers Grove, IL: InterVarsity, 1997.

Ware, Kallistos. *The Inner Kingdom*. Crestwood, NY: St. Vladimir's Seminary Press, 2000.

Wright, N. T. *Jesus and the Victory of God*. Minneapolis: Fortress, 1996.

Zacharou, Archimandrite Zacharias. *Hesychasm: The Bedewing Furnace of the Heart*. Essex: Stavropegic Monastery of St. John the Baptist, 2022.

# Scripture Index

## HEBREW BIBLE/ OLD TESTAMENT

### Genesis

## Genesis *(cont.)*



## Exodus



## Leviticus



## Numbers

## NEW TESTAMENT

### Matthew

## Mark



## Luke



## John

## Acts



## Romans



## 1 Corinthians



## 2 Corinthians

www.ingramcontent.com/pod-product-compliance
Lightning Source LLC
LaVergne TN
LVHW050629100826
845148LV00011B/1800

*9798385263035*